NOLO *Your Legal Companion*

"In Nolo you can trust." —THE NEW YORK TIMES

OUR MISSION

Make the law as simple as possible, saving you time, money and headaches.

Whether you have a simple question or a complex problem, turn to us at:

NOLO.COM

Your all-in-one legal resource

Need quick information about wills, patents, adoptions, starting a business—or anything else that's affected by the law? **Nolo.com** features free articles in our Nolopedia, legal updates, resources and all of our books, software, forrms and online applications.

NOLO NOW

Make your legal documents online

Creating a legal document has never been easier or more cost-effective! Create an online will or trust, form an LLC, or file a Provisional Patent Application! Check it out at **http://nolonow.nolo.com**.

NOLO'S LAWYER DIRECTORY

Meet your new attorney

If you want advice from a qualified attorney, turn to Nolo's Lawyer Directory—the only directory that lets you see hundreds of in-depth attorney profiles so you can pick the one that's right for you. Find it at **http://lawyers.nolo.com**.

ALWAYS UP TO DATE

Sign up for NOLO'S LEGAL UPDATER

Old law is bad law. We'll email you when we publish an updated edition of this book—sign up for this free service at **nolo.com/legalupdater**.

Find the latest updates at NOLO.COM

Recognizing that the law can change, we post legal updates during the life of this edition at **nolo.com/updates**.

Is this edition the newest? ASK US!

To make sure that this is the most recent edition available, just give us a call at **800-728-3555**.

(Please note that we cannot offer legal advice.)

Please note

We believe accurate, plain-English legal information should help you solve many of your own legal problems. But this text is not a substitute for personalized advice from a knowledgeable lawyer. If you want the help of a trained professional—and we'll always point out situations in which we think that's a good idea—consult an attorney licensed to practice in your state.

5th edition

Patent Searching Made Easy

How to Do Patent Searches on the Internet & in the Library

By David Hitchcock

FIFTH EDITION	APRIL 2009
Editor	RICHARD STIM
Cover Design	SUSAN PUTNEY
Proofreading	SUSAN CARLSON GREENE
Index	ELLEN SHERRON
Printing	DELTA PRINTING SOLUTIONS, INC.

Hitchcock, David, 1956-

Patent searching made easy : how to do patent searches on the Internet and in the library / by David Hitchcock ; edited by Richard Stim. -- 5th ed.

p. cm.

Includes indexes.

ISBN-13: 978-1-4133-1036-8 (pbk.)

ISBN-10: 1-4133-1036-2 (pbk.)

1. Patent searching. 2. Patent literature. 3. Patent searching--Computer network resources. I. Title.

T210.H58 2007

608--dc22

2009000962

Quantity sales: For information on bulk purchases or corporate premium sales, please contact the Special Sales Department. For academic sales or textbook adoptions, ask for Academic Sales. Call 800-955-4775 or write to Nolo, 950 Parker Street, Berkeley, CA 94710.

Acknowledgements

All screen shots from United States Patent and Trademark Office website are courtesy of the USPTO. All screen shots from the European Patent Office website are courtesy of the EPO. All screen shots from the Defense Technical Information Center are courtesy of DTIC. The author gratefully acknowledges and thanks the Thomas Register, Google, Medical Informatics Engineering, the Intellectual Property Office of Singapore, and the Microsoft Corporation for granting permission to use various screen shots in this book.

Table of Contents

Part III: Resources

Appendixes

Index

Your Legal Companion

Okay, you've come up with what seems like a new way to solve a problem or accomplish a task. But you're wondering whether somebody has already trod this ground before you. And if they have, you're wondering whether they succeeded in obtaining a patent … or proving that the idea isn't feasible.

Perhaps you've been told that the answers to your questions can only come from a patent search performed by a lawyer or professional patent searcher at a cost of $500 or more—possibly much more. You can't afford to spend that much money on an idea, especially if someone else may have thought of it already. Maybe you should just forget about it?

Think again. You can do your own patent search with only a reasonable amount of effort, and this book will show you how. Even better, you can do your searching without spending more than a few dollars. Even if your invention is not patentable, you will have saved time and money and learned skills that will help with your next great idea. If it turns out that your idea has never before been addressed in a patent, your invention—should it issue as a patent—could provide you with satisfaction and financial benefits.

This book will help you achieve your goals by showing you how to:

- quickly check out any new idea, to see if anyone else has already patented it
- verify the patent status of ideas submitted to you for development (if you are a potential developer), and
- save lots of money in legal fees.

This book is arranged in three parts:

In Part I, we explain the relationship between your search and the patentability of your invention. We also help you come up with words to describe your invention—also known as keywords or search words. Once you come up with these words, you can use your computer to search the U.S. patent database for patents that contain these words. In addition to searching for isolated occurrences of your individual search terms, you can also search for combinations of search terms.

In Part II, we help you perform simple and advanced Internet patent searches. We also introduce you to the U.S. Patent and Trademark Office (PTO) classification system—the categories that the PTO uses to classify or sort the various types of inventions. We will also help you discover what category the PTO will most likely use for your invention. Then, we will show you how to search for other patents within the same category. Part II also explains searching at the European Patent Office (EPO) using a translation service to translate foreign language patents and searching nonpatent resources.

In Part III, we cover the resources available at the nationwide network of Patent and Trademark Depository Libraries (PTDLs), including the *Index to the U.S. Patent Classification System*, *Manual of Classification,* and *Classification Definitions.* We also explain how to use CASSIS—the Classification And Search Support Information System.

In summary, this book will help you to:

- understand how the PTO classifies different types of inventions
- assign your idea to the right class
- compare your idea to other similar ideas in the same class, and
- tentatively conclude whether your idea is new enough to qualify for a patent.

Part I:

The Basics

In Chapter 1, we discuss what a patent is, the basic principles of searching, and the relationship between your search and the patentability of your invention. In Chapter 2, we introduce you to word-based patent searches and the resources you will need for patent searching.

CHAPTER 1

Patents and Patent Searching

In order to receive a patent, your invention must be both new (novel) and surprising in light of prior developments (not obvious). Both of these standards are judged not only against all previously issued patents, but also against all previous developments in the same field, whether or not they were ever patented. For instance, the grooves in an automobile steering wheel were deemed to be a nonpatentable invention because of the traditional use of grooves in sword handles.

So, the key to assessing the patentability of your new idea is understanding what previous developments—known in the trade as prior art—the U.S. Patent and Trademark Office (PTO) will consider when deciding whether to issue a patent on your idea. In order to proceed, you must first understand the nature of patents and prior art.

What Is a Patent and What Does It Do for Me?

A patent is a right, granted by the government, to a person or legal entity (partnership or corporation). A patent gives its holder the right to exclude others from making, using, or selling the invention "claimed" in the patent deed for 20 years from the date of filing (for patents issued before June 8, 1995, 17 years from the date the patent was issued by the PTO). Once the patent expires, the invention covered by the patent enters the public domain and can be used by anyone. The scope of a U.S. patent is limited to the borders of the United States and its territories.

The right of exclusion given to a patent owner is referred to as an offensive legal right—meaning that the owner must go on the offensive to protect patent rights. That may mean filing a lawsuit in federal court against an infringer (anyone who violates the right of exclusion). Because the right of exclusion is not a defensive legal right, the patent owner can't rely on law enforcement agencies to automatically prosecute someone who infringes (copies) his or her patented invention.

In the sense that a patent gives the patent holder the right to sue anyone who tries to develop, use, or manufacture the invention covered by the patent, the patent can be a valuable commodity. It can be sold outright or licensed in exchange for a royalty. Additionally, the patent owner may choose to manufacture and distribute the invention, thereby keeping all the proceeds for him- or herself.

What Is Prior Art?

Some inventors mistakenly believe that finding prior art automatically kills the chances of obtaining a patent. This is not true. Prior art refers to *all* information existing or publicly available either before the date of invention or more than one year prior to your earliest patent application date. As long as you can demonstrate that your innovation differs physically in some way from all prior developments and concepts, the prior art will not affect your ability to patent your invention.

On the other hand, if prior art is uncovered by a patent examiner that demonstrates somebody already came up with the same idea as you—that is, all of the significant elements in your innovation were embodied in an existing innovation—you will be unable to obtain a patent and you'll lose the thousands of dollars spent on application or attorney fees. (This is referred to as "prior art anticipation.") In order to avoid this fate, and to help you improve your invention's chance of acquiring patent rights, we strongly recommend searching for prior art.

Since prior art is defined by time limits related to your date of invention, you must first determine this date. Most inventors think it's the date on which one files a patent application. However, the date of invention is the earliest of the following dates:

- the date an inventor filed the patent application (provisional or regular)
- the date an inventor can prove that the invention was built and tested (known as "reduction to practice") in the United States, or
- the date an inventor can prove that the invention was conceived (date of conception), provided the inventor can also prove diligence in building and testing it or filing a patent application on it.

As noted, an inventor who maintains proper records and is diligent afterwards in the invention process will be able to use the date of conception, which is usually several months before the filing date. Once the date of invention is determined, the relevant prior art comprises everything available before that date or anything available about the invention more than one year prior to filing the application.

The definition of prior art—everything available before the date of invention or anything available about the invention more than one year prior to filing the application—can also be summarized as including:

- any published writing (including any patent) that was publicly available either (1) before your date of invention, or (2) over one year before you filed your patent application
- any U.S. patent that has a filing date earlier than your date of invention
- any relevant invention or development (whether described in writing or not) existing prior to the date your invention was conceived, or
- any public or commercial use, sale, or knowledge of the invention more than one year prior your application filing date.

For your purposes, it's best to spread as wide a prior art search net as possible, and to spread this net, you will eventually need to go beyond the database of patents at the PTO and examine *all* written references and all real-life items that may embody your idea.

However, for now, we'll begin your research with a basic and inexpensive search of the U.S. patent database. That's because if someone has thought of your idea before and deemed it valuable, chances are good that the idea will show up in one or more patents. Keep in mind, however, that pending patent applications (patent applications that have already been submitted, but for which no patent has yet been issued) cannot be searched until 18 months after the application was filed. (We explain more about this later in this chapter.)

CAUTION

Do not publish or publicly use your invention more than one year prior to applying for a patent. If you do, you will not be able to claim patent rights.

What Is the PTO Patent Database?

Much of your patent searching will be accomplished by searching the U.S. patent database which contains all the patents issued by the PTO. These patents are stored in patent file folders at the PTO in Virginia, and the PTO has created a computer database of patent images and text.

The traditional method of searching the patent database is to hire a search professional to travel to the PTO's offices in Virginia and conduct the search there. While very effective, this process is also very expensive. Instead of starting with this approach, you can save yourself some money by performing a preliminary search. If your search reveals that your idea has already been described in one or more previous patents, you will have saved yourself the expense of hiring a search professional.

The PTO provides an online database where you simply type in words which describe your invention—called keywords—to search for patents as far back as 1971 that contain those same words. Pre-1971 patents can also be searched on a much more limited basis. By the way, the search engine company Google goes one step further: The company has scanned all U.S. patents in the PTO database and permits you to search even pre-1971 patents using keyword searching techniques at its Google Patent Search website.

In addition, a great resource for patent searching is a network of special libraries called Patent and Trademark Depository Libraries (PTDLs—see Appendix A for a list). At a PTDL you can perform computer searches of the PTO's electronic database.

As you search the PTO patent database, you also will learn how to think about your ideas in the same way that the examiners at the PTO would think of them, were you to apply for a patent. This knowledge will enable you to search for ideas that are not only the same as yours, but similar to yours. This process will allow you to determine not only if your invention is the first, but also whether it is the best. And if it is not, the search may inspire you to refine your idea in ways that will qualify it for a patent.

As you will also see, searching the PTO patent database is a great way to become familiar with patent terminology. This will come in handy during all aspects of the patent search as well as the patent application process itself. In particular, when dealing directly with the patent examiner who is reviewing your application, it helps if you are both speaking the same language.

Patent Searching and Patent Eligibility

In order to search properly, you will need a short primer on what qualifies for a patent. This primer will help you decide—once you complete your search—whether you should go through the effort and expense of filing a patent application. Keep in mind that this is a brief, simple explanation of patentability. Before filing a patent (and for a more thorough analysis of patentability), we recommend you peruse a more detailed analysis. A good way to start would be by reviewing *Patent It Yourself* by attorney David Pressman (Nolo).

In order to get a utility patent (as opposed to a design patent), your patent application has to satisfy four legal criteria:

- It must fit into an established statutory class.
- It must be useful.
- It must be novel—that is, have some physical difference from any similar inventions in the past.
- It must be unobvious (also referred to as nonobvious) to someone who is skilled in the appropriate field.

The Easy Part: Statutory Subject Matter and Usefulness

Two patent standards, statutory subject matter and usefulness, are easy to achieve. The first requirement—statutory subject matter—means that your invention must be a process, a machine, an article of manufacture, a composition of matter, or a new use invention. It's not necessary to decide which applies to your invention—and many inventions overlap—as long as your invention is covered by at least one of them.

Statutory Subject Matter	
Subject Matter	**What Is It?**
Process	A process is the performance of a series of operations on something—for example, electroplating or a process for scanning election results.
Machine	A machine is a device consisting of a series of fixed or moving parts that direct mechanical energy towards a specific task—for example, an automobile engine, turbine, or drill press.
Article of Manufacture	These are relatively simple inventions with few or no moving parts—for example, a screwdriver, rake, pencil, or mirror.
Composition of Matter	Compositions are a unique arrangement of items—for example, glue and plastics.
New Use Invention	A new use is a new way of using an invention that fits in one of the first four statutory classes—for example, using birth control pills to limit acne or a method of converting a video game controller into a laser pointer.

The second requirement is utility—that is, is your invention useful? If your invention is operable (if it functions), it will satisfy this requirement. Perpetual motion machines or other devices that violate an established law of physics are examples of inventions that fail this requirement.

Novelty: Is Your Invention New?

At the heart of patent searching—and the goal of this book—is demonstrating that your invention is novel. Demonstrating novelty means that you must be able to prove that no single prior art item describes all of your invention's significant elements. If your search uncovers inventions that perform the same or similar functions, you will need to somehow distinguish your innovation from these previous inventions (whether patented or not). You can distinguish your invention based on:

- physical differences
- combinatorial differences, or
- new uses.

Physical Differences

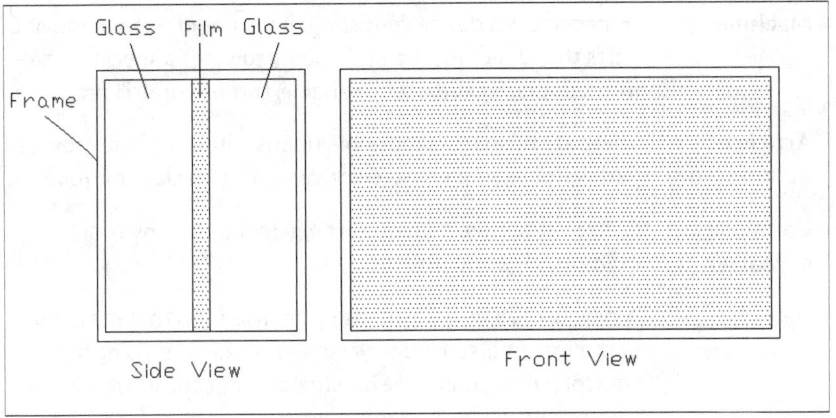

Figure 1.1

An example of a physical difference between your invention and a previously patented product would be the elimination, replacement, or functional modification of a component of the previous device.

Consider the invention shown in Figure 1.1. The figure shows a side and front view of a fire safety glass window. It consists of four elements.

- Element #1. Left-hand side glass segment
- Element #2. A thermal conduction film
- Element #3. Right-hand side glass segment
- Element #4. Heat-conducting metal frame

In order for this invention to work, a heat-conducting film is sandwiched between two glass plates. When a sharp temperature rise occurs on either side of the glass, the film conducts the heat away from the window to the metal frame.

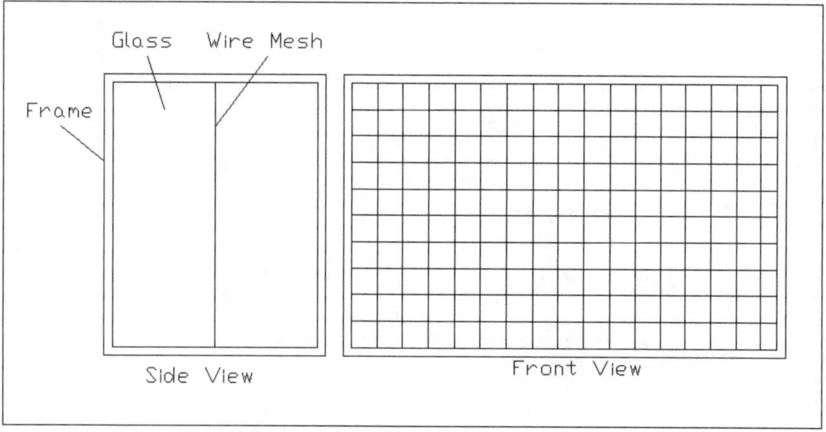

Figure 1.2

Now consider the invention shown in Figure 1.2. This figure is also a side and front view of a safety glass window. In this case there are three elements:

- Element #1. Thermal-conducting wire mesh
- Element #2. Glass segment enclosing the wire mesh
- Element #3. Heat-conducting metal frame

The wire mesh conducts heat away from the glass and into the frame, just as the first invention does. But now, instead of two separate glass elements, there is only one continuous glass element (in which the wire grid is embedded).

As an example of a replacement physical difference, consider the centrifugal water pump shown in Figure 1.3. Centrifugal pumps use impellers to impart energy to the water. For the sake of simplicity, we will identify four essential elements.

- Element #1. Pump intake
- Element #2. Metal impeller
- Element #3. Pump casting
- Element #4. Pump discharge

Suppose the impeller is made out of metal and you design a new impeller for this pump that performs as well, but with a different design and made out of plastic. This replacement physical difference would satisfy the novelty requirement.

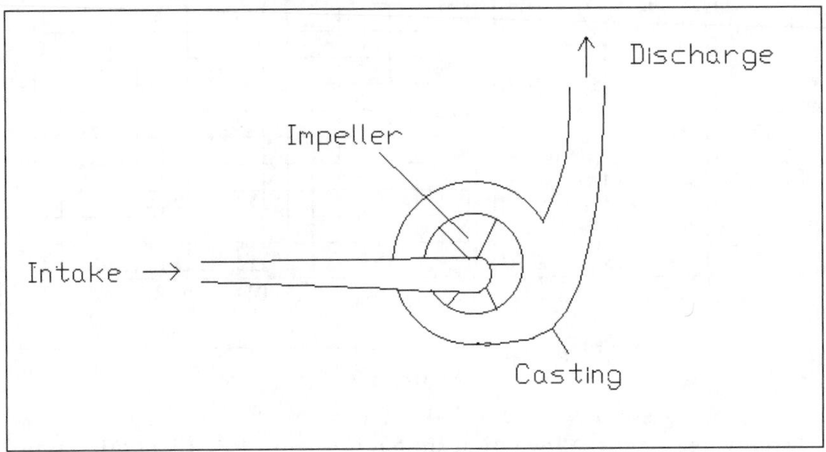

Figure 1.3

As an example of a functional modification, suppose our water pump vibrates at high pressure (high impeller speed) due to water turbulence. You redesign the blades of the impeller by increasing their pitch. This solves the turbulence problem and allows the pump to operate at high pressure. You have therefore made a functional modification.

Combinatorial Differences

A new combination of two different inventions can also be used to satisfy the novelty requirement—for example, the combination of a hot air balloon (an old invention) and a new high-strength lightweight fabric. The lightweight fabric replaces the older balloon material, making the balloon lighter. This provides more lift and lets the balloon carry more cargo.

New Uses

A new use of an old invention can also satisfy the novelty requirement. As an example, suppose during World War II, a sonar engineer developed a sonar receiver that detects the sound of a ship's propeller. Several years later, an independent inventor designs a pool alarm that uses the same technology to sound an alarm if a child accidentally falls into a pool. Even though the pool alarm uses the same electronics, it would pass the new use test.

A Systematic Approach to Novelty

A four-step systematic approach can be made for assessing novelty.

1. Analyze your invention for elements.
2. Analyze each prior art reference for its elements.
3. Compare the elements of each prior art reference to the elements of your invention.
4. If no one prior art reference contains all of the same elements used in the same way and for the same purpose as your invention, then it is novel.

Nonobviousness: Is Your Invention Obvious?

This is the most challenging patent requirement to fulfill. Essentially, it means that if a skilled worker who is thoroughly familiar with developments in the area of your invention would consider the idea obvious, you would fail this test. As an example, consider the balloon made with new lightweight fabric from the previous page. While this invention qualifies as novel, it would be obvious to a person skilled in the art of balloon making to try using new lightweight materials.

The Patent Application Process

When you submit your completed patent application and filing fee to the PTO, you will be assigned a filing date. After a waiting period (commonly 6 to 18 months), a patent examiner will review the application. It is extremely rare that an application will be allowed as is. More often than not, the patent examiner will object to one or more of your claims or require changes to your patent drawings or specification. This result is what is known as an Office Action (or OA). The OA is an official communication from the PTO, outlining the objections to your original patent application. You then have the choice of either modifying the application or convincing the examiner that your application is correct as written—that is, the examiner is in error.

After you successfully respond to the OA, the patent examiner will allow your application and you will have to pay an issue fee. After a few more months' delay, your patent will finally issue. The entire process, from initial patent application submission to issued patent, usually takes from 16 to 36 months.

RESOURCE

For more information about how to complete and file a patent application, see *Patent It Yourself,* by attorney David Pressman (Nolo).

Types of Patents

There are three types of patents: utility patents, design patents, and plant patents. In this book, we focus on searching for utility patents, the most common of the three, and, unless otherwise indicated, when we speak of a patent, we are referring to a utility patent. (Note: The rules for searching all types of patents are similar.)

A **utility patent** covers the functional aspects of an invention. As an example, assume that the hammer hasn't been invented. Ivan Inventor conceives of the hammer as an invention after he accidentally smashes his thumb with a rock he was using to pound a square peg into a round hole. If Ivan applies for a patent and his patent application describes his hammer invention in general enough terms, the patent would cover all variations of the hammer as a utilitarian device. It would cover common household hammers, sledge hammers, rubber hammers, and the like. Perhaps even hydraulic hammers could be covered.

A **design patent** only protects the appearance of an invention. In our example, Ivan might apply for a design patent for a hammer with a horsehead etched into the shaft of the hammer. Removal of the horsehead would not affect the usefulness or functioning of the hammer. It is easy to create a fairly similar design without infringing a design patent (referred to as designing around the patent). A competitor could design a hammer with a slightly different horsehead (longer mane or bigger eyes), and the new hammer design most likely would not infringe on the original design patent.

Plant patents are for new types of plants. We don't discuss them in this book.

First-to-File vs. First-to-Invent and Pending Patent Applications

One of the pitfalls of any patent search is that there is no way to search pending patent applications prior to 18 months from filing. Another inventor may have already filed a patent application on essentially the same invention as you. Because pending patent applications are kept confidential (prior to 18 months), if the patent hasn't been issued yet you have no way of knowing about it. This is one of the occupational hazards involved in applying for a patent.

If you have a patent application pending and a patent is issued that covers the essential aspects of your idea, you may still be able to get a patent. How? You do it by proving that you conceived of the invention prior to the inventor listed in the opposing patent.

While most of the world uses what is known as a first-to-file system (the first person to file a patent application is legally recognized as the inventor), the United States uses a first-to-invent system. This means that the inventor who can prove to have conceived of the idea first gets the patent.

To prove when you first conceived of your invention idea, you have to keep legally acceptable records. Nolo publishes an excellent workbook called *The Inventor's Notebook*, where you can record the conception, building, and testing of your invention. The notebook walks you through the due diligence process and helps you prove the earliest possible date of invention. It can also help you if your first-to-invent status is ever challenged by another inventor.

The Patent Document

Although we have explained some patent basics—for example, the PTO issues patents; patents provide certain affirmative rights; and a patent expires in 20 years—the idea of a patent is still an abstraction.

A patent manifests itself in its most "real" form in a document called a patent deed. This is the document issued by the PTO after your patent application has been approved and your patent rights have issued. The patent deed, commonly referred to as a patent or patent reference—is a collection of words and drawings that summarize how to make and use your invention. This document also defines the boundaries of your rights, known as the claims. The PTO's patent database comprises hardcopy, microfiche, or electronic copies of these patent documents.

Every patent has several identifiable fields or sections. Understanding the different parts of the patent will be especially important when we cover computer searching. This is because we will conduct our search in certain subsections of the patent, and it helps to know what sort of information to expect to find there.

We have prepared a table showing the typical sections that appear in a patent, along with a brief description. The table introduces you to several terms commonly used in the patent world. These include:

Classification (class and subclass). These refer to the system used by the PTO to categorize each patent. Conceptually, the system is similar to an alphabetical library index file. For example, to search a library for a book about baseball, one would first go to the subject card index. In the file drawer for subjects beginning with the letter S, you would most likely find a sports section. under the sports section, you would go to the subsection for baseball. There you would find the titles of several books related to baseball. The PTO currently has more than 100,000 classes and subclasses.

Abstract. An abstract is a summary of the most important features of the invention covered by the patent. The abstract appears on the front page of the issued patent. Patent searchers consult the abstract to get a quick overview of the invention. This, in turn, helps them decide whether it is worthwhile to review the entire patent. The abstract is the searcher's way to separate the wheat from the chaff. A typical abstract—from Pat. No. 5,712,618—is shown below.

Sample abstract for an automatic turn signaling device for vehicles

> An automatic signaling device for a vehicle which automatically initiates a method and apparatus for an automatic signaling device warning signal to pedestrians and to other vehicles in connection with lane changes and upon turns. The present invention is activated and deactivated automatically, providing significant safety advantages for all of those using the roads and highways.
>
> 15 Claims, 2 Drawing Figures

Background of the invention. This is a discussion of previous inventions that are related in some way to the current invention. These inventions are known as the prior art. The prior art may embody some of the same or similar elements as the current invention. For example, sprinkler systems and fireproof blankets are two vastly different products. However, they are both related by the fact that they are fire suppressant devices. So, if you invented a modern-day fire suppression device (for instance, one using nanotechnology—tiny microscopic machines—to deprive the fire of oxygen), both sprinkler systems and fireproof blankets would be considered prior art related to your invention.

The first two paragraphs from the background section of Pat. No. 5,712,618 are shown below. The first paragraph is a general summary of the background of the invention. The next paragraph begins the discussion of the advantages of the current invention over previously patented inventions.

Patent Fields and Sections	
Section/Field	**Description**
Title	This is the name or title of the invention.
Inventor Information	This is the inventor's identifying information—that is, name and address.
Patent Number	This is the number assigned by the PTO to the issued patent.
Patent Filing Date	This is the date that the patent application was filed with the PTO.
Patent Issue Date	This is the date that the patent was issued by the PTO.
Classification	These are the categories (the class and subclass) that the PTO uses to classify or sort the various types of inventions.
Referenced Patents	These are the patent numbers of previous patents referred to in the patent application, along with their classes and subclasses.
Abstract	Usually one concise paragraph, the abstract summarizes the invention in layperson terms. The abstract appears on the front page of the patent and is the most frequently referenced section.
Drawings	These are black-and-white drawings of the invention as seen from different perspectives.
Background of the Invention	This is a discussion of any previous inventions that were related to this invention (known as prior art).
Summary of the Invention	Here is a discussion of the invention that captures its essential functions and features.
Brief Description of Drawings	These are one-sentence descriptions of each patent drawing figure.
Detailed Description of the Preferred Version of the Invention	This is an in-depth discussion of the various aspects of the invention and in which painstaking references to the patent drawings are made.
Claims	This section defines the legal scope of the patent (in the way that a deed describes the boundaries of real estate).

Sample background of the invention for an automatic turn signaling device for vehicles

> The invention disclosed herein relates to preferred methods and apparatuses for an automatic signaling device which automatically activates a warning signal. The following patents form a background for the instant invention. None of the cited publications is believed to detract from the patentability of the claimed invention.
>
> U.S. Pat. No. 3,771,096 issued to Walter on Nov. 6, 1973, discloses a lane changing signaling device for vehicles employing a rotary electrical connector joined to the steering wheel. The principal disadvantage of the device is that it fails to measure the angle of rotation of the steering wheel.

Detailed description of the preferred version of the invention. This is a detailed description of an actual, "nuts and bolts" version of the current invention ("embodiment" in patent terms). It is essentially the inventor's best-guess (preferred embodiment) description of the product at the time the patent application is written. By reading the detailed description, a person who is familiar with similar products should be able to build and operate the current invention. It is important to note that the legal scope of the patent is not defined (the language of patents calls it "limited") by the details of the description of the preferred embodiment. Rather, the scope of the patent is actually determined by the claims.

The first paragraph of the detailed description of the preferred embodiment for Pat. No. 5,462,805 is shown below. Reading through the description, we see that specific numbered elements of Figure 1.1 (from Pat. No. 5,462,805) are referenced. This figure is shown as Figure 1.4 below. Here we have a glass plate (Element 10), another glass plate (Element 11), an intermediate resin layer (Element 12), and first and second adhesive layers (Elements 13 and 14). By following along with the detailed description, and matching the numbered elements of the description with the labeled elements of the drawing, a person familiar with fire safety glass would be able to construct this invention.

Description of the preferred embodiment for a fire safety glass panel

Referring to FIG. 1, a fire-protection and safety glass panel according to a preferred embodiment of this invention comprises a first glass plate 10, a second glass plate 11 opposite to the first glass plate, and an intermediate resin layer between the first and second glass plates 10 and 11. At least one of the first and the second glass plates 10 and 11 is a heat-resistant glass plate. The intermediate resin layer comprises a polyethylene terephthalate film (namely, a PET film) 12 and first and second adhesive agent layers 13 and 14 and has a thickness which is not greater than 200 μm. The first adhesive agent layer 13 adheres the PET film 12 to the first glass plate 10.

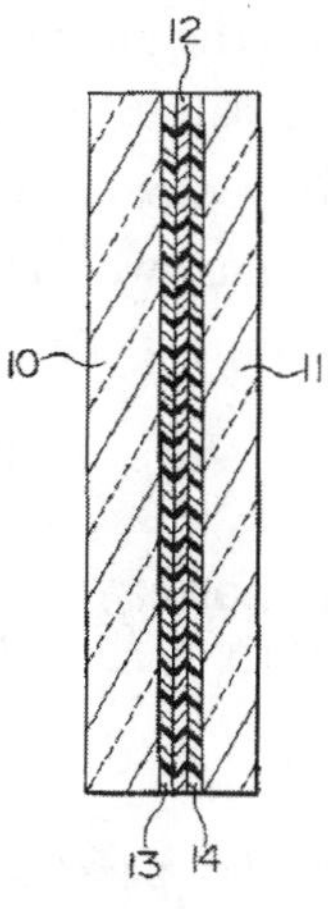

FIG. 1

Claims. Patent claims are a series of carefully worded statements that precisely describe and define the underlying invention. Patent claims operate in much the same way as real estate deeds—they precisely delimit the scope of the patent in the same way as the real estate deed describes the precise location of the property.

From the patent applicant's viewpoint, the claims should be as broad as possible, thus covering many possible versions of the same basic invention. Broad claims make it difficult for someone to defeat the patent by making a minor change to the invention. On the other hand, if patent claims are too broad, there is always the possibility of someone finding a previous invention (prior art reference) that falls within the patent's scope. This could make the patent susceptible to being ruled invalid if the patent holder ever finds it necessary to bring an infringement case.

The first claim from the fire safety glass patent (5,462,805) is shown below. While calling out the same elements of the invention as described in the preferred embodiment, the specific element references have been omitted. This is because the claim is meant to be general enough to include different designs based upon the same invention concept.

You will note that here that the glass plates are referred to as "low-expansion crystallized glass." This is broad enough to include many types of glass that do not readily expand when exposed to heat. If a specific type of low-expansion glass were claimed, then the patent could be "worked around" by simply claiming a different type of low-expansion glass.

Claims for a fire safety glass panel

What is claimed is:

1. A fire-protection and safety glass panel comprising a first glass plate, a second glass plate opposite to said first glass plate, and an intermediate resin layer between said first and said second glass plates, at least one of said first and said second glass plates being a low-expansion crystallized glass plate of a low-expansion crystallized glass, wherein said intermediate resin layer comprises a polyethylene terephthalate film, a first adhesive agent layer for adhering said polyethylene terephthalate film to said first glass plate, and a second adhesive agent layer for adhering said polyethylene terephthalate film to said second glass plate, said intermediate resin layer having a thickness which is not greater than 200 μm.

The Prior Art Aspect of a Previously Issued Patent Is Larger Than the Patent's Claims

Every patent includes claims. Novice inventors often confuse the claims of a patent with the concept of prior art anticipation. Don't make the mistake of thinking that if an aspect of your invention hasn't been "claimed" in a prior patent, you can claim it. The claims of the patent only define the legal scope of the inventor's intellectual property, and if a claim is violated (infringed upon), an inventor has offensive legal rights and can sue the infringer.

In general, incremental changes are considered obvious since the results could be easily predicted by someone skilled in the related field, whereas changes that produce new and unexpected results are considered nonobvious. Oftentimes, new inventions combine elements from two or more previous inventions. Here, the end result must also produce a new and unexpected outcome.

For example, electrical circuits can carry alternating currents. A square piece of iron has certain magnetic field properties due to its composition. By combining the two via electrical windings on opposite legs of the iron square, you can create a transformer. By varying the number of turns in the primary and secondary windings (the primary winding is on the voltage supply side of the iron core) you obtain either a voltage increase or decrease (a step-up or a step-down transformer). This is a new and unexpected result.

Patents Are Intellectual Property

A patent falls under the larger umbrella of intellectual property which also includes trademarks, trade secrets, and copyrights. Intellectual property refers to anything of value created by the human mind. Depending on your invention, one of these other forms of intellectual property may give you additional and/or greater offensive legal rights.

A **trademark** is any symbol, word, or other signifier that consumers associate with a particular product or service. Often, trademarks become as valuable as the innovation itself—for example, the Club, the Segway, or the Hula Hoop.

A **trade secret** is any information that, by being kept a secret, gives its owner a competitive business advantage. There may be elements, formulas, or methods associated with your invention that are not part of your patent application that are your trade secrets—for example, you may have a secret method of creating tooling for the manufacture of your innovation.

Copyright law protects the expressive works of authors, computer programmers, movie producers, and other artistic creators. Certain elements associated with your invention may be copyrightable—for example, artwork affixed to the exterior, software programs used in the creation of the device, or the commercial for your product that you may eventually post online.

CHAPTER

2

Understanding Patent Databases

In order to get the most benefit from a word-based computer search, it is useful to first understand how searchable databases are put together. Creating a computer database is basically a two-step process. First, the information has to be entered into the computer. Then, the information has to be processed by a special kind of computer program so that the information can be easily retrieved in a meaningful form.

How Information Is Entered Into the Database

Information is commonly entered into a computer in two ways: Someone physically types the data in using a keyboard, or someone uses a scanner. A scanner is similar to the everyday copy machine. A page is placed on a surface and a machine records an image of what's on the page and stores that image on the hard disk of the computer. When a document is scanned into a computer, the result is either an image of text, or text that has been extracted from the scanned document by optical character recognition software (OCR).

For the purpose of searching by computer, there is a big difference between an image of a document and actual text. The contents of an image can't be searched; after all, it's just a picture. The computer has no way of knowing what the picture contains. You can pull up the patent on your computer screen the same as any other graphical image, but you can't search for the patent according to the words contained in it. However, if the text in the patent document has been converted by an OCR program before it makes its way into the database, the text can be indexed so that a user can pull up the patent document based on a search of words used in the text.

In this way, a text-based patent database is essentially a huge lookup table. The database program builds this table by searching through all the entered text and extracting all the meaningful words. When you use a computer program to perform a word-based search, the program matches the search words you type in with words stored in its lookup table. The search words that you enter are called "keywords" and the search process is called a keyword search. If the computer finds a match, the program will report back to you the document in which the word was found and, in some cases, the location of the word within the document.

The lookup table ("database" in computer talk) is similar to indexes found in the back of many books. In book indexes, words are listed alphabetically, along with a comma-separated list of each page in the book where the word was used.

Understanding Keyword Searching

When you use a computer program to search for patents, you often must search for them by entering words into a "query" box and asking the search program to match your words with words stored in its database.

As you might expect, performing keyword searches is a skill with a learning curve. Sure, anyone can put one or two words into a box and pull up all the patents with those words. No skill there. But the overall number of patents you pull up is likely to be huge and the number of the patents that are relevant to your search is likely to be low. To pull up a manageable number of patents and to assure that most of them will have some relevance to your own invention, you will need to know at least some of the basic techniques for choosing your search terms and combining them into meaningful search queries.

The Role of Wildcards in Keyword Searching

One powerful tool that is often used during keyword searching is called the wildcard. A wildcard is a special character inserted into your keyword. This character tells the computer search program to do something special with the keyword within which it's used. The two most often used wildcard symbols are the dollar sign "$," and the question mark "?."

The dollar sign wildcard is used at the end of a word root to take the place of any number of additional letters that may come after that root. For example, assume you have invented a new type of dance shoe.

The shoe can be used for ballroom, ballet, and tap dancing. In addition to the keywords "ballroom," "ballet," and "tap," you will certainly want to search for the word "dance." But there are several variations of the word "dance," such as "dancing," "dancer," "danced," and even "danceable." By using "danc$" as your keyword, the dollar sign replaces any other possible characters that would follow the four letters, "danc."

Figure 2.1 shows the search results from searching the titles of U.S. patents issued in the years 1997–1998 for the word "dance." The patent titles that have the word "dance" in them are listed and numbered. As you can see, there are four patents that have the word "dance" in the title. The first title relates to a dance practice slipper, the second title concerns the sole of a dance shoe, the third title relates to a type of dance, and the fourth title relates to a portable dance floor.

Refine Search

ISD/1/1/1997->12/31/1998 and ttl/dance

	PAT. NO.		Title
1	D388,592	**T**	Dance practice slipper
2	5,682,685	**T**	Dance shoe sole
3	PP9,938	**T**	Peach tree "Snow Dance"
4	5,634,309	**T**	Portable dance floor

Figure 2.1

Figure 2.2 contains the search results from searching the titles of U.S. patents issued in the years 1997–1998 for the word "danc$." As you can see, we now have nine patents listed. The first patent listed (Pat. No. 5,827,107) contains the word "dancing" as opposed to "dance."

Refine Search | ISD/1/1/1997->12/31/1998 and ttl/danc$

	PAT. NO.		Title
1	5,827,107	T	Spinning dancing top
2	D388,592	T	Dance practice slipper
3	5,682,685	T	Dance shoe sole
4	5,669,117	T	Buckle for line dancing
5	D382,902	T	Unit for teaching dancing
6	5,659,229	T	Controlling web tension by actively controlling velocity of dancer roll
7	PP9,938	T	Peach tree "Snow Dance"
8	5,634,309	T	Portable dance floor
9	5,602,747	T	Controlling web tension by actively controlling velocity of dancer roll

Figure 2.2

The first four letters (danc) are the same as in the word "dance," but the wildcard ($) was used for the letters "ing." The next two titles are the same ones that we obtained before. However, titles numbered 4 and 5 also contain the word "dancing" as opposed to "dance." Similarly, titles numbered 6 and 9 contain the word "dancer," as opposed to "dance." Here, the wildcard ($) was used for the letters "er."

The question mark (?) wildcard can be used to replace any single character in a word. Continuing with our dancing example, the words "foot" or "feet" could be searched by using "f??t" as our keyword. Obviously, you would not want to use the keyword "f$," as this would return every word that started with the letter "f." By using "f??t," every four-letter word that starts with "f" and ends with "t" would be searched for by the computer. For example, along with the words "feet" and "foot," the words "flat" and "fast" would also be reported to you in the search results.

In Figure 2.3, we show the search results obtained from searching the titles of U.S. patents issued on December 19, 1997 for the word "f??t." The first two patents listed (Pat. Nos. 5,696,609 and 5,696,529), contain the word "flat" in their titles. The next two patents listed (Pat. Nos. 5,696,435 and 5,695,530) contain the word "fast" in their titles.

The fifth and sixth patents listed (Pat. Nos. 5,695,527 and 5,695,526), contain the word "foot" in their titles. The seventh, eighth, ninth, and tenth patents listed (Pat. Nos. 5,695,360; 5,695,359; 5,694,834; and 5,695,792), contain the word "flat" in their titles. Finally, the eleventh patent listed (Design Pat. No. D387,428) contains the word "foot" in the title.

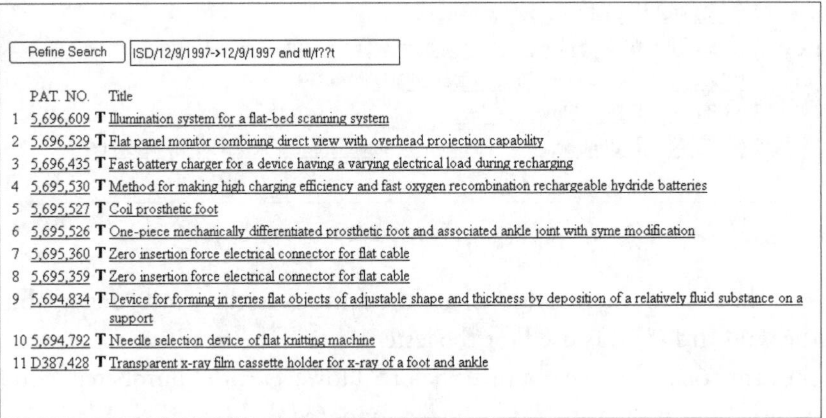

Refine Search | ISD/12/9/1997->12/9/1997 and ttl/f??t

PAT. NO. Title

1 5,696,609 T Illumination system for a flat-bed scanning system
2 5,696,529 T Flat panel monitor combining direct view with overhead projection capability
3 5,696,435 T Fast battery charger for a device having a varying electrical load during recharging
4 5,695,530 T Method for making high charging efficiency and fast oxygen recombination rechargeable hydride batteries
5 5,695,527 T Coil prosthetic foot
6 5,695,526 T One-piece mechanically differentiated prosthetic foot and associated ankle joint with syme modification
7 5,695,360 T Zero insertion force electrical connector for flat cable
8 5,695,359 T Zero insertion force electrical connector for flat cable
9 5,694,834 T Device for forming in series flat objects of adjustable shape and thickness by deposition of a relatively fluid substance on a support
10 5,694,792 T Needle selection device of flat knitting machine
11 D387,428 T Transparent x-ray film cassette holder for x-ray of a foot and ankle

Figure 2.3

The Role of Boolean Logic in Keyword Patent Searching

A search technique known as Boolean logic can be used to combine individual keywords into powerful searches. Boolean logic uses a total of four words (called "logical operators") to define the search: AND, OR, XOR, and ANDNOT. The AND operator is by far the most useful. A graphical representation known as a Venn diagram will help you to understand how these operators work.

In Figure 2.4, we have a circle that has been shaded. The area inside the circle represents all of the patents that contain the keyword represented by the letter A. The area outside the circle represents all the other patents that do not contain the keyword represented by A. In other words, if we were to search a database of patents for all the occurrences of the keyword A, our search results would be contained in the shaded circle.

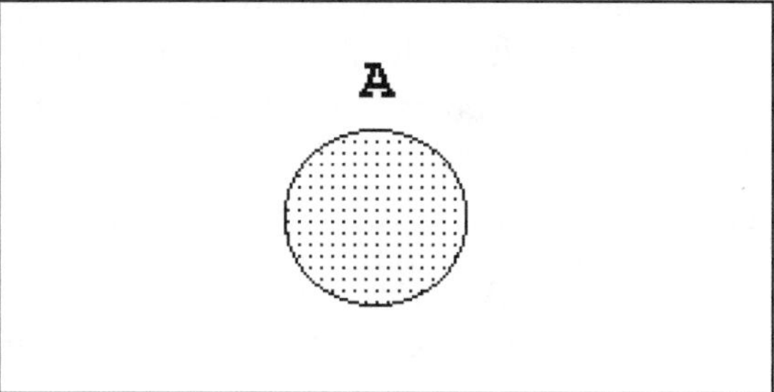

Figure 2.4

In Figure 2.5, we have two keywords represented by the circles A and B. Searching for individual occurrences of the keywords A or B would result in a lot of search results. It would take a long time to review these results and most of them would be irrelevant.

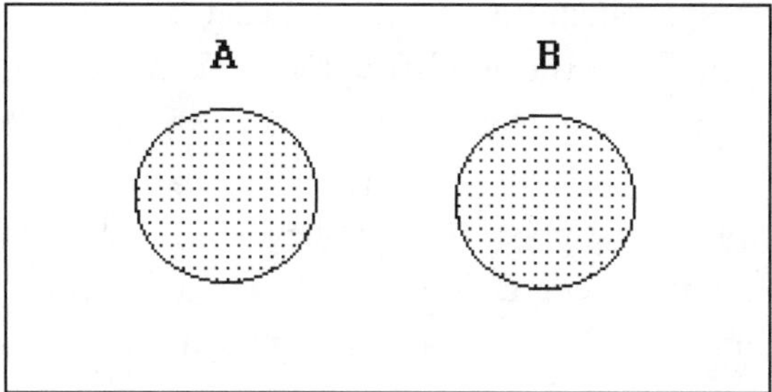

Figure 2.5

For example, let's suppose we have an invention idea for a new type of telephone cable. A search for the keyword "telephone" would return numerous references to different types of telephones. Similarly, a keyword search for the word "cable" would return patents related to cable television, bridge support cables, cable cars, and so on. What we need is a way to search for both the keywords "telephone" and "cable" within the same patent. This is where Boolean operators come into the picture.

The AND Boolean Operator

In Figure 2.6, we have used the Boolean operator AND to combine the keywords A and B. The shaded area where the circles overlap represents the search results that contain both keywords A and B. As you can see, the AND operator is a great way to narrow the scope of the search.

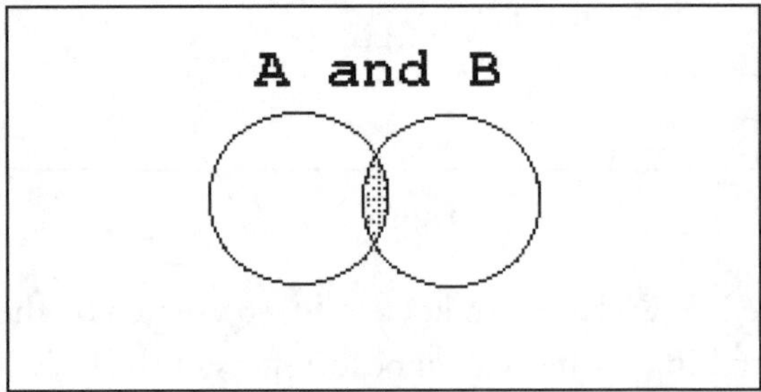

Figure 2.6

When a match is found between a keyword (or a combination of keywords) and a patent, the result is called a "hit." When patent searches are conducted, the number of hits, or occurrences, of a keyword match is usually reported to the user. By using the AND operator, the user reduces the quantity of hits that need to be reviewed.

For example, let's suppose that you have invented a new type of steam engine. A steam engine is a machine for converting the heat energy in steam into mechanical energy by means of a piston moving in a cylinder.

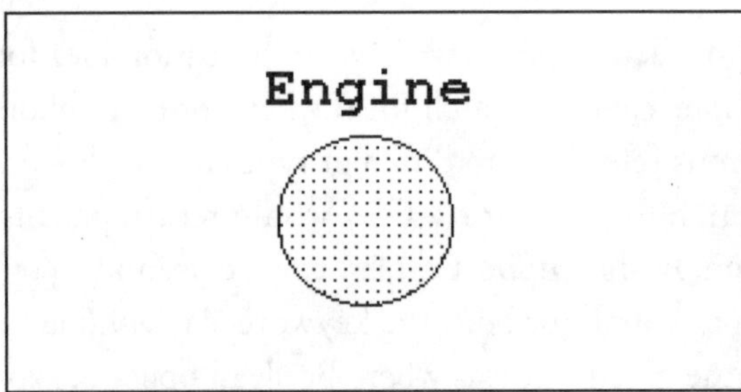

Figure 2.7

The search results using the keyword "engine" are shown in Figure 2.7. The shaded circle represents all of the patents that contain the word "engine." This could be quite an extensive list. For example, all the various types of internal combustion engines would be included in this list. A steam-powered vehicle is an external combustion device; the steam is usually obtained from an external boiler. However, if we only searched for the word "engine," we would have to review search results that contained references to gasoline-powered engines for cars, trucks, trains, and all other engine-powered devices.

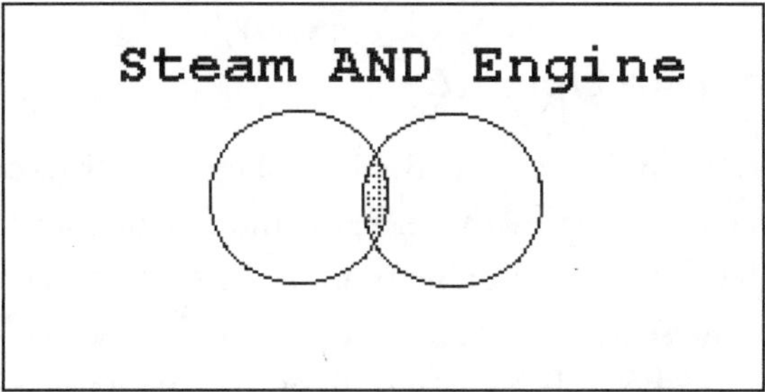

Figure 2.8

Figure 2.8 shows the search result obtained when using the Boolean AND operator to combine the keywords "steam" and "engine." The resulting number of hits is represented by the small shaded area in the diagram, where the two circles overlap. We can see at once why AND is the most often used Boolean operator. It allows the searcher to narrow the scope of the search and obtain more meaningful results.

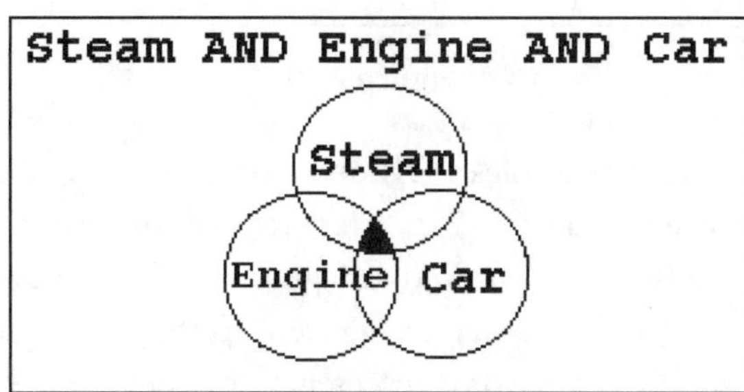

Figure 2.9

In Figure 2.9, we see the results of a search using the keywords "steam," "engine," and "car." In this case, the overlapping area is even more precisely defined. It would be necessary for a patent to contain all three keywords before being reported as a match.

TIP

The more keywords you use with the AND operator, the smaller the number of matches you will obtain, and the more meaningful each match.

The OR Boolean Operator

In Figure 2.10, we have used the Boolean operator OR to combine the keywords represented by the letters A and B. The shaded area within the circle labeled A represents all of the patents that contain the keyword represented by the letter A. Similarly, the shaded area within the circle labeled B represents all of the patents that contain the keyword represented by the letter B.

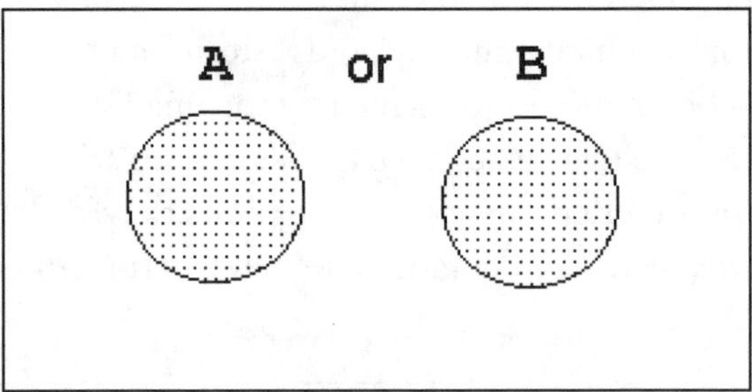

Figure 2.10

When you use the Boolean OR operator, you can't tell from your search results whether a particular reference contains just one of your key words or both. Using our Venn diagrams to represent one possible set of search results, we see that in Figure 2.10 there were no hits that contained both of the keywords represented by the letters A and B. If the search results did have some patents that contained both keywords, the resulting Venn diagram would look like Figure 2.11.

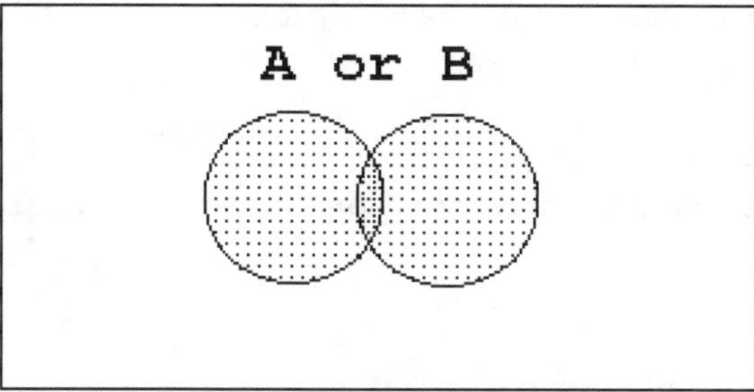

Figure 2.11

In Figure 2.11, we have the two circles A and B, with a small overlapping area. The lightly shaded areas of A and B that do not overlap represent patents that contain only one of our keywords. The heavily shaded, overlapping area represents patents that contain both keywords.

Returning to our steam engine example, Figure 2.12 represents the number of hits returned when we use "steam OR engine" to search the patent database. What this means is that any patent that contained the word "steam" or the word "engine" would be returned as a match. The lightly shaded areas of the circles represent patents that contain the keyword "steam" or the keyword "engine" but not both.

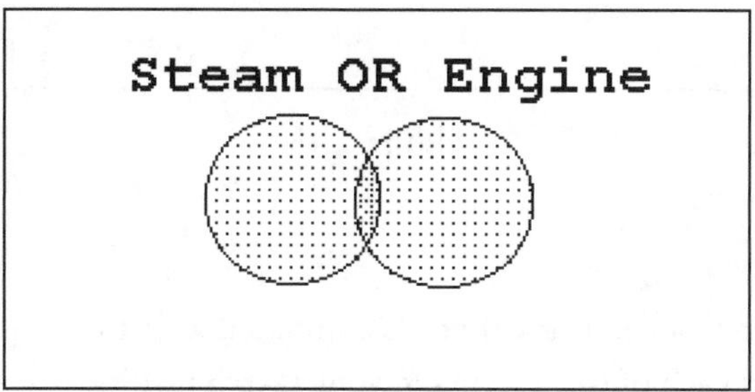

Figure 2.12

The heavily shaded area where the two circles overlap represents patents that contain both keywords. Keep in mind, however, that you couldn't tell this from your research results; the Venn diagrams are only being used to explain what happens in fact.

TIP

Use the OR operator to widen the scope of the search results.

The XOR Boolean Operator

The EXCLUSIVE OR operator is symbolized by the letters XOR. This operator is very similar to the OR operator, but with one important difference: The overlapping area is not included in the search results. So, if we used "steam XOR engine" to search our database, we would obtain a list of patents that contained the word "steam" or the word "engine," but not both.

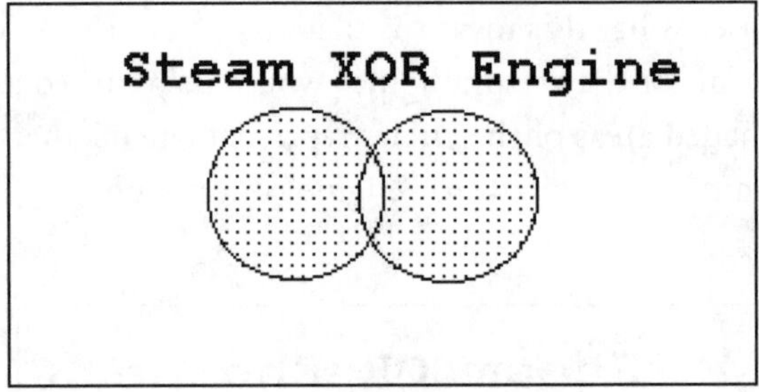

Figure 2.13

TIP

Only one of the keywords combined with the XOR operator will appear in each of the patents in your search results.

The ANDNOT Boolean Operator

The final Boolean operator we will be reviewing is ANDNOT. The ANDNOT operator is actually a combination of the AND and NOT operators. The NOT operator, by itself, simply finds all the patents that do not contain the keyword used. The reason the NOT operator is combined with the AND operator can be seen in Figure 2.14. If you were to use the NOT operator by itself with just the keyword "engine," your search results would include all the patents that do not contain the word "engine"—a very large search result indeed.

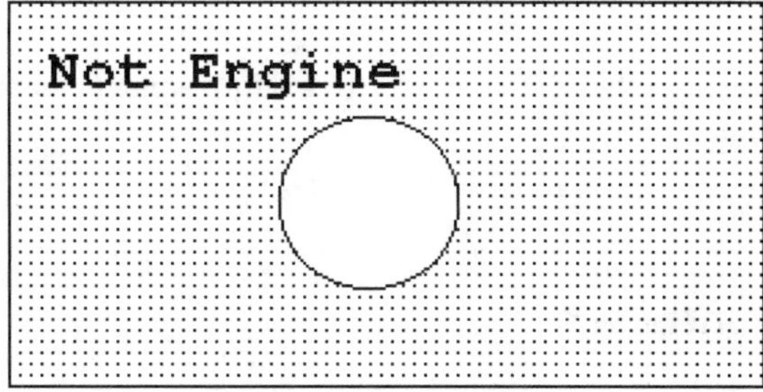

Figure 2.14

An example of the correct use of the ANDNOT operator is shown in Figure 2.15. If you wanted to search for steam engines used in all devices except trains, you could compose this query: (steam AND engine) ANDNOT train.

This would return a list of patents related to steam engines but it would not return patents with the word "train" (regardless of whether train was used as a verb or noun). This is true even if the words "steam" and "engine" were contained within a train-related patent. Figure 2.15 shows the search results obtained when using this query. The resulting number of hits is again represented by the small shaded area in the diagram where the circles representing the keywords "steam" and "engine" overlap. However, a small section of that overlapping area has been excluded. This excluded area represents the patents that contain the keyword "train."

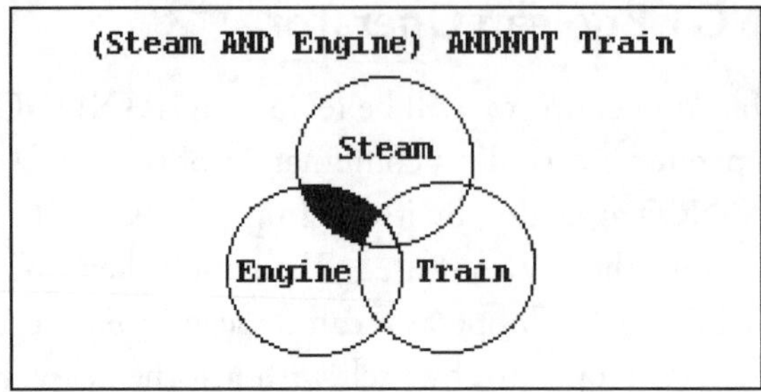

Figure 2.15

TIP

Use the ANDNOT operator to exclude specific keywords from the search results.

Use of Parentheses

In the previous query, you may have noticed that we have made use of left and right parentheses—( )—around the words "steam AND engine." This means that the words within the parentheses are evaluated first, then the ANDNOT condition is applied.

You can also combine wildcards with Boolean operators. Returning to our dance shoe example, we can combine the keyword "danc$," with the keyword "shoe," and exclude the keyword "tap" with the following query: (danc$ AND shoe) ANDNOT tap.

The resulting patents would have the words "shoe" and one or more words like "dancing," "dancer," or "dance," but not the word "tap."

What You Need to Search Patent Databases

In order to carry out your preliminary patent search, you will need a computer that is connected to the Internet. Typically, most people connect to the Internet either by residential phone lines or through faster broadband systems. A broadband system uses either a cable connection or a DSL connection. Ideally, you would want access to the speediest Internet connection possible, but any Internet connection speed will work if you have patience. As you are probably aware, you connect to the Internet using a software program called a browser, the most popular of which is Microsoft's Internet Explorer.

What If You Know Nothing About Computers?

Even if you don't own a computer and don't know anything about how computers operate, you can still perform the basic searches described in this book. All it takes is access to a computer and a lesson or two from someone who can show you the basics of Internet surfing. To put it bluntly, it does not require much brain power to surf the Net (as you will soon realize once you are connected). A great place to start the learning process is your local public library, which probably offers Internet access as well as basic instructions in use.

Also, although not essential for patent searches, you should have a professional word processing program installed on your system. Later in this book, we will be using a word processor to assemble a summary of our patent search results. Although small word processing programs, such as *Notepad* and *Wordpad*, usually ship with Windows, these programs lack the tools that a full-blown word processing application has. We recommend installing Microsoft *Word for Windows* or *WordPerfect*. Both of these programs have spell-checking capability and a thesaurus. A thesaurus comes in handy when you're trying to think of words that describe your invention.

An essential (and free) program that you should use for patent searching is the Adobe *Reader*. As we shall see later in this book, the Adobe format is widely used by many U.S. patent database systems and by the European PTO (EPO) website. The Adobe *Reader* can be freely downloaded from www.adobe.com.

Using a PTDL as an Alternative to Searching on the Internet

As an alternative to using the Internet, if you happen to live near Alexandria, Virginia, you can perform patent searches at the PTO itself. The patent search room is located at: Madison East, 1st Floor, 600 Dulany Street, Alexandria, Virginia, 22314. The hours of business are: weekdays (except holidays) from 8:00 a.m. to 8:00 p.m. For information, call 571-272-3275. For the rest of us, there is the PTDL System. A network of more than 80 PTDLs are located in 49 states, the District of Columbia, and Puerto Rico. (See Appendix A for a list of PTDLs, showing locations and telephone numbers.) The PTDL system provides access to many of the same products and services offered at the PTO in Arlington, Virginia. The scope of the various patent collections, the hours of operations, and available services vary from location to location. In Part III of this book, we show you how to use the PTDL and its many useful resources.

Part II:

Simple and Advanced Searching

Part II consists of five chapters. The first two chapters—Chapters 3 and 4—explain how to perform preliminary patent searches at the PTO website. Chapter 5 discusses the European Patent Office (EPO) website. Chapter 6 provides information about Google's patent search engine and the patent searching capabilities available at the Intellectual Property Office of Singapore. Finally, Chapter 7 explores some other important prior art search resources such as Internet search engines and government websites.

CHAPTER

3

Patent Searching at the PTO Website

Okay, it's time to try some actual patent searches at the PTO's patent search website, which—although you can get to it from the PTO's general website—is actually a separately maintained website.

Simple Keyword Searches at the PTO's Website

We'll start with a simple keyword search at the PTO's patent search website. This site allows you to search the full text and drawings of all patents issued since 1976. The full-page images of patents since 1790 are also available for viewing. Furthermore, you can search patent applications published since March 15, 2001.

Connecting to the PTO's Website

In order to get to the PTO's patent searching website, type www.uspto.gov/patft in the address window of your web browser. You should soon see the homepage for the PTO's patent searching site, as shown in Figure 3.1.

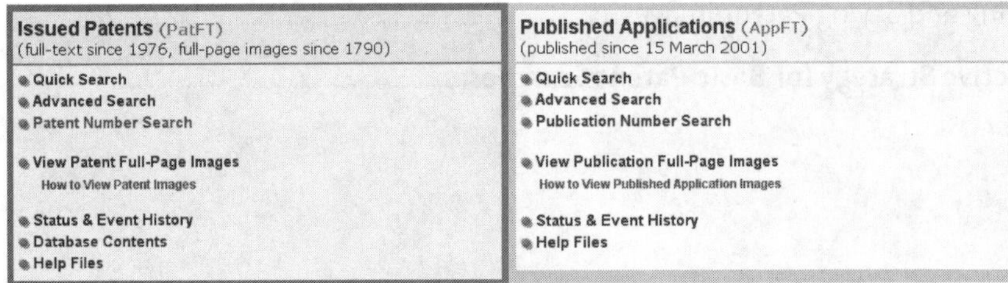

Figure 3.1

There are two databases available for searching at the PTO's patent search website: the PatFT (Patent Full Text) database and the AppFT (Patent Applications Full Text). In this chapter, we will be dealing with the PatFT database. The PatFT database is actually a combination of two separate databases—one, which lets you search the full text of patents issued since 1976, and another, which lets you search the full-page images of patents issued from 1790 through 1975.

Understanding the PTO's Quick Search Page

To perform a quick search of the PatFT database, click on the "Quick Search" link illustrated in Figure 3.1. You will then be presented with the Web page shown in Figure 3.2. As you can see from Figure 3.2, there are several fields that can be filled in. We will discuss them one at a time.

Query [Help]

Term 1: in Field 1: All Fields

AND

Term 2: in Field 2: All Fields

Select years [Help]

1976 to present [full-text] Search Reset

Patents from 1790 through 1975 are searchable only by Patent Number and Current US Classification!

Figure 3.2

The first area that we want to address is the "Select years" dropdown menu (seen in the lower left of Figure 3.2). To make a selection, click on the dropdown arrow (v). The result is shown in Figure 3.3. There are two selections to choose from:

- **1976 to present [full-text].** The current selection is set to "1976 to present [full-text]." Using this setting will allow you to search through every word contained in every patent issued since January 1, 1976.
- **1790 to present [entire database].** This selection will allow you to search through the full text of patents since 1976, and the images of patents from 1790 through 1975.

Note that for patent image data from 1790 through 1975, only three fields can be searched. These three fields are the issue date, patent number, and the current classification. Issue date can be in the form of month/day/year. Patent numbers must be seven characters in length, excluding commas, which are optional.

What this effectively means is that your keyword search for this range of years will only be applied to the Current US Classification field.

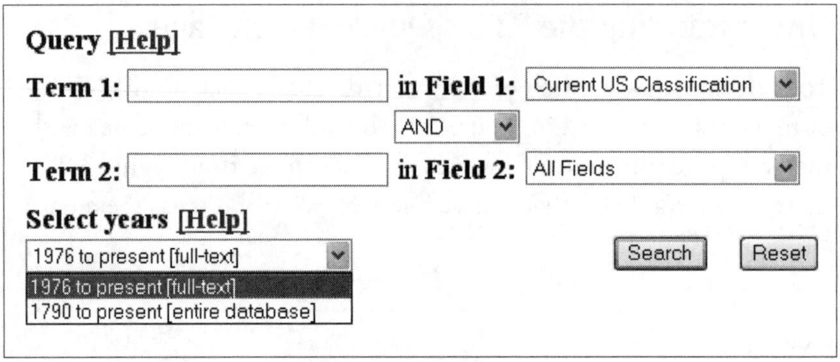

Query [Help]

Term 1: **in Field 1:** Current US Classification

AND

Term 2: **in Field 2:** All Fields

Select years [Help]

1976 to present [full-text]

1976 to present [full-text]

1790 to present [entire database]

Search Reset

Figure 3.3

On the right side of Figure 3.3 are two field selection dropdown menus. By positioning your mouse over the arrow and clicking once, you can see all of the searchable fields of the patent database that are available. This action is shown in Figure 3.4.

With these field selections you can limit the scope of your search to a particular section of the issued patent. For example, if you only wish to search the abstract of the patent, you can scroll down with your mouse to that entry point. The item will be highlighted, and you can then click to select it.

To search the entire text of all the issued patents in the years 1976 to the present, select the entry 'All Fields' (as shown in Figure 3.4) and leave the "Select years" dropdown set to the default selection, "1976 to present [full-text]."

Limiting your search to certain sections of the issued patent has several advantages, the most significant being that you can precisely define your search in order to find just the patents you are looking for and nothing extra.

In the center of Figure 3.4 is the operator selection dropdown menu. To see the available Boolean operators that can be used to combine your search keywords, select this menu. This action is shown in Figure 3.5. By clicking the down arrow, you will be able to choose among the three Boolean operators (AND, OR, and ANDNOT) that we discussed in Chapter 2. For the purposes of this first search, let's select the AND operator, which is the default.

Query [Help]

Term 1:		in Field 1:	All Fields
		AND	All Fields Title Abstract Issue Date Patent Number Application Date Application Serial Number Application Type Assignee Name Assignee City Assignee State Assignee Country International Classification Current US Classification Primary Examiner Assistant Examiner Inventor Name Inventor City Inventor State Inventor Country Government Interest Attorney or Agent PCT Information Foreign Priority Reissue Data Related US App. Data Referenced By Foreign References Other References Claim(s)
Term 2:		in Field 2:	

Select years [Help]

1976 to present [full-text]

Patents from 1790 through 1975 are searchable only b... US Classification!

Figure 3.4

Query [Help]

Term 1:		in Field 1:	All Fields
		AND AND OR ANDNOT	
Term 2:			All Fields

Select years [Help]

1976 to present [full-text]

Search | Reset

Figure 3.5

Doing the Search

To the left of the operator selection dropdown in Figure 3.5 are the search term entry boxes. Here is where you enter your search words (keywords). For example, let's suppose that your invention is related to a device that is involved in fire protection. You could type in "fire" for the first search term, select the logical operator AND, and enter "protection" for the second search term. The field selections could be set to All Fields and the Select years dropdown set to 1976 to present. This is shown in Figure 3.6.

Query [Help]

Term 1: fire in **Field 1:** All Fields

AND

Term 2: protection in **Field 2:** All Fields

Select years [Help]

1976 to present [full-text] Search Reset

Figure 3.6

Now we are ready to begin our search. The search program will search for the terms "fire" and "protection" in all the fields of all the patents issued between the years 1976 and the present. To start the search, click on the button labeled Search, located at the lower right of the screen (as shown in Figure 3.6). Adjacent to the Search button is the Reset button. Clicking on this button will clear all of the entries and selections that you have made. This comes in handy when starting a new search. You should receive your search results within 30 seconds, depending on your connection speed and the Internet traffic.

Understanding the Search Results

The results of our search are shown in Figure 3.7. Under the heading "US Patent Collection Results of Search db for: fire AND protection," the system has reported 23,442 hits or patents in which our two search terms were found. Keep in mind that with the use of the AND Boolean operator, both search terms—"fire" and "protection"—must be present for the system to report a match.

Results of Search in US Patent Collection db for:
fire AND protection: 23442 patents.
*Hits **1** through **50** out of **23442***

Next 50 Hits

Jump To

Refine Search   fire AND protection

	PAT. NO.		Title
1	7,426,437	T	Accident avoidance systems and methods
2	7,426,436	T	High-performance server architecture, methods, and software for spatial data
3	7,426,429	T	Smart seatbelt control system
4	7,426,422	T	Wood tracking by identification of surface characteristics
5	7,426,190	T	System and method for a communication protocol for wireless sensor systems including systems with high priority asynchronous message and low priority synchronous message
6	7,425,780	T	Safety interface system
7	7,425,677	T	Closed electrical enclosure
8	7,425,676	T	Coaxial cable for exterior use
9	7,425,670	T	Methods and compositions for protein production in tobacco plants with reduced nicotine
10	7,425,631	T	Compounds and methods of use
11	7,425,545	T	Modulation of C-reactive protein expression
12	7,425,544	T	Modulation of eIF4E expression

Figure 3.7

Why so many hits? The reason is that because we selected All Fields in our Field settings. Therefore, the search results reflect any patent in which the terms "fire" and "protection" occur anywhere in the issued patent.

Figure 3.7 illustrates a major source of frustration for novice patent searchers. How do you search through such a large number of patents? However, this frustration can quickly be eliminated with a more focused search.

In Figure 3.8, we changed the All Fields settings to Title. The results of our new search are shown in Figure 3.9. Here we see that by limiting our keyword search to the Title field only, the number of hits has been reduced from 23,442 to 237.

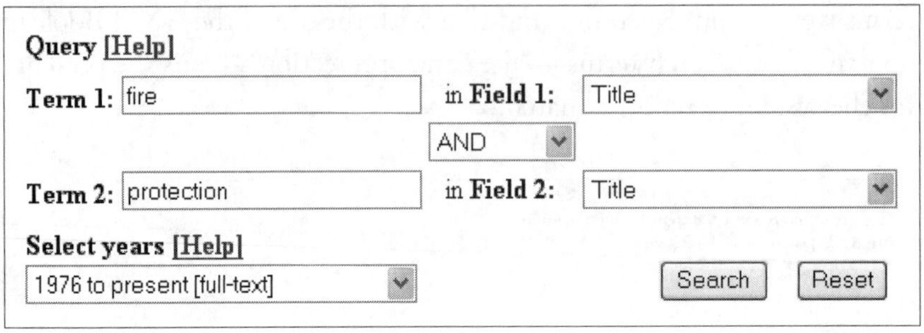

Query [Help]

Term 1: fire in **Field 1:** Title

AND

Term 2: protection in **Field 2:** Title

Select years [Help]

1976 to present [full-text] Search Reset

Figure 3.8

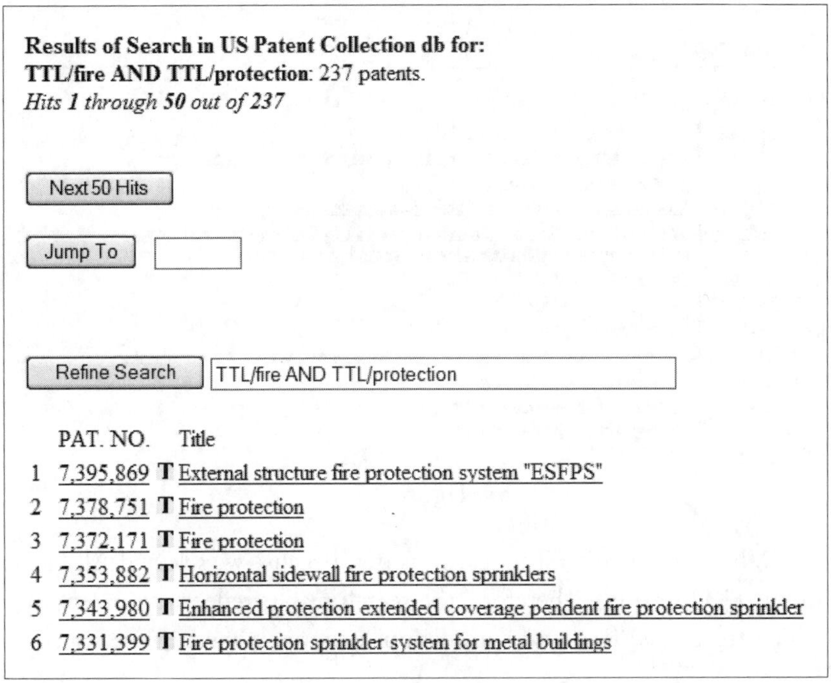

Results of Search in US Patent Collection db for:
TTL/fire AND TTL/protection: 237 patents.
Hits 1 through 50 out of 237

Next 50 Hits

Jump To

Refine Search TTL/fire AND TTL/protection

	PAT. NO.		Title
1	7,395,869	T	External structure fire protection system "ESFPS"
2	7,378,751	T	Fire protection
3	7,372,171	T	Fire protection
4	7,353,882	T	Horizontal sidewall fire protection sprinklers
5	7,343,980	T	Enhanced protection extended coverage pendent fire protection sprinkler
6	7,331,399	T	Fire protection sprinkler system for metal buildings

Figure 3.9

Reading the search summary, we see that hits 1 through 50 of 237 are listed. Looking below the "PAT. NO." and "Title" headings in the middle of Figure 3.9, we see the matching patents. Notice that the patent numbers start with the most recently issued (highest number) patent first and then proceed back in time.

Each of these listed patent numbers is accompanied by a patent title. If you don't find what you are looking for in the first 50 hits, you can select the Next 50 Hits button (shown at the top of Figure 3.9) to see the next 50 matches. Note that only the first seven patents are shown in Figure 3.9.

Saving and Printing the Search Results

You can get a printout of the displayed patent numbers and titles by using your browser's print feature. Simply move your mouse to the File menu item at the upper-left corner of your browser and click once, then scroll down and select the Print function. This action is demonstrated in Figure 3.10.

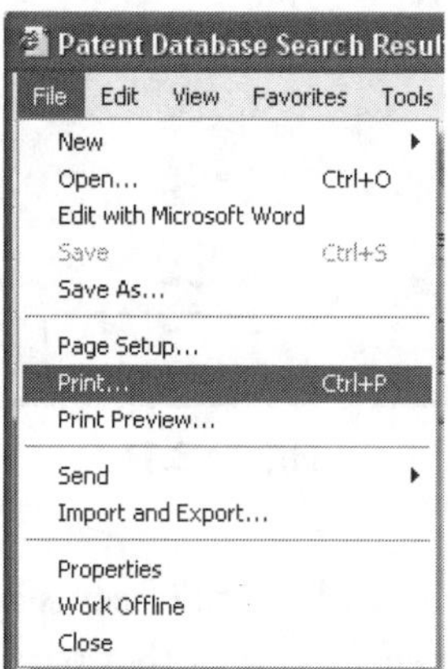

Figure 3.10

When you select the Print function, a printer control window similar to the one shown in Figure 3.11 will open up. To obtain your printout, just click the Print button at the bottom of the window.

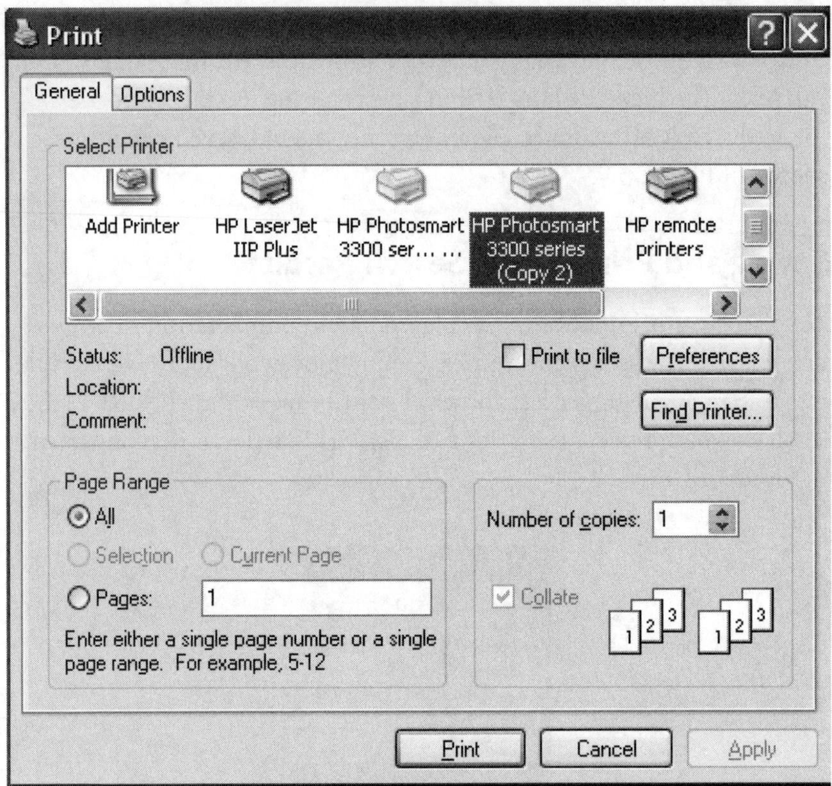

Figure 3.11

When you find a patent whose title seems appropriate to your search, you can view the entire text of that patent by simply clicking on that title. This is because the search result displayed is actually a list of hypertext links. Let's suppose that after selecting the Next 50 Hits button a couple of times, we see that Pat. No. 5,462,805 is one that we are interested in. This is Item 132 as shown in Figure 3.12. To view the front page of this patent, just select the link with the mouse and click once.

127 5,524,616 **T** Method of air filtration for fire fighter emergency smoke inhalation protection
128 5,518,638 **T** Fire extinguishing and protection agent
129 5,505,383 **T** Fire protection nozzle
130 5,495,894 **T** Fire protection filter
131 5,467,923 **T** Method and device for the monolithic application of a thermal-insulation and/or fire-protection compound to a surface
132 5,462,805 **T** Fire-protection and safety glass panel
133 5,433,991 **T** Reinforcement system for mastic intumescent fire protection coatings comprising a hybrid mesh fabric
134 5,423,150 **T** Automated exterior fire protection system for building structures
135 5,396,715 **T** Microwave clothes dryer and method with fire protection
136 5,392,993 **T** Fire protection nozzle
137 5,378,530 **T** Device for protection against fire, made of endothermic flexible material

Figure 3.12

The full text of the patent will then be displayed, as shown in Figure 3.13. Here, you can review the inventor's name, patent issue date, and patent abstract. By scrolling down the page, you can see the current classification of this patent. This is shown in Figure 3.14. Scrolling down further, we see a list of referenced patents (Figure 3.15). These are the patents that were determined to be the prior art for Pat. No. 5,462,805.

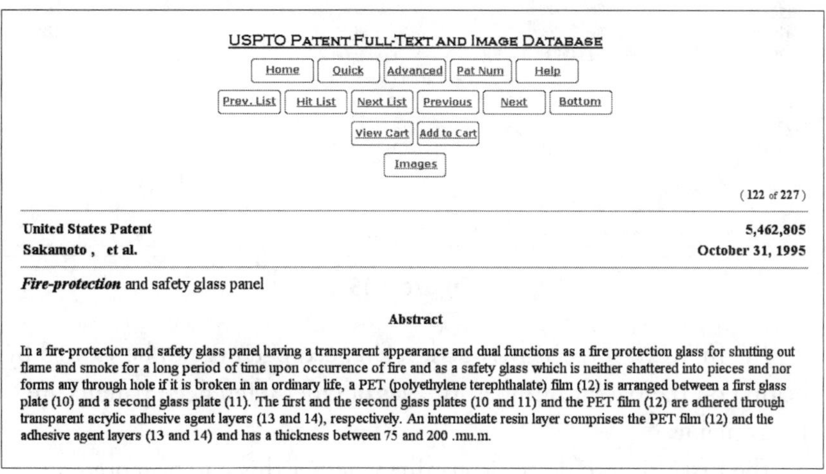

USPTO PATENT FULL-TEXT AND IMAGE DATABASE

Home | Quick | Advanced | Pat Num | Help

Prev. List | Hit List | Next List | Previous | Next | Bottom

View Cart | Add to Cart

Images

(122 of 227)

United States Patent **5,462,805**
Sakamoto , et al. **October 31, 1995**

Fire-protection and safety glass panel

Abstract

In a fire-protection and safety glass panel having a transparent appearance and dual functions as a fire protection glass for shutting out flame and smoke for a long period of time upon occurrence of fire and as a safety glass which is neither shattered into pieces and nor forms any through hole if it is broken in an ordinary life, a PET (polyethylene terephthalate) film (12) is arranged between a first glass plate (10) and a second glass plate (11). The first and the second glass plates (10 and 11) and the PET film (12) are adhered through transparent acrylic adhesive agent layers (13 and 14), respectively. An intermediate resin layer comprises the PET film (12) and the adhesive agent layers (13 and 14) and has a thickness between 75 and 200 .mu.m.

Figure 3.13

Inventors:	**Sakamoto; Akihiko** (Shiga, JP); **Takahashi; Tadashi** (Shiga, JP); **Ninomiya; Masayuki** (Shiga, JP)
Assignee:	**Nippon Electric Glass Co., Ltd.** (Otsu, JP)
Appl. No.:	**099226**
Filed:	**July 29, 1993**

Foreign Application Priority Data

Jul 30, 1992[JP]	4-223470

Current U.S. Class:	**428/430**; 428/215; 428/410; 428/426; 428/480; 428/911; 428/913; 428/920
Intern'l Class:	B32B 009/00
Field of Search:	428/458,432,437,141,524,480,215,412,410,426,911,913,920 526/87

Figure 3.14

References Cited [Referenced By]

U.S. Patent Documents			
3900673	Aug., 1975	Mattimoe et al.	428/339.
4358329	Nov., 1982	Masuda	156/106.
4382996	May., 1983	Mori et al.	428/442.
4910074	Mar., 1990	Fukawa et al.	428/215.
4911984	Mar., 1990	Parker	428/428.
4952460	Aug., 1990	Beckmann et al.	428/429.
5002820	Mar., 1991	Bolton et al.	428/215.
5091258	Feb., 1992	Moran	428/437.
5091487	Feb., 1992	Hori et al.	526/87.
5145746	Sep., 1992	Tomoyuki	428/458.
5219630	Jun., 1993	Hickman	428/38.
5230954	Jul., 1993	Sakamoto et al.	428/332.
Foreign Patent Documents			
684017	Jul., 1966	BE.	
1905619	Aug., 1970	DE.	
480276	Dec., 1969	CH.	

Primary Examiner: Ryan; Patrick J.
Assistant Examiner: Krynski; William A.
Attorney, Agent or Firm: Hopgood, Calimafde, Kalil & Judlowe

Figure 3.15

The full text of recently issued, referenced patents can be viewed by clicking on the patent number. Images of older referenced patents are also available.

The first thing to do to determine whether this patent represents relevant prior art is to read the abstract of the patent. If it is germane to your invention, then you will want to save this information. Again, you can obtain a hard-copy printout, as discussed above. However, you can also save an electronic copy. To do this, go to the File menu in the upper-left corner of your browser, click once, and scroll down to Save As, as shown in Figure 3.16.

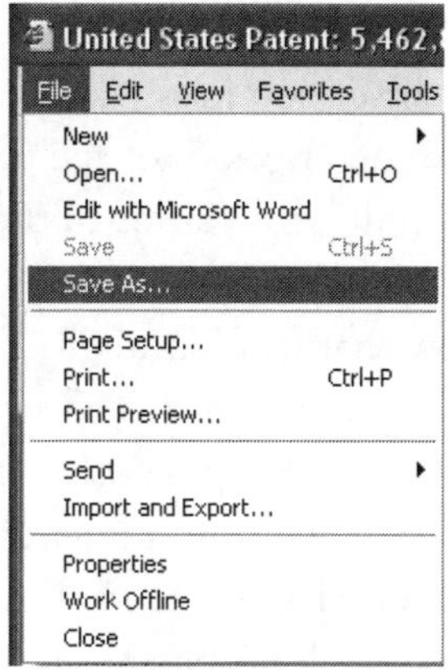

Figure 3.16

When you click Save As, you will have the choice of whether to save the file as an HTML document or a TXT document. An HTML document has special codes in it that allow browser programs to display and link the document with other documents on the Internet. Saving the document in HTML format will preserve the hypertext links. However, you will most likely not need these links since you will be assembling your patent search results in a word processor. Therefore, you should save the file in a TXT format. A TXT format is a common format that any word processor can read.

In addition to the patent abstract, you can determine the class and subclass of the patent from Figure 3.14. The PTO uses classifications to group patents according to their subject matter. In short order, we will see how to use this classification system to jump-start your patent search.

The classes and subclasses of the referenced patents are shown in Figure 3.15. These are arranged in columns. From left to right, the columns represent patent number, issue date, inventor, and major class/subclass—for example, for the referenced Pat. No. 5,230,954, also by Sakamoto, Class 428 and Subclass 332 are listed. Class 428 is also shown in Figure 3.14 as the current classification for this patent.

Searching the *Manual of Classification*

In the previous section, you searched the full text of recently issued patents. You may have gathered information about patented inventions that were similar to your invention idea. This information includes the one-paragraph abstract (or description) of the patent, the class/subclass that the patent was filed under, the claims of the patent, and a detailed description of the patent.

But how do you know that you found all of the relevant classes and patents? The search results that you obtained so far depended entirely on the keywords that you used. Suppose other inventors used different words to describe similar patented inventions. In that case, you may have missed entire classes of related patents. One way to help prevent this from happening is to search for patents according to how they've been grouped by the PTO—that is, by class and subclass.

The document that summarizes all the classes used by the PTO is called the *Manual of Classification*. To search this document, type the following address in the address bar of your Web browser: www.uspto.gov/go/classification (Figure 3.17).

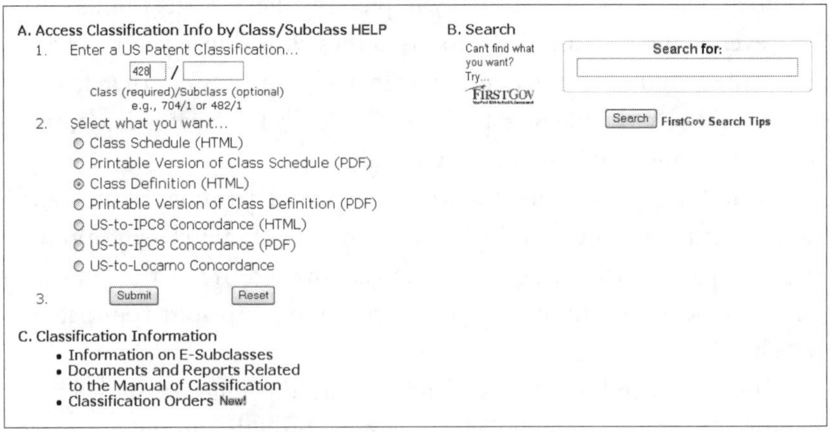

A. Access Classification Info by Class/Subclass HELP
1. Enter a US Patent Classification...
428 /
Class (required)/Subclass (optional)
e.g., 704/1 or 482/1
2. Select what you want...
Class Schedule (HTML)
Printable Version of Class Schedule (PDF)
Class Definition (HTML)
Printable Version of Class Definition (PDF)
US-to-IPC8 Concordance (HTML)
US-to-IPC8 Concordance (PDF)
US-to-Locarno Concordance
3. Submit Reset

B. Search
Can't find what you want? Try...
FIRSTGOV
Search for:
Search FirstGov Search Tips

C. Classification Information
- Information on E-Subclasses
- Documents and Reports Related to the Manual of Classification
- Classification Orders New!

Figure 3.17

Previously, we discovered that the current classification of the Sakamoto patent (Pat. No. 5,462,805) was Class 428. In Figure 3.17, you will notice there is a Section A: Access Classification Info by Class/ Subclass. Under Item 1 (Enter a US Patent Classification), we entered 428 into the Class text entry box. Under Item 2 (Select what you want…) we selected the third radio button (Class Definition (HTML)).

This will allow us to view the class definition for Class 428 as an interactive HTML document in a browser window. To view the *Manual of Classification* entry for Class 428, click the Submit button under Item 3. The results are shown in Figure 3.18.

CLASS 428,STOCK MATERIAL OR MISCELLANEOUS ARTICLES
Click here for a printable version of this file

SECTION I - CLASS DEFINITION

This class accommodates certain products of manufacture which are not provided for in classes devoted primarily to manufacturing methods and apparatus. The bulk of the documents are directed to stock material composites, that is, materials having two or more distinct components which are more ordered than a mere random mixture of ingredients.

Certain finished articles, generally of an ornamental or readily disposable nature, are placed herein when this class specifically provides for them. Unfinished articles, e.g., blanks requiring further significant shaping to be suitable for ultimate use, and stock materials from which an indefinite number of usable portions may be cut, are placed herein unless specifically provided for elsewhere. The determination whether a product is a finished article or a stock material is made on the basis of the amount of structure included in the body of the claims.

Figure 3.18

Figure 3.18 shows the very top of a lengthy document which describes the types of inventions that are classified under Class 428. If you were to print out this class description, it would generate more than 200 pages. That's a lot of pages to print and read! In the next section we will show you how to use the Find feature of your Web browser to greatly simplify this task.

One of the reasons for the length of the class description is the large number of subclasses contained in Class 428. However, we already know that the current classification of the Sakamoto patent is Class 428, subclass 430. Therefore, we can quickly locate the description for subclass 430 by entering 430 into the Subclass text entry box shown in Figure 3.19.

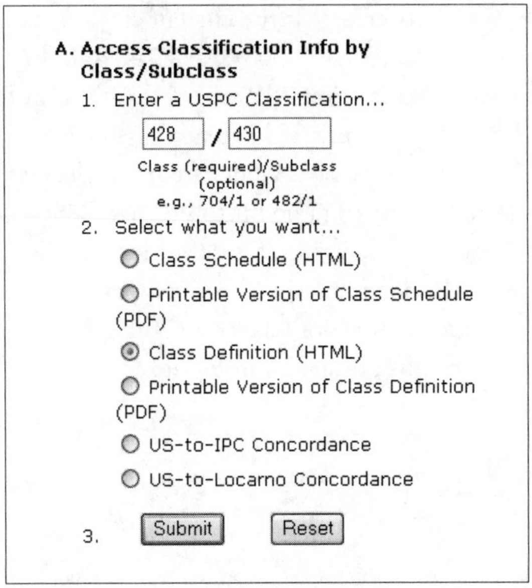

A. Access Classification Info by Class/Subclass

1. Enter a USPC Classification...

428 / 430

Class (required)/Subclass (optional)
e.g., 704/1 or 482/1

2. Select what you want...

- ○ Class Schedule (HTML)
- ○ Printable Version of Class Schedule (PDF)
- ◉ Class Definition (HTML)
- ○ Printable Version of Class Definition (PDF)
- ○ US-to-IPC Concordance
- ○ US-to-Locarno Concordance

3. Submit Reset

Figure 3.19

After clicking the Submit button shown in Figure 3.19 (Item 3), the class/subclass description shown in Figure 3.20 will be displayed. This class description is quite brief, but special notation is made that the subclass is actually indented under a broader subclass numbered 426. In your browser window, the notation of subclass 426 is actually a hypertext link. To see this subclass description, click on the link. The results are shown in Figure 3.21. Reading this further description we can clearly see that subclass 426 is germane to the Sakamoto fire-resistant glass patent.

430Next to polyester (e.g., alkyd)
This subclass is indented under **subclass 426**. Product in which a layer contiguous with quartz or glass contains polyester*.

Figure 3.20

426 **Of quartz or glass**
This subclass is indented under **subclass 411.1**. Product in which at least one layer contains fused silica (i.e., quartz), or a mixture of (1) fused silica, and (2) alkali and alkaline silicates, commonly known as glass.

(1) Note. The glass may be in the form of fibers or as a fiber glass mat.

(2) Note. Such materials as waterglass, isinglass and plexiglass are not considered as glass.

(3) Note. Vitreous enamel or vitreous ceramic, per se, is considered to be glass.

SEE OR SEARCH THIS CLASS, SUBCLASS:

38, for stained glass elements in an aperture or frame.
49, for a unilayer of plural glass sections extending in both lateral and longitudinal directions.
174+, for corrugated fiber glass web or sheet.
312, 317, 325, 392, 406+, 415, and 417, as appropriately entitled, for other products containing glass, in the form of particles, a layer, foam, or fibers.

Figure 3.21

Web Page Locations

The location and content of the PTO's Web pages often changes. The Web address of the *Manual of Classification* is current as of the publication date of this text. However, by the time you read this, the address may have changed. One way to keep abreast of these changes is to go to the main PTO website at www.uspto.gov and look for a link called Site Index. This is usually an updated listing of the location of the PTO's online resources.

Browsing the U.S. Patent Classes

At the top of the PTO's *Manual of Classification* Web page (www.uspto.gov/go/classification) above the Section A entries are a series of navigation aids. To browse through the various major patent classifications, click on the link labeled "Class Numbers & Titles" shown at the top of Figure 3.22. You will then be presented with the Web page illustrated in Figure 3.23.

Class Numbers & Titles | Class Numbers Only

A. Access Classification Info by Class/Subclass

1. Enter a USPC Classification...

[ ] / [ ]

Figure 3.22

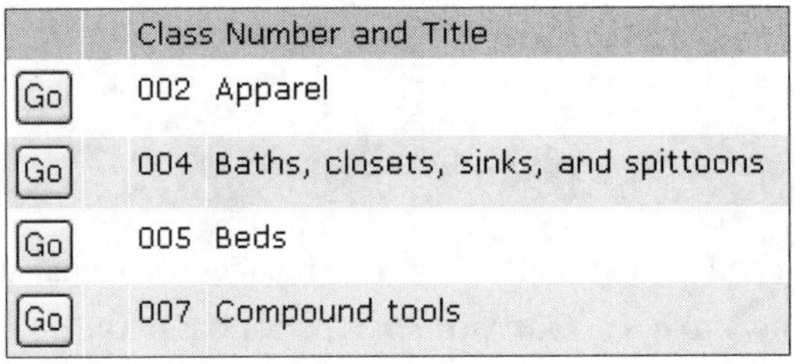

	Class Number and Title
Go	002 Apparel
Go	004 Baths, closets, sinks, and spittoons
Go	005 Beds
Go	007 Compound tools

Figure 3.23

Adjacent to each class number within the listing shown in Figure 3.23 is a "Go" button. This button is actually a link to a description of the referenced class. By scrolling down this Web page, you could read the titles of the various classes until you encountered one or more relevant classes. But, as we explained earlier, there are more efficient methods.

Before continuing, let's stop and ask: What good is this classification information? Suppose you came up with a new idea for a nightlight. Since many nightlights are used in bathrooms, you reason that shining a light off the reflective surfaces of porcelain fixtures (sinks and toilet bowls) would help light up the bathroom. You design your bathroom nightlight to mount to a wall fixture. In order to have the nightlight shine at the appropriate angle, you position the bulb at the end of a flexible support.

It seems simple enough to search for a classification called "lights" or "light." You would think that the PTO should have a huge listing of subclasses under the Class Light. To check this assumption, we will use the Find feature of our browser.

To activate the Find feature, just click on the Edit menu at the top of the browser, then click Find (on This Page), as seen in Figure 3.24 (or, in most browsers, you can simply type CTRL-F).

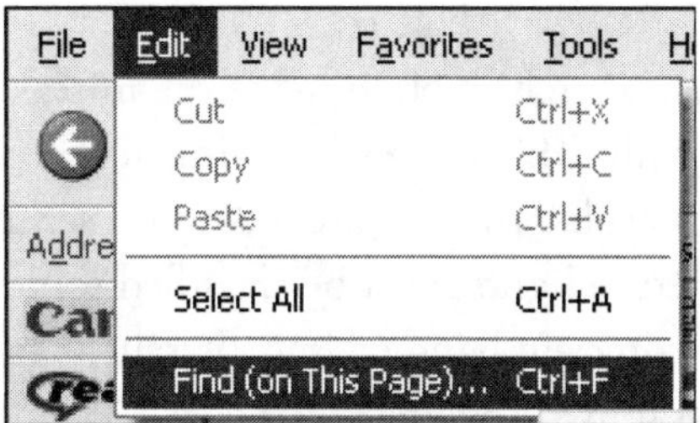

Figure 3.24

After clicking on Find (on This Page), a window similar to the one shown in Figure 3.25 will pop up. This utility will allow you to search for any word occurring in the list of class titles.

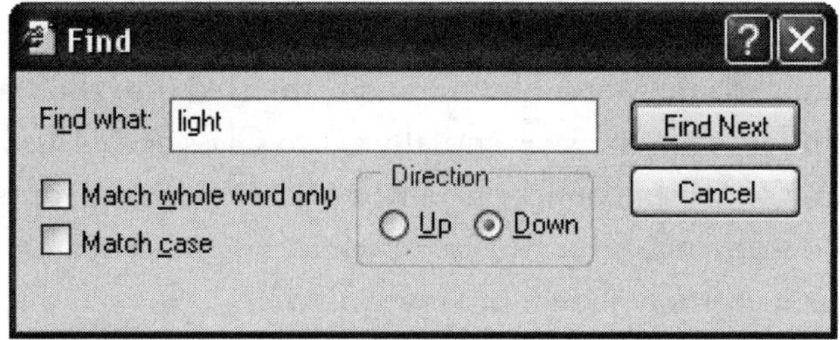

Figure 3.25

To search for the word "light" in the title of any of the classes, enter the word "light" into the Find What box, as shown in Figure 3.25. Make sure the direction radio button is set to "Down" and click "Find Next." Each time the Find function encounters the word "light" in a class title, the word will be highlighted. After viewing each occurrence of the word "light" in a classification title, you can proceed to the next occurrence by clicking "Find Next."

You may be surprised to learn that while there are classifications for lasers (Class 372 Coherent Light Generators) and lights used in Surgery

(Class 607 Light Surgery), there is no major classification using the word "light." How can this be? Isn't the light bulb the universal symbol for a new idea or invention? The case of the word "light" should serve as a warning that the PTO may use a term you don't expect to see for a class title.

First-time patent searchers often make the mistake of searching for obvious keywords only. This has a serious impact on the reliability of their patent search results. In this case, common sense tells us that all of the patents related to lights must be classified somewhere else. This is where a thesaurus comes in handy. Use a thesaurus to find alternatives for the keywords you used the first time.

TIP

Since the PTO may use a term you don't expect for a class/subclass title, always use a thesaurus to find alternative descriptive words for your class titles.

One alternative to the word "light" is "illumination." Trying our search again with the word "illumination" inserted into the search box, as shown in Figure 3.26, we eventually get to Class 362. This is shown in Figure 3.27. (When conducting a new search, position yourself at the top of the document again. Be sure to select the proper search direction with the radio buttons shown in Figure 3.26.)

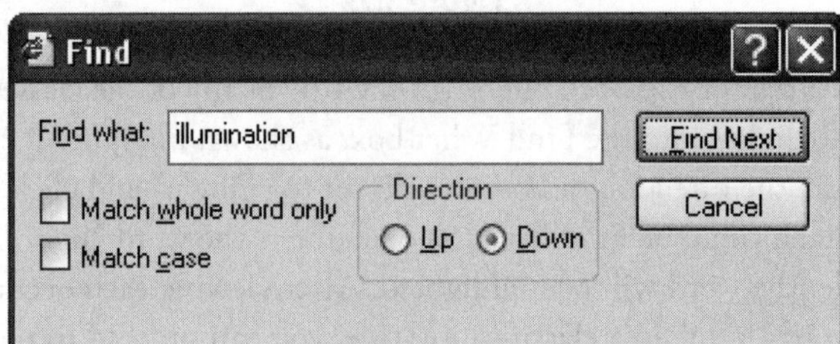

Figure 3.26

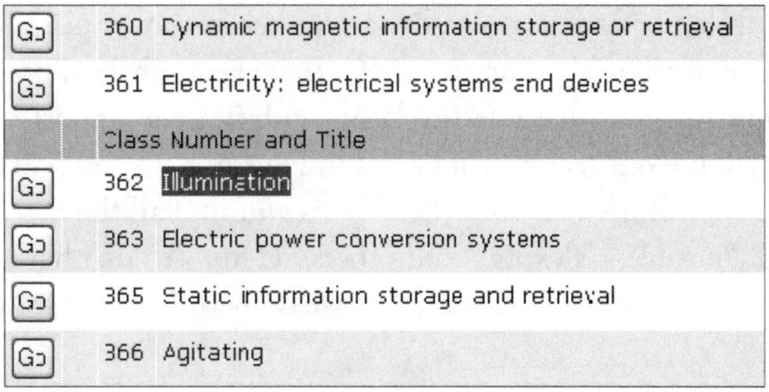

Go	360 Dynamic magnetic information storage or retrieval
Go	361 Electricity: electrical systems and devices
	Class Number and Title
Go	362 Illumination
Go	363 Electric power conversion systems
Go	365 Static information storage and retrieval
Go	366 Agitating

Figure 3.27

Adjacent to each class number within the listing of Figure 3.27 is a "Go" button. As previously stated, this button is actually a link to a description of the referenced class. Therefore, to view a description of the Class 362: Illumination, just click on the adjacent "Go" button. The result is shown in Figure 3.28.

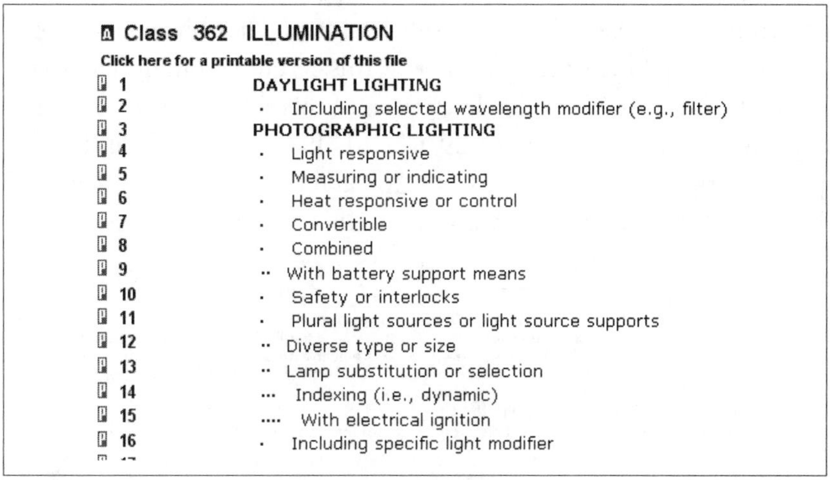

Class 362 ILLUMINATION

Click here for a printable version of this file

1	DAYLIGHT LIGHTING
2	· Including selected wavelength modifier (e.g., filter)
3	PHOTOGRAPHIC LIGHTING
4	· Light responsive
5	· Measuring or indicating
6	· Heat responsive or control
7	· Convertible
8	· Combined
9	·· With battery support means
10	· Safety or interlocks
11	· Plural light sources or light source supports
12	·· Diverse type or size
13	·· Lamp substitution or selection
14	··· Indexing (i.e., dynamic)
15	···· With electrical ignition
16	· Including specific light modifier

Figure 3.28

This Web page shows an indented list of all the subclasses that can be found under Class 362. Reading this entire Web page to see if there is a subclass title that might pertain to your invention could be very time consuming. Instead, we will again make use of your browser's Find feature.

Recall that besides having a light, another feature of our invention was the use of a flexible support. Might there be a subclass, under the class "Illumination," that refers to lights with flexible supports? To find out, we will use our search window as in Figures 3.25 and 3.26, but this time we will use the word "flex." This will find all the derivatives of the word ("flexible," "flexing," and others). Here, we don't have to use a wildcard such as the dollar sign ($), as we do with Boolean searching.

194	· Battery supported separable lamp assembly
195	·· Battery terminal sole support of lamp
196	· Mating-halves type flashlight casing
197	· Lamp bulb or lamp support axis adjustable or angularly fixed relative to axis of flashlight casing
198	·· Flexibly or extensibly mounted lamp bulb or lamp support
199	·· Separate lamp housing or lamp support pivoed to flashlight casing
200	· Flat flashlight casing
201	·· Lamp terminal directly contacts a battery terminal

Figure 3.29

Eventually, our Find function will bring us to subclass 198, as shown in Figure 3.29. This is the subclass titled, "flexibly or extensibly mounted lamp bulb or lamp support." This certainly sounds like what we are looking for. To read a description of this subclass, click on the link on the left side of Figure 3.29, labeled "198." This will load the Web page description for the entire Class 362 and position you at the exact location of the subclass 198 description. This is shown in Figure 3.30.

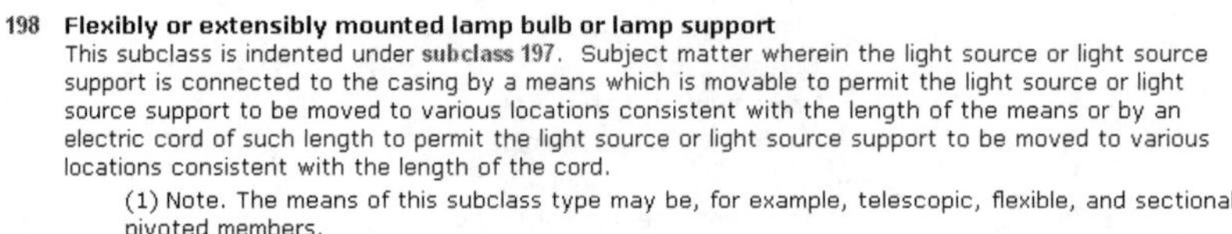

198 Flexibly or extensibly mounted lamp bulb or lamp support

This subclass is indented under **subclass 197**. Subject matter wherein the light source or light source support is connected to the casing by a means which is movable to permit the light source or light source support to be moved to various locations consistent with the length of the means or by an electric cord of such length to permit the light source or light source support to be moved to various locations consistent with the length of the cord.

(1) Note. The means of this subclass type may be, for example, telescopic, flexible, and sectional pivoted members.

Figure 3.30

At this point, we seem to have identified one of the primary classes and subclasses of our invention—namely, Class 362, subclass 198. Wouldn't it be nice to be able to get a comprehensive list of all the patents issued in this class/subclass combination? Well, we can, by using the Quick Search page.

Finding All the Patents Under a Particular Class and Subclass

If we return to the PTO's patent searching website (www.uspto.gov/patft), we can perform our class/subclass search. First, select the Quick Search link (shown at the beginning of this chapter in Figure 3.1).

To search for all the patents in a particular class and subclass, we click the arrow for Field 1 and change the setting from "Any Field" to "Current US Classification." In the Term 1 entry box, we type "362/198." That is, the class 362, followed by a slash, and then the subclass 198.

Next, we need to specify a range of years to search. In this case, for the Select years dropdown menu, let's select "1790 to present" to search the entire patent database. Note that since we are searching the patent classification we can also search through the collection of patent images that are searchable by classification and patent number. These selections and entries are shown in Figure 3.31.

Query [Help]

Term 1: 362/198 in **Field 1:** Current US Classification

AND

Term 2: in **Field 2:** All Fields

Select years [Help]

1790 to present [entire database]

Search Reset

Patents from 1790 through 1975 are searchable only by Patent Number and Current US Classification!

Figure 3.31

After clicking the Search button, the list of patents shown in Figure 3.32 (first three patents only) will be returned. As shown in the figure, there were 166 patents issued between the years 1790 and the present (as of the time of printing of this book) in the Class 362, subclass 198. These are patents issued for inventions that involve a light with a flexible support. Recall that our invention involves a nightlight for the bathroom that casts reflections off the porcelain fixtures.

Results of Search in US Patent Collection db for:
CCL/362/198: 166 patents.
Hits 1 through 50 out of 166

Next 50 Hits

Jump To

Refine Search | CCL/362/198

	PAT. NO.		Title
1	7,419,283	**T**	Electrical decoration lighting device and set of such devices
2	7,399,100	**T**	Pistol adaptation with flashlight attachment
3	7,390,105	**T**	Illuminating book light

Figure 3.32

In reviewing the list of patents (after selecting Next 50 Hits), we see that Item 102, Pat. No. 5,136,476, "Toilet bowl illuminator," sounds similar to our idea (Figure 3.33).

	PAT. NO.		Title
101	5,136,477	**T**	Miniature battery-powered lighting device
102	5,136,476	**T**	Toilet bowl illuminator
103	5,012,394	**T**	Hand portable light with extendable lamp housing
104	4,931,913	**T**	Portable sirening and illumination device

Figure 3.33

To get a listing of the text of this patent, just click on the patent number or title. We are then presented with the text of Pat. No. 5,136,476, issued to D. Horn on August 4, 1992. By reading the patent abstract, as shown in Figure 3.34, we see that some aspects of our idea have been anticipated by the Horn patent. Clearly, Pat. No. 5,136,476 requires further study.

(85 of 149)

United States Patent **5,136,476**
Horn **August 4, 1992**

Toilet bowl illuminator

Abstract

An easily-installed, portable illuminator for the illuminating of toilet bowls is disclosed. More specifically, the illuminator of this disclosure hangs on the rim of a toilet bowl by a tubular conduit through which electrical conductors carry current from a battery pack or other power source external to the bowl and to a light source suspended within the bowl. Light-sensitive and manual switches and current-regulating circuitry are options on advanced embodiments.

Figure 3.34

Searching With a Keyword Query

Another method of finding relevant classes for our invention is to directly search the class descriptions. You can accomplish this by searching the *Manual of Classification* on its Web page, www.uspto.gov/go/classification.

Section B of this Web page is shown in Figure 3.35. This section allows us to search for keywords within the class descriptions. To search for occurrences of the word "illumination" within the various class descriptions, just type the word "illumination" into the query box, as shown in the figure, and click on the Search button.

B. Search

Can't find what you want? Try...

FIRSTGOV

Search for:

illumination

Search **FirstGov Search Tips**

Figure 3.35

A portion of the results are shown in Figure 3.36. After you have collected the most relevant classes, you can return to the Quick Search page and search for all the patents within those classes.

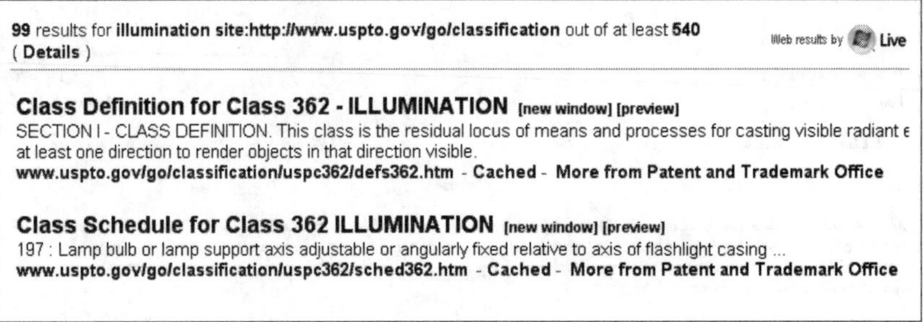

99 results for illumination site:http://www.uspto.gov/go/classification out of at least 540
(Details)
Web results by Live
Class Definition for Class 362 - ILLUMINATION [new window] [preview]
SECTION I - CLASS DEFINITION. This class is the residual locus of means and processes for casting visible radiant e
at least one direction to render objects in that direction visible.
www.uspto.gov/go/classification/uspc362/defs362.htm - Cached - More from Patent and Trademark Office
Class Schedule for Class 362 ILLUMINATION [new window] [preview]
197 : Lamp bulb or lamp support axis adjustable or angularly fixed relative to axis of flashlight casing ...
www.uspto.gov/go/classification/uspc362/sched362.htm - Cached - More from Patent and Trademark Office

Figure 3.36

Search by Patent Number

Let's suppose that you have a patent number and wish to quickly look up a description of that patent. This can come in handy for sudden inspirations or for detailed product research. For example, suppose you are doing some interior decorating and you are working with a stud finder. (Stud finders are used to find the wooden studs hidden behind plasterboard on interior walls.)

After missing a stud and driving a nail through the wall, you decide that there has to be a better design for a stud finder. A quick look at the back of the device you are using reveals a patent number in raised plastic. Wouldn't it be great if you could review a patent document just by typing in a patent number?

The PTO provides just such a feature. Here's how it works. After returning to the main PTO patent search page at www.uspto.gov/patft, you will see the links shown in Figure 3.37. To search by patent number, select the Patent Number Search link.

Issued Patents (PatFT)
(full-text since 1976, full-page images since 1790)

- Quick Search
- Advanced Search
- Patent Number Search

- View Patent Full-Page Images
  How to View Patent Images

- Status & Event History
- Database Contents
- Help Files

Figure 3.37

You will then be presented with the page shown in Figure 3.38. To review a particular patent, just enter the patent number into the query box as shown in the figure, and click on "Search." The results are shown in Figure 3.39.

Enter the patent numbers you are searching for in the box below.

Query [Help]

5,148,108 [Search] [Reset]

All patent numbers must be seven characters in length, excluding commas, which are optional. Examples:

Utility -- 5,146,634 6923014 0000001
Design -- D339,456 D321987 D000152
Plant -- PP08,901 PP07514 PP00003
Reissue -- RE35,312 RE12345 RE00007
Defensive Publication -- T109,201 T855019 T100001
Statutory Invention Registration -- H001,523 H001234 H000001
Re-examination -- RX29,194 RE29183 RE00125
Additional Improvement -- AI00,002 AI000318 AI00007

Figure 3.38

United States Patent	*5,148,108*
Dufour	**September 15, 1992**

Stud finder with level indicator

Abstract

A stud finder includes a magnetic subassembly for detecting the presence of a ferrous metal object, such as the head of a nail or screw, in a wall, with the magnetic subassembly being mounted at one end of a base member. A level vial is mounted at the other end of the base member, and a slot is formed in the base member between the magnetic subassembly and the level vial. When the base member is placed against a wall and the presence of a stud is detected by the magnetic subassembly, the base member is moved to a position in which the level vial indicates level. The slot has its longitudinal axis oriented perpendicular to the longitudinal axis of the level vial, so that the user can place a vertical mark on the wall through the slot. The slot is oriented so as to be in vertical alignment with the nail or screw head, when the base member is moved such that the magnetic subassembly is directly over the nail or screw head. With this arrangement, the mark made on the wall by the user is vertically aligned with the nail or screw head.

Figure 3.39

Working With Patent Images

In addition to searching through the full text of all patents issued since January 1, 1976, you can look at images of each page. Viewing scanned images of issued patents allows you to review the patent drawings. The detailed descriptions of patents contain painstaking references to these patent drawings. By reading the detailed description and referring to each of the numbered elements of the patent drawings, a reviewer can gain a detailed understanding of the patent.

Loading the Image Viewer

The first step to viewing patent images on the PTO's website is to load a separate image viewer program into your computer. The good news is that the program is free and can be downloaded over the Internet. At the main PTO patent search Web page (www.uspto.gov/patft) there is a link titled "How to Access and View Full-Page Images" (Figure 3.40).

Important Notices and Policies -- *Please read!*
How to Access and View Full-Page Images
Problems Using the Databases?
Report Errors in Data Content

Figure 3.40

By clicking on this link, you will be presented with a Web page that provides some background information about PTO-compatible image-viewing programs. Currently, there are two freely available image-viewing programs that will work with the PTO's online database. By scrolling through the above-mentioned Web page you will see links to these programs. These links are shown in Figure 3.41.

The only free, unlimited time TIFF plug-ins offering full-size, unimpeded patent viewing and printing unimpeded by any advertising on **Windows® x86 PCs** of which we are aware are:

- AlternaTIFF: http://www.alternatiff.com/ (tested: IE, Netscape, Opera)
- interneTIFF: http://www.internetiff.com/ (tested: IE, Netscape)

Figure 3.41

To demonstrate how this works, we will install the AlternaTIFF program. Click on the link labeled "AlternaTIFF: …" shown in the center of Figure 3.41. You will then be presented a Web page that will allow you to download the actual image-viewing program. The actual link that you want to click on is about halfway down the Web page (Figure 3.42).

1. ActiveX control, auto-install
For Internet Explorer 4.x and higher.

<Click here to go to the installation page>

Figure 3.42

After clicking this link, you should see the AlternaTIFF installation Web page shown in Figure 3.43. To install the viewer, click on the "Auto-install AlternaTIFF ActiveX control" link shown at the bottom of Figure 3.43.

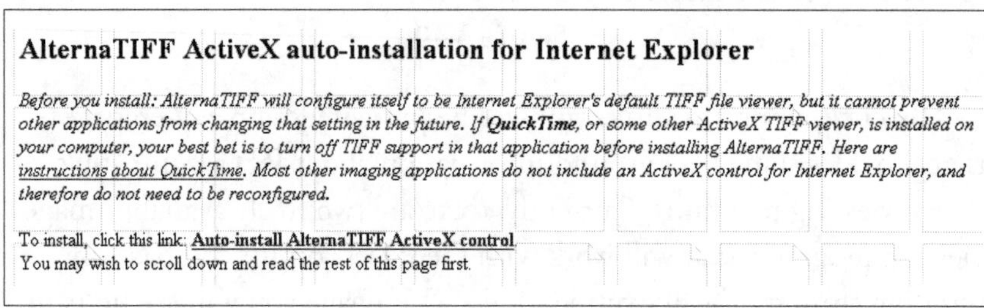

AlternaTIFF ActiveX auto-installation for Internet Explorer
Before you install: AlternaTIFF will configure itself to be Internet Explorer's default TIFF file viewer, but it cannot prevent other applications from changing that setting in the future. If QuickTime, or some other ActiveX TIFF viewer, is installed on your computer, your best bet is to turn off TIFF support in that application before installing AlternaTIFF. Here are instructions about QuickTime. Most other imaging applications do not include an ActiveX control for Internet Explorer, and therefore do not need to be reconfigured.
To install, click this link: Auto-install AlternaTIFF ActiveX control.
You may wish to scroll down and read the rest of this page first.

Figure 3.43

After clicking on the Auto-install link shown in Figure 3.43, you should see a small pop-up warning window similar to Figure 3.44.

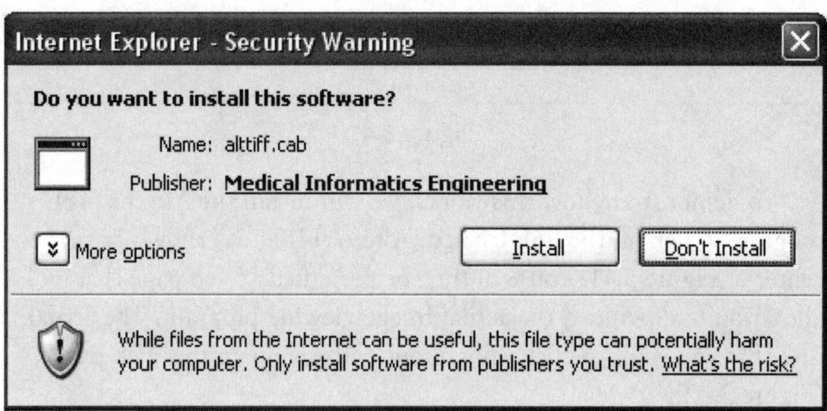

Figure 3.44

Click on the Install button to install the viewer. If the AlternaTIFF viewer is properly installed on your computer, you should see a confirmation message similar to the one shown in Figure 3.45.

Figure 3.45

Using the Image Viewer

After successfully installing the AlternaTIFF image viewer, we can return to the PTO's patent search website and view the scanned images of each page of our relevant patents. At the PTO patent search homepage, click on Patent Number Search (Figure 3.37). For example, let's look at the scanned images of Pat. No. 5,462,805, the fire-protection and safety glass panel. After entering the patent number and clicking on "Search," you will see the Web page shown in Figure 3.46.

USPTO PATENT FULL-TEXT AND IMAGE DATABASE

Home | Quick | Advanced | Pat Num | Help

Bottom

View Cart | Add to Cart

Images

(1 of 1)

United States Patent — *5,462,805*
Sakamoto , et al. — **October 31, 1995**

Fire-protection and safety glass panel

Abstract

In a fire-protection and safety glass panel having a transparent appearance and dual functions as a fire protection glass for shutting out flame and smoke for a long period of time upon occurrence of fire and as a safety glass which is neither shattered into pieces and nor forms any through hole if it is broken in an ordinary life, a PET (polyethylene terephthalate) film (12) is arranged between a first glass plate (10) and a second glass plate (11). The first and the second glass plates (10 and 11) and the PET film (12) are adhered through transparent acrylic adhesive agent layers (13 and 14), respectively. An intermediate resin layer comprises the PET film (12) and the adhesive agent layers (13 and 14) and has a thickness between 75 and 200 .mu.m.

Figure 3.46

Figure 3.46 shows the abstract for Pat. No. 5,462,805. Note that across the top of Figure 3.46 are several navigation buttons. The center button labeled "Images" is an activation button for our patent image-viewing program. To start the viewer, click on the "Images" button. You will then see the Web page shown in Figure 3.47.

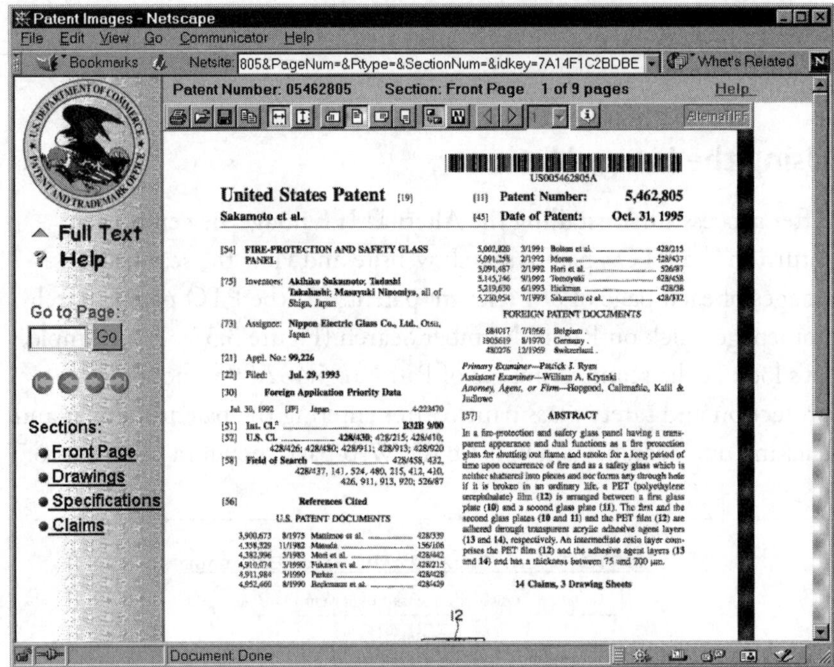

Figure 3.47

Figure 3.47 shows the image-viewing program with the first page of Pat. No. 5,462,805 already loaded. The left side of Figure 3.47 shows several controls for the image viewer. We will discuss these one by one.

Towards the center left of Figure 3.47 there is an entry box labeled "Go to Page." You can make the image viewer display any selected page of the patent by typing in the page number and clicking on the small button labeled "Go" immediately to the right.

Below the "Go to Page" box are a series of arrows. They work in a similar fashion to the indicators on a tape recorder. The left-most arrow will rewind the image viewer to the beginning or first page of the patent. The next arrow reduces the page number currently displaying, one page at a time. Similarly, the third arrow from the left advances the displayed patent page, one page at a time. Finally, the fourth arrow advances the displayed page to the last page of the patent.

Below the arrows, hypertext links have been set up for the major sections of the displayed patent. As shown in the figure, these sections are Front Page, Drawings, Specifications, and Claims. Clicking on any of these links will cause the respective section of the patent to be immediately displayed in the viewer. This can come in handy if, for example, you want to jump directly to the patent specifications section. This way you don't have to search for it by advancing one page at a time through the entire patent.

One of the primary reasons for using the image viewer is to review the patent drawings. Figure 3.48 shows the image viewer display after the "Drawings" link has been selected. As you can see from the top of the display, this particular patent has three drawing pages. The image viewer has jumped to the first drawing page.

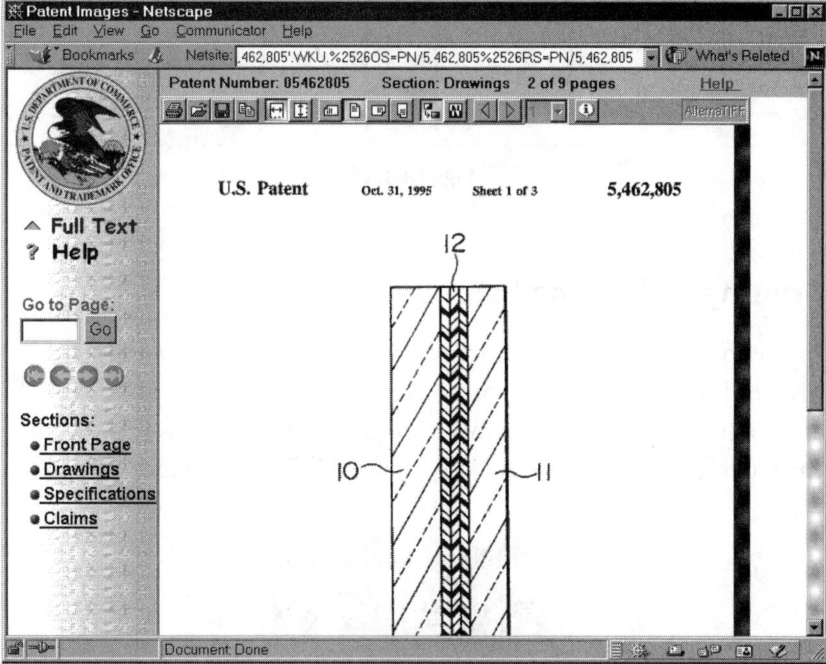

Figure 3.48

Enlarged images of the patent drawings can be displayed by moving the mouse's cursor over the displayed area. The shape of the cursor will change from an arrow to a magnifying glass. An enlarged display of a section of a patent drawing can be obtained by positioning the cursor over the selected area and clicking once. An enlarged display of the top area of the patent drawing number is shown in Figure 3.49. This clearly shows where Drawing Element 12 is used in this patent. The image is returned to normal size by clicking it once again.

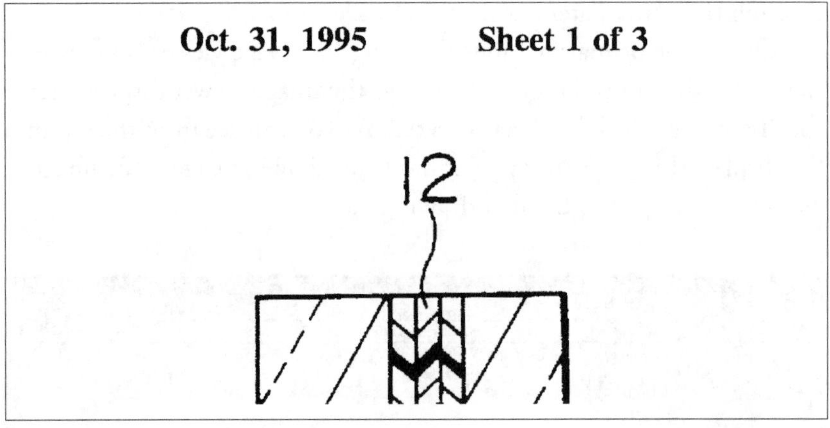

Figure 3.49

Printing and Saving Patent Images

Images of any displayed patent page can be printed or saved to hard disk for future reference. To print the currently displayed page, just click on the button with the small image of a printer. This is shown in the top left of Figure 3.47. A close-up view is shown in Figure 3.50.

Figure 3.50

To save the displayed patent page to the hard disk, click on the second button from the left. This is the button with the small image of a floppy disk shown in Figure 3.50.

An Effective Strategy for Basic Patent Searches

When searching the patent database, there are two goals that you must keep in mind. The first goal is to find the most relevant classes and subclasses for your invention. Relevancy is determined by reading the class descriptions and applying them to your invention. The second goal is to review all of the issued patents within those classes and determine if your idea has been anticipated by the prior art. Anticipation means that all the main aspects of your idea have been documented in previously issued patents or other sources of prior art.

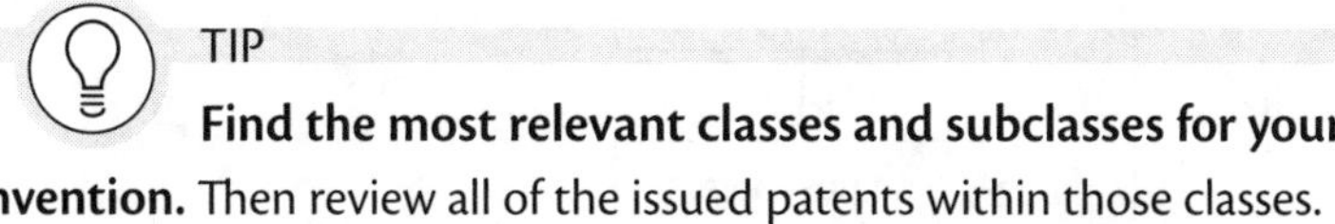

TIP

Find the most relevant classes and subclasses for your invention. Then review all of the issued patents within those classes.

You can approach this problem in one of two ways. First, you start from a keyword search of the patent classes. By reviewing the class descriptions, you determine where your invention might fit in. Then you review all of the issued patents within those classes. Alternately, you can start from keyword searches of the patents themselves and, after reviewing the matching patents, extract the relevant patent numbers and classes.

Starting from a keyword search of the classes first is usually more efficient. However, we recommend using both methods. That way, you are less likely to miss an important prior art reference. Figure 3.51 shows a flowchart for searching the patent classes. Notice that you can start from keyword searches of the class titles or of the class descriptions. Figure 3.52 shows a flowchart for searching the text of the patents themselves.

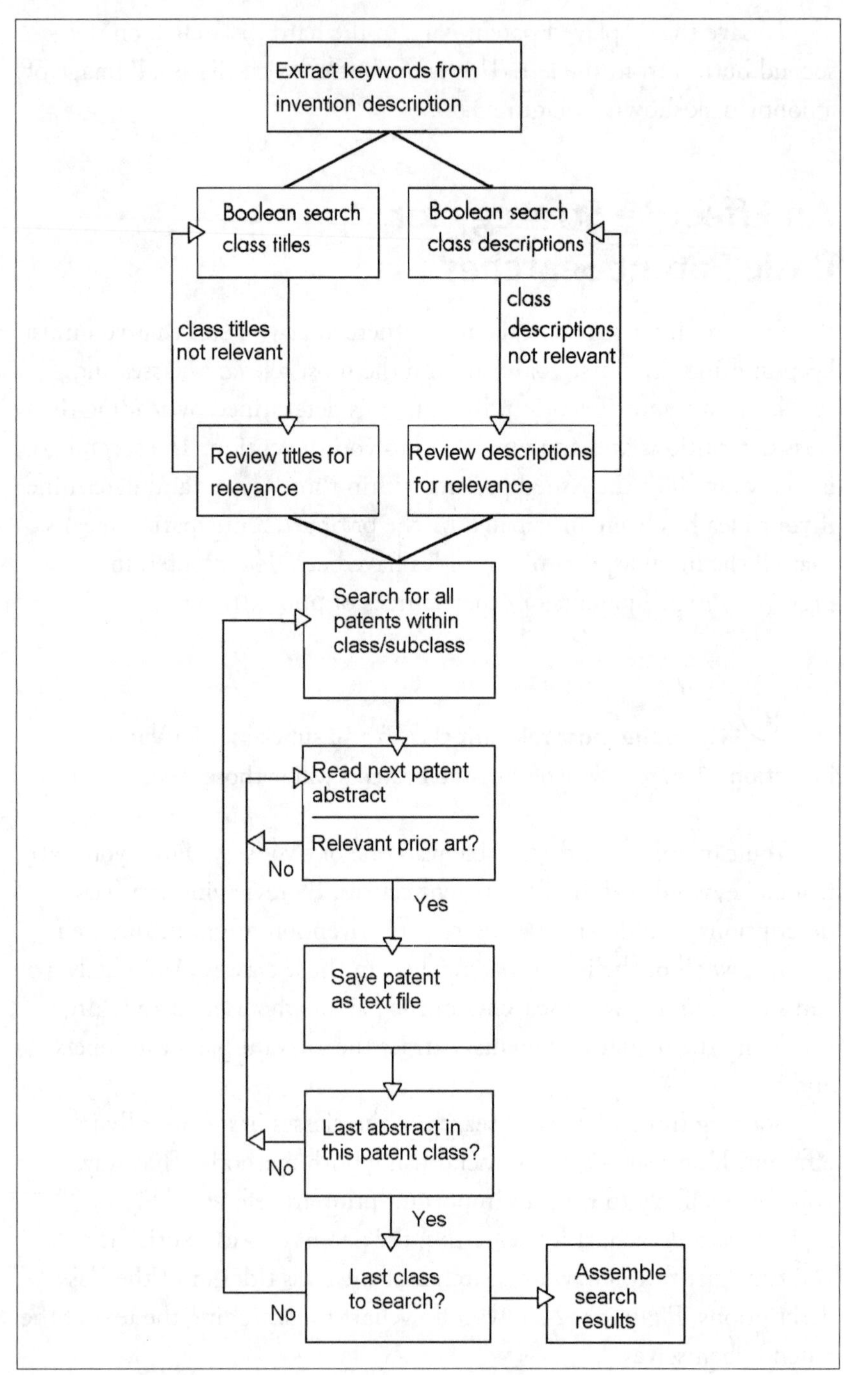
Extract keywords from invention description
Boolean search class titles
Boolean search class descriptions
class titles not relevant
class descriptions not relevant
Review titles for relevance
Review descriptions for relevance
Search for all patents within class/subclass
Read next patent abstract
Relevant prior art?
No
Yes
Save patent as text file
Last abstract in this patent class?
No
Yes
Last class to search?
No
Assemble search results

Figure 3.51

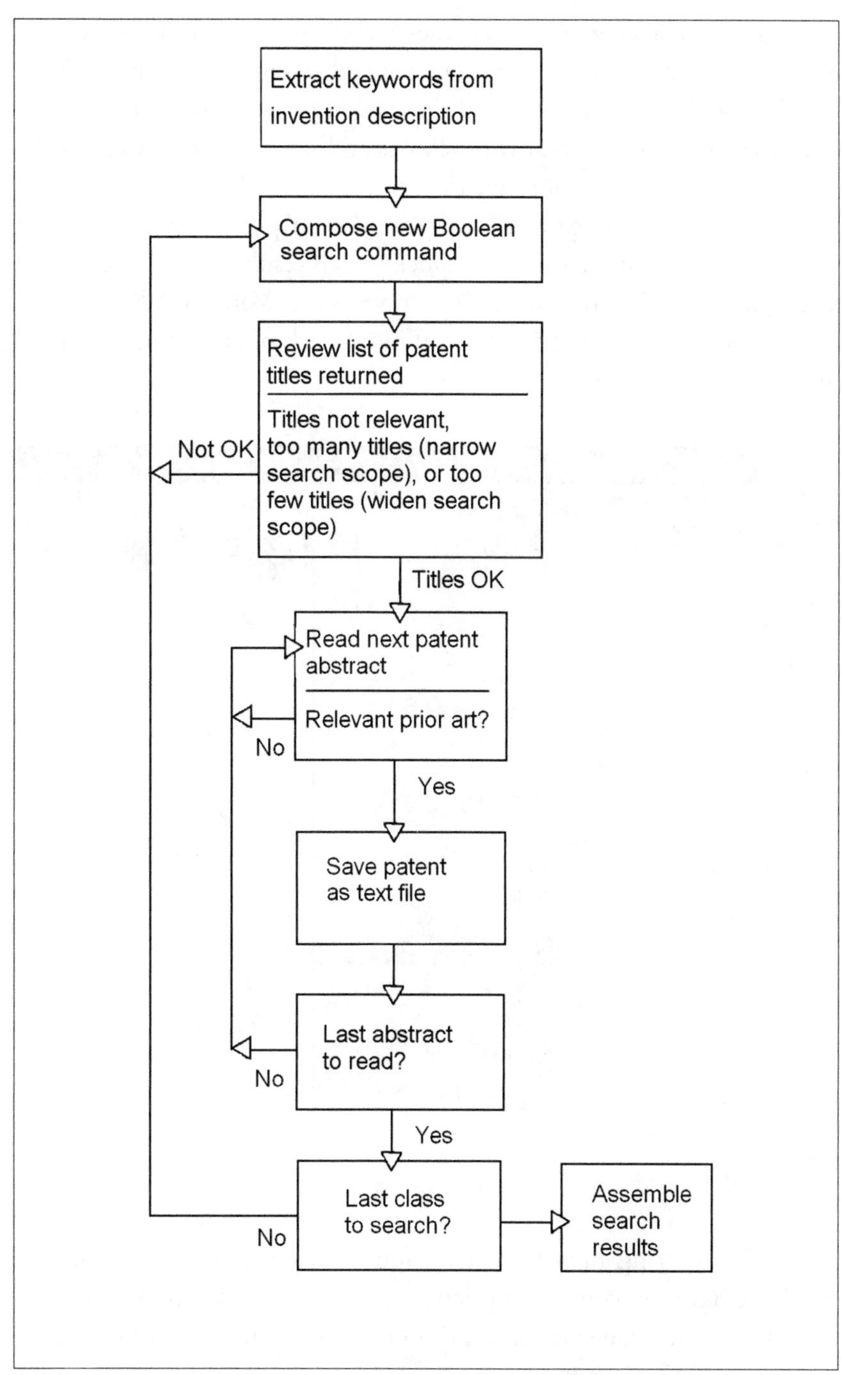
Extract keywords from invention description
Compose new Boolean search command
Review list of patent titles returned
Titles not relevant, too many titles (narrow search scope), or too few titles (widen search scope)
Not OK
Titles OK
Read next patent abstract
Relevant prior art?
No
Yes
Save patent as text file
Last abstract to read?
No
Yes
Last class to search?
No
Assemble search results

Figure 3.52

This is what we would call a one-level-deep search. In other words, you have made one pass of your keywords through the Internet PTO database and hopefully extracted some relevant prior art; you have probably also found two or three classes and several patents that speak to different aspects of your invention.

After saving the text of all relevant prior art patents, you can assemble these documents into a quick search results report. For example, using the "Insert/File" function of the Word for Windows word processor (Figure 3.53), we can insert each of our saved patents into a single document.

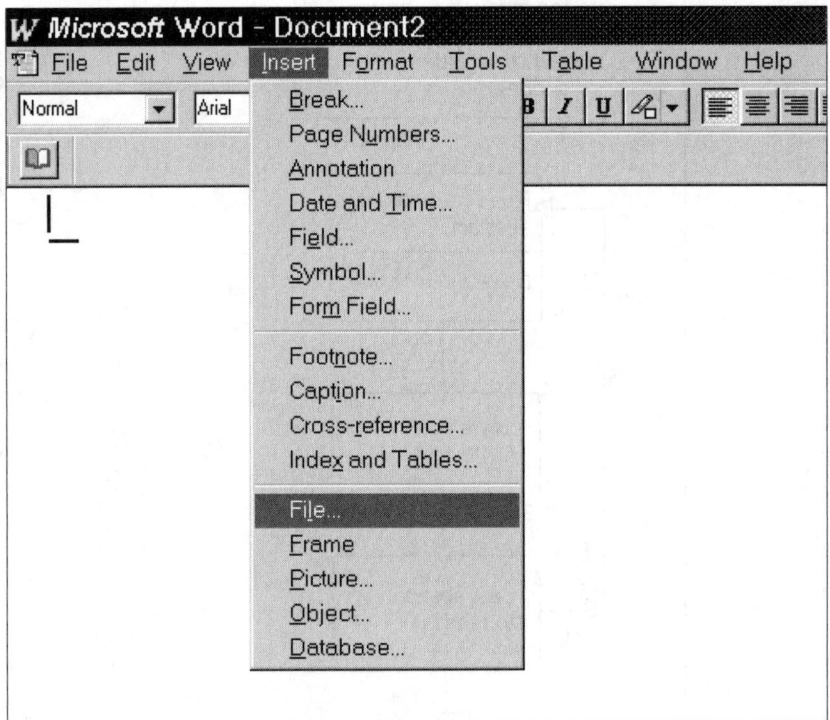

Figure 3.53

After inserting all of the patents into your new document, just use the "File/Save As" command (Figure 3.54) and give the file a name. Use the patent image viewer to print out and save images of each page of the pre-1976 relevant patents.

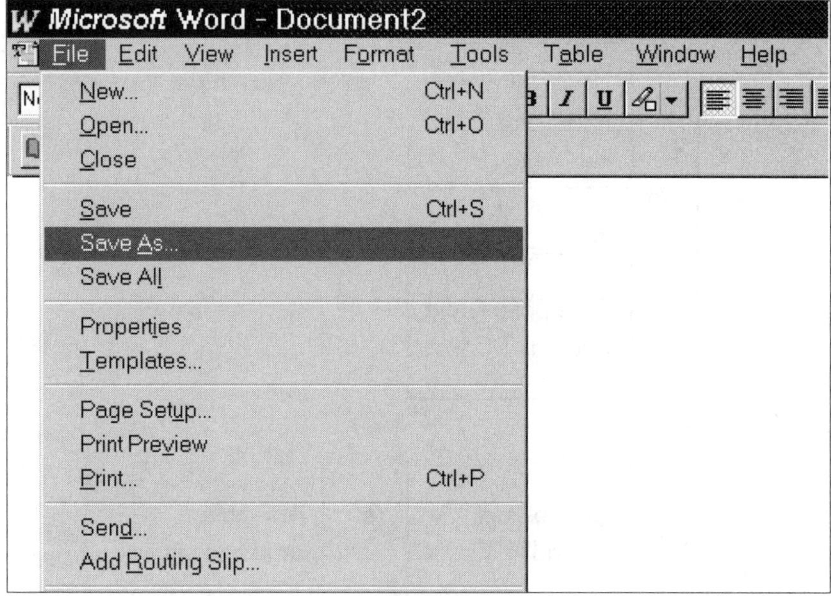

Figure 3.54

In order to do a reasonably thorough patent search, you should make a second-level pass through your results. This means reviewing the referenced patents listed on the front of each of those prior art patents. This action is shown in Figure 3.55. This can lead to a lot of reading. For example, if you found ten patents related to yours and each of these referenced ten older patents, then you have an additional one hundred patents to review. It's worth the effort, however, because this may lead you to an important class or patent that you might have otherwise overlooked.

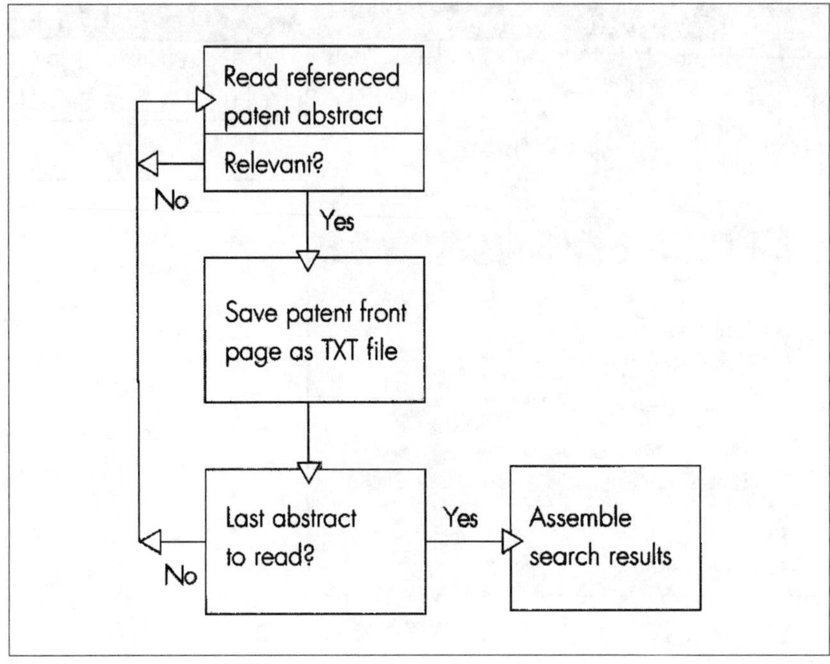
Read referenced patent abstract
Relevant?
No
Yes
Save patent front page as TXT file
Last abstract to read?
No
Yes
Assemble search results

Figure 3.55

CHAPTER

4

Advanced Search Techniques

Previously, we discussed basic Boolean and keyword searching principles. In this chapter, we're going to expand on those principles and explain how to apply more advanced search methods at the PTO website.

How to Accomplish an Advanced Patent Search at the PTO Website

Okay, you know how to search using keywords and you understand the principles of searching by class number. (If you don't, you should review Chapter 3.) Now that you grasp these basics, it's time to improve your skills.

Using Multiple Boolean Operators

Simple Boolean expressions are generally understood to mean the use of two keywords connected by a single Boolean operator. For example the query "fire AND protection," would return all of the patents that contained both of the words "fire" and "protection." By requiring both of the keywords to be present, we reduce the size of our search results.

The query "building OR structure" would return all of the patents that contained the word "building" or the word "structure." By requiring only one of the keywords to be present, we enlarge the size of our search results.

An advanced Boolean query involves the use of more than one operator and sometimes the use of parentheses.

Consider the query "fire AND protection AND (building OR structure)."

This Boolean search command would return only patents that contained the words "fire," "protection," and the word "building" or "structure." The first two keywords — "fire AND protection"—use a logical AND operation to narrow the search results.

Then the logical AND operation is applied to the expression contained within the parentheses—"building OR structure." The use of the parentheses around the keywords "building OR structure" means that patents are searched for either of these words (this widens the size of the search results because either keyword can cause a hit).

However, the result of the search for the keywords "building OR structure" is then further narrowed because these two words must occur in combination with the words "fire AND protection." The flow chart of Figure 4.1 illustrates this process. The correct placement of parentheses is important because this determines how the keywords are combined.

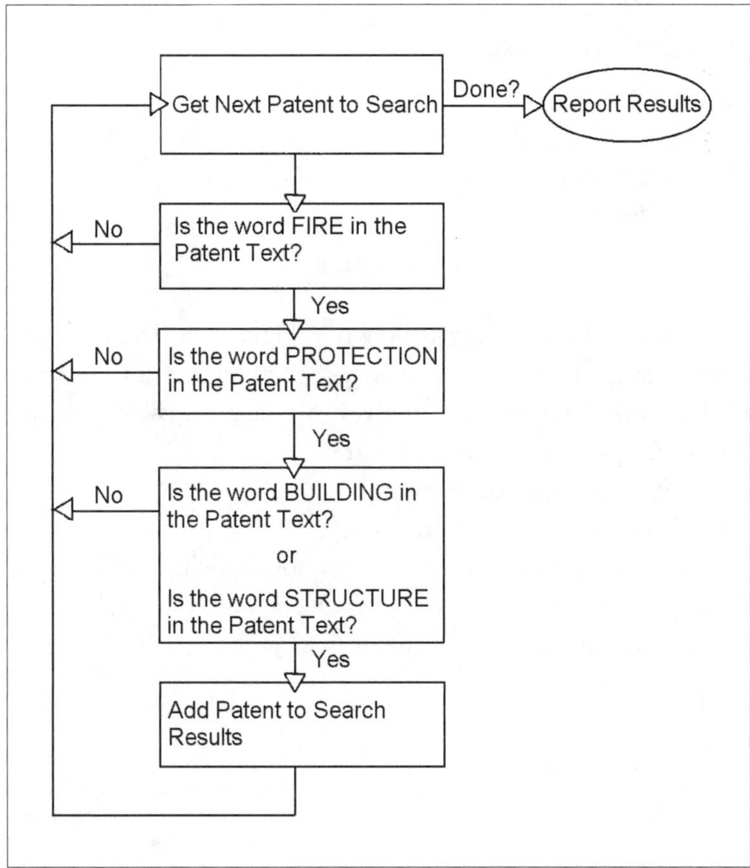

Figure 4.1

Let's try some Advanced Search commands at the PTO patent database website (www.uspto.gov/patft) and examine the results.

To get to the advanced search page, click on the Advanced Search link shown in Figure 4.2.

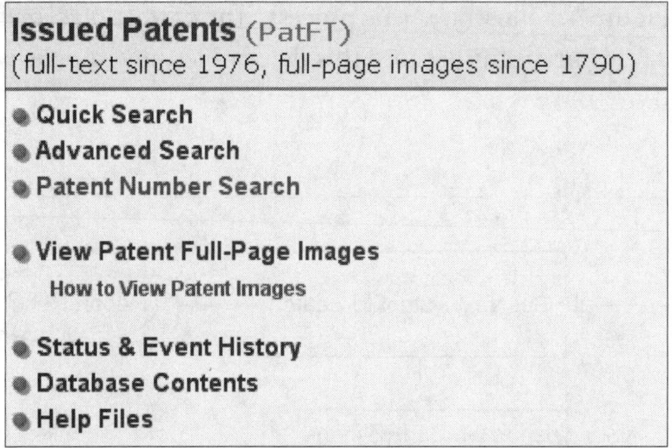

Figure 4.2

The advanced search page is shown in Figure 4.3. There are several similarities to the basic Boolean search page discussed in Chapter 3. The Select Years dropdown menu gives you the same two ranges as the Quick Search page. These selections are:

- 1976 to present [full-text]
- 1790 to present [entire database]

For now, we will use the default selection, which is "1976 to present [full-text]." Using this setting will allow us to search through every word contained in every patent issued since January 1, 1976.

Query [Help]

fire AND protection AND (building OR structure)

Examples:
ttl/(tennis and (racquet or racket))
isd/1/8/2002 and motorcycle
in/newmar-julie

Select Years [Help]

1976 to present [full-text]

Search Reset

Figure 4.3

The Query box of the Advanced Search page is quite different from the previous basic Boolean search page. We no longer have the two keyword entry fields separated by a Boolean operator field, as shown in Chapter 3, Figure 3.6. Instead, we are faced only with a challenging blank box. It is here that we enter our advanced Boolean expressions. Let's type in the search command "fire AND protection AND (building OR structure)," as shown in the figure. To start the search, just click on the Search button shown in the lower middle of Figure 4.3.

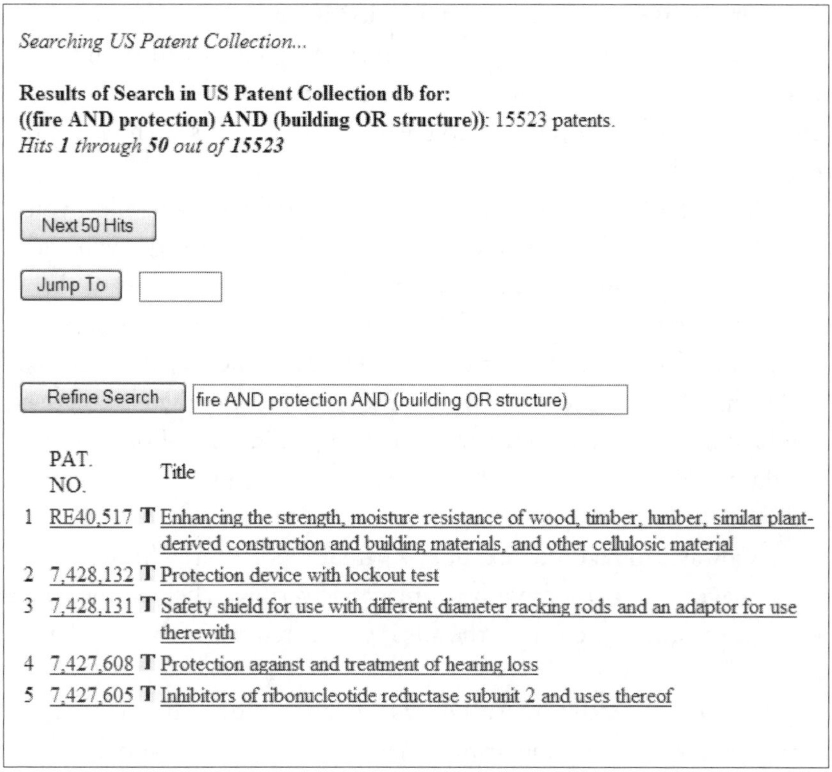

Searching US Patent Collection...

Results of Search in US Patent Collection db for:
((fire AND protection) AND (building OR structure)): 15523 patents.
*Hits **1** through **50** out of **15523***

Next 50 Hits

Jump To

Refine Search | fire AND protection AND (building OR structure)

	PAT. NO.		Title
1	RE40,517	T	Enhancing the strength, moisture resistance of wood, timber, lumber, similar plant-derived construction and building materials, and other cellulosic material
2	7,428,132	T	Protection device with lockout test
3	7,428,131	T	Safety shield for use with different diameter racking rods and an adaptor for use therewith
4	7,427,608	T	Protection against and treatment of hearing loss
5	7,427,605	T	Inhibitors of ribonucleotide reductase subunit 2 and uses thereof

Figure 4.4

First, note that under "Results of Search in US Patent Collection db for:" in Figure 4.4 your search query was modified slightly by the search engine to enclose your first two search terms in parentheses. It also enclosed your entire query in parentheses. Below, we explain what these parentheses mean and when you can use the same approach to perform your search.

You may recall that in Chapter 3, we executed the simple Boolean search command "fire AND protection" for patents issued in the years 1976 to the present. The results showed 23,442 hits. Now, by using a more complex Boolean expression, we were able to add the requirement for the keywords "building OR structure." The results of our new search are shown in Figure 4.4. From the figure, you can see that the number of matching patents has been reduced from 23,442 to 15,523.

Why are we still getting so many hits? Keep in mind that we are searching through the entire text of every patent issued from the year 1976 to the present for a match to our search query. Later in this chapter, we will show you how to greatly narrow your search results by the use of field codes.

The Query entry box of the Advanced Search page will allow you to type in any valid Boolean search command. This provides you with the ability to precisely define your search requirements. It means that your search results will be more relevant and that there will be less material to read over. Of course, the downside to the advanced Query box is that if you are too narrow in your search requirements, you may overlook patents that are relevant. For example, instead of the words "building OR structure," a relevant patent may contain the words "edifice," "palace," or "skyscraper."

As always, to read the text of any patent reported as a hit (or to view images of the patent with an image viewer) just click on the patent number or title. To return to the advanced search page, click the back arrow of your browser.

As you may recall, the ANDNOT operator allows you to exclude certain keywords from the search results. Let's suppose that our invention is a fire protective device used in various buildings but does not involve sprinklers. To exclude sprinklers from the search results we add "ANDNOT sprinkler" to our search command and compose the following query (shown in Figure 4.5): fire AND protection AND (building OR structure) ANDNOT sprinkler.

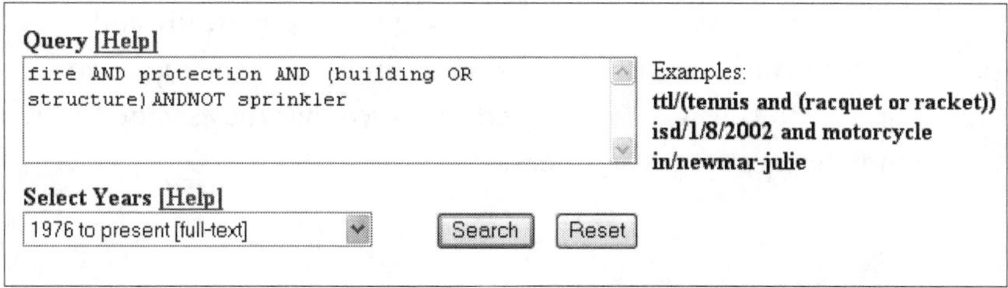

Figure 4.5

Using Parentheses to Organize Your Search Query

When using multiple Boolean operators, it's important to keep in mind the order in which the terms will be evaluated. Proceeding from left to right in the query shown in Figure 4.5:

- First, the AND operator will be used to locate results combining the two terms "fire AND protection."
- Second, the expression within the parentheses—(building OR structure)—will be evaluated because it is enclosed in parentheses with the OR operator.
- Third, the AND operator will be used to evaluate and combine the results of the first two steps "fire AND protection" and "(building OR structure)."
- Finally, the ANDNOT operator will be used to exclude any results that contain the term "sprinkler."

If you are in doubt about the order of evaluation of a complex Boolean expression, you can always add more parentheses. For example, consider the following expression: ((fire AND protection) AND (building OR structure)) ANDNOT sprinkler

- First, the inner parentheses around "fire AND protection" causes these two terms to be AND-ed together.
- Next, the parentheses around "building OR Structure" cause these two terms to be OR-ed together.
- Finally, the outer parentheses cause the results of both operations to be AND-ed together.

In fact, the PTO's patent search server will automatically add parentheses to your search command and display it at the top of your search results. In this way, you can check to see that the executed search command matches what you intended.

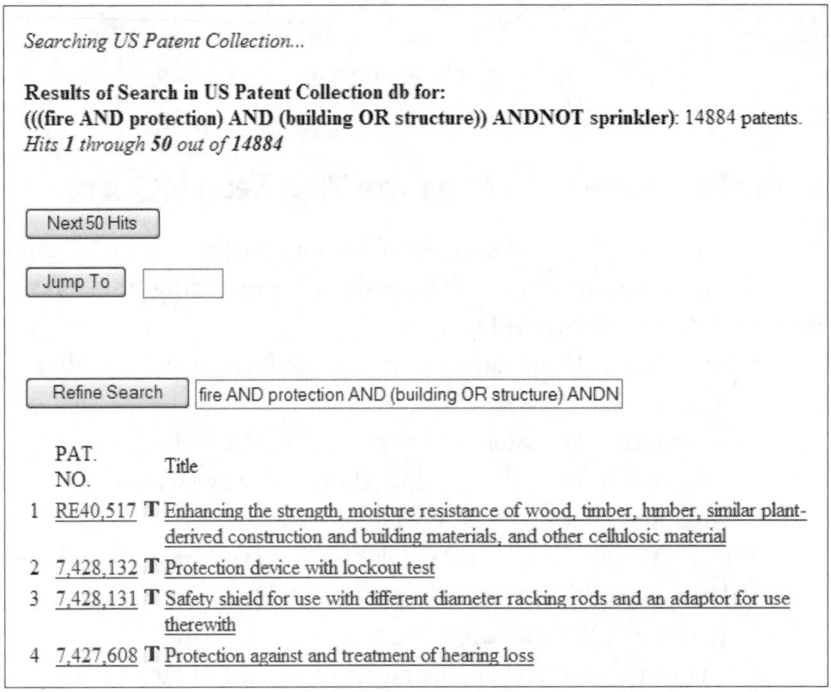

Searching US Patent Collection...

Results of Search in US Patent Collection db for:
(((fire AND protection) AND (building OR structure)) ANDNOT sprinkler): 14884 patents.
*Hits **1** through **50** out of **14884***

Next 50 Hits

Jump To

Refine Search | fire AND protection AND (building OR structure) ANDN

	PAT. NO.		Title
1	RE40,517	T	Enhancing the strength, moisture resistance of wood, timber, lumber, similar plant-derived construction and building materials, and other cellulosic material
2	7,428,132	T	Protection device with lockout test
3	7,428,131	T	Safety shield for use with different diameter racking rods and an adaptor for use therewith
4	7,427,608	T	Protection against and treatment of hearing loss

Figure 4.6

Figure 4.6 shows the result of our search that excludes sprinklers. Notice that the executed search command is displayed at the top of the search results: (((fire AND protection) AND (building OR structure)) ANDNOT sprinkler). The total number of resulting hits has been further reduced from 15,523 to 14,884.

TIP

If you are in doubt about the order of evaluation in complex patent search commands, use parentheses to explicitly set the order. Then check the output command at the top of the results report.

Using Field Codes to Narrow Your Search

So far, we have been searching the entire text of issued patents with the Advanced Search mode of the PTO's patent search database. We can, however, limit our searches to certain sections of the issued patents through the use of field codes.

Why limit your search to only selected sections? Because by always searching through the maximum amount of patent text, you will often get thousands of matching patents that don't really have any bearing on your invention. Selected keywords like "fire" and "protection" can occur in many contexts. They are used in literally thousands of different types of inventions. Constructing queries that blindly look for any use of these keywords will often return many irrelevant hits. This fact is well illustrated by the results shown in Figure 4.6, where 14,884 hits were returned.

Field Code	Field Name	Field Code	Field Name
PN	Patent Number	IN	Inventor Name
ISD	Issue Date	IC	Inventor City
TTL	Title	IS	Inventor State
ABST	Abstract	ICN	Inventor Country
ACLM	Claim(s)	LREP	Attorney or Agent
SPEC	Description/Specification	AN	Assignee Name
CCL	Current US Classification	AC	Assignee City
ICL	International Classification	AS	Assignee State
APN	Application Serial Number	ACN	Assignee Country
APD	Application Date	EXP	Primary Examiner
PARN	Parent Case Information	EXA	Assistant Examiner
RLAP	Related US App. Data	REF	Referenced By
REIS	Reissue Data	FREF	Foreign References
PRIR	Foreign Priority	OREF	Other References
PCT	PCT Information	GOVT	Government Interest
APT	Application Type		

Figure 4.7

At the bottom of the Advanced Search page is a table showing all the available field codes (Figure 4.7). Next to each field code is the name of the field (actually a hypertext link). To get a further description of any particular field code, just click its name. For example, to read a description of the Patent Abstract field code (ABST), just click on "Abstract" (fourth from the top on the left-most column) as shown in Figure 4.7. The resulting description is shown in Figure 4.8.

Abstract (ABST)

This field contains a brief summary of the patented invention.

TIP: The abstract contains many of the relevant words of a patent.

Figure 4.8

As described, the patent abstract is a brief summary of the patented invention that contains many of the relevant words of a patent. As a learning exercise in how to use field codes to improve the relevancy of our search results, let's limit our patent search to the patent abstract only—that is, use the ABST field code shown in Figure 4.7.

Let's further suppose that we wish to apply our previous search using the words "fire" and "protection" in the abstracts of issued patents. We would then compose the query shown in Figure 4.9.

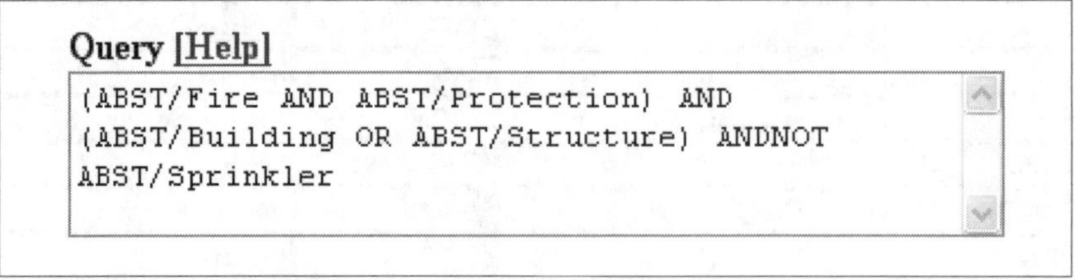

Figure 4.9

Notice how each keyword is preceded by the characters "ABST/." This tells the patent search program to look for that keyword in the patent abstract only. The results of our search are shown in Figure 4.10. The reduction in the number of reported hits is quite dramatic. Comparing Figure 4.6 with Figure 4.10, we see that the number of reported hits has been reduced from 14,884 to a much more manageable 81 patents.

Searching US Patent Collection...

Results of Search in US Patent Collection db for:
(((ABST/Fire AND ABST/Protection) AND (ABST/Building OR ABST/Structure)) ANDNOT ABST/Sprinkler): 81 patents.
*Hits **1** through **50** out of **81***

Final 31 Hits

Jump To

Refine Search (ABST/Fire AND ABST/Protection) AND (ABST/Buildi

	PAT. NO.		Title
1	7,399,520	**T**	Fibre-reinforced building article and manufacturing method thereof
2	7,395,869	**T**	External structure fire protection system "ESFPS"
3	7,349,891	**T**	Site integration management system for operational support service in an internet data center
4	7,273,634	**T**	Coatings and additives containing ceramic material

Figure 4.10

There's a shorthand way of composing this query. When you are using parentheses you can place the field code characters (in this case "ABST") outside the parentheses. The patent search program will then apply the field code to the entire contained expression. In this case, we can recompose our query as is shown in Figure 4.11 and obtain the same result.

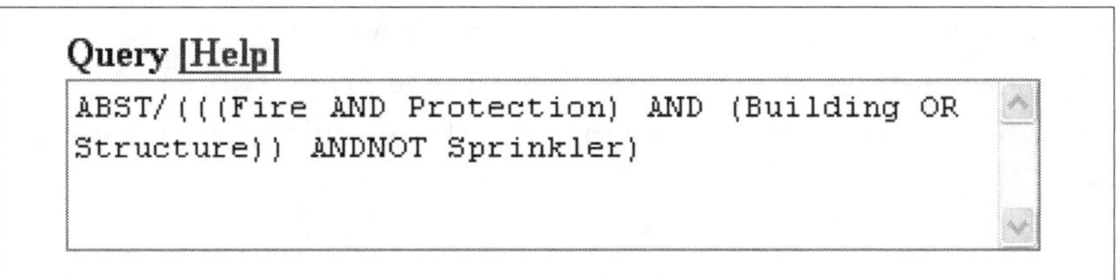

Figure 4.11

TIP

By placing a field code outside a set of parentheses in complex Boolean queries, you can apply that field code to every keyword in the contained expression.

Searching for a Phrase

Another way that we can use the Advanced Search page is through the use of a quoted phrase. This is helpful when specific words are commonly found adjacent to each other in certain technology—for example, in biotechnology, the phrase "absorption spectroscopy" is often encountered. (Absorption spectroscopy is the use of a spectrophotometer to determine the ability of solutes to absorb light through a range of specified wavelengths.) To search for this phrase, just enclose the words in double quotes as shown in Figure 4.12, then click the Search button. The results are shown in Figure 4.13.

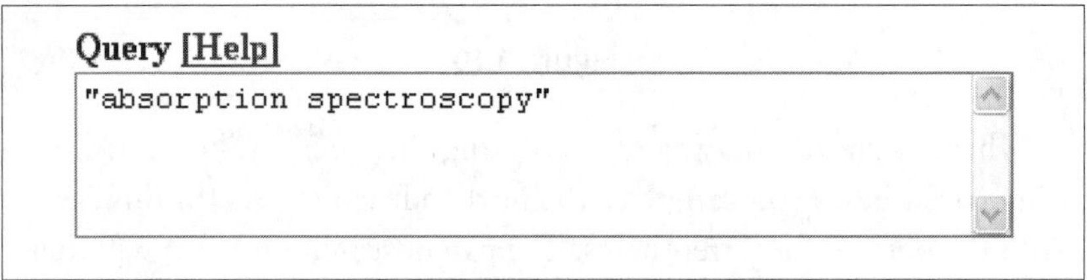

Figure 4.12

You can see that there have been 5,174 patents issued since 1976 that include the phrase "absorption spectroscopy." Note that if your sequence of words does not exactly match the way they are used in the patent text to be searched—for example, "absorption 3-D spectroscopy"—you won't get a match and you could miss a relevant prior art patent.

Limiting the Range of Years Searched

As you can see in Figure 4.13, we obtained 5,174 hits from our previous search query. That's an awful lot of results to read through. We could reduce this number by limiting our search to specific sections of the issued patent, specifically the abstract. But what if we missed a relevant prior art reference?

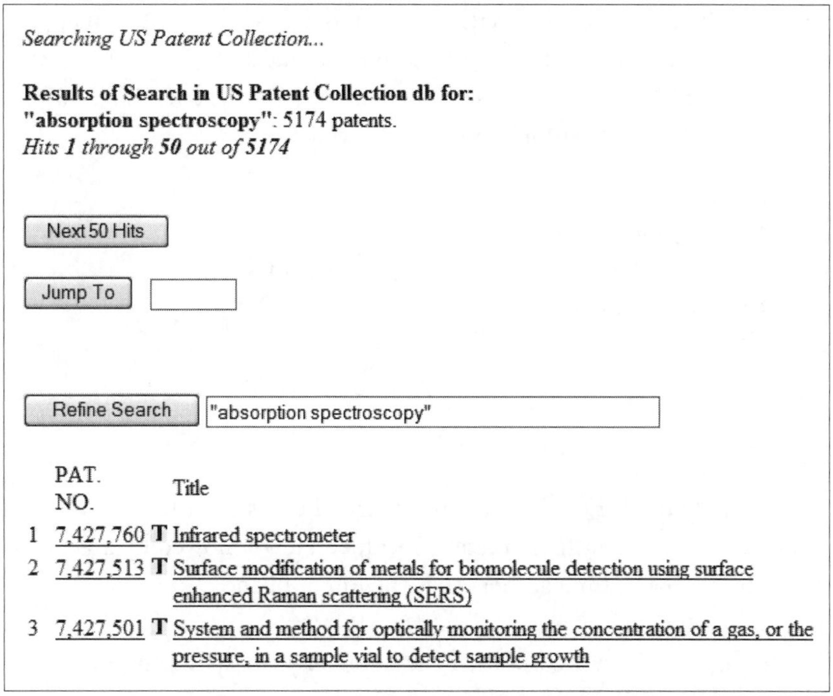

Searching US Patent Collection...

Results of Search in US Patent Collection db for:
"absorption spectroscopy": 5174 patents.
*Hits **1** through **50** out of **5174***

Next 50 Hits

Jump To

Refine Search "absorption spectroscopy"

	PAT. NO.		Title
1	7,427,760	T	Infrared spectrometer
2	7,427,513	T	Surface modification of metals for biomolecule detection using surface enhanced Raman scattering (SERS)
3	7,427,501	T	System and method for optically monitoring the concentration of a gas, or the pressure, in a sample vial to detect sample growth

Figure 4.13

Our search for "absorption spectroscopy" leads us to another important way of refining our search queries. The "Select Years" dropdown menus on both the Quick Search and Advanced Search web pages only allow for "1976 to present [full-text]" and "1790 to present [entire database]."

But often, you may want to limit the range of years searched to a smaller value. For example, suppose that you are a biotechnology researcher and you have come up with an improvement to a spectrophotometer. The improvement is not only limited to the field of absorption spectroscopy, but also depends on recent technological developments. Therefore, you could reasonably assume that any relevant patents would have been issued quite recently—say, in the past three years. But how do you limit the range of years to be searched?

You will see (Figure 4.7) that one of the specified field codes is the issue date (ISD). This code is used to search for a patent that was issued on a specific date. We can use this code and a special operator to apply our patent search query to a discrete range of dates.

In Figure 4.14, we composed the following query: ISD/1/1/2003 ->12/31/2005 AND "absorption spectroscopy"

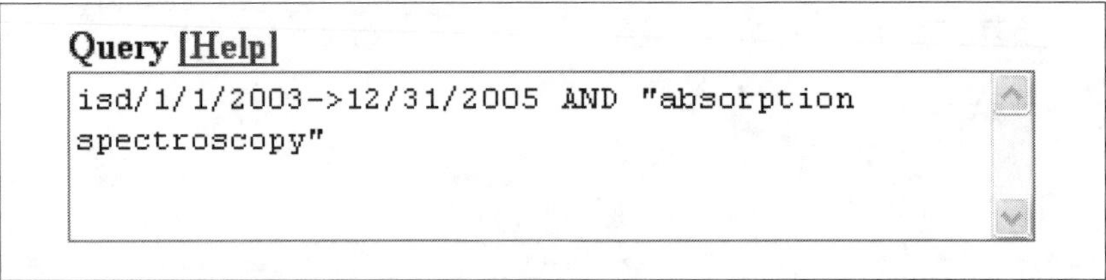

Figure 4.14

To apply the ISD field code to a range of dates, we use the (->) operator; that is, a dash character (-) immediately followed by a greater-than character (>). One gathers that the intent of the -> operator is to resemble an arrow.

In Figure 4.14, we combined the range of years with our search phrase using the Boolean AND operator. The results are shown in Figure 4.15.

Results of Search in US Patent Collection db for:
(ISD/20030101->20051231 AND "absorption spectroscopy"): 814 patents.
*Hits **1** through **50** out of **814***

Next 50 Hits

Jump To

Refine Search isd/1/1/2003->12/31/2005 AND "absorption spectrosco

	PAT. NO.		Title
1	6,980,285	T	Method in quality control of a spectrophotometer
2	6,979,538	T	Directed evolution of novel binding proteins
3	6,979,530	T	Peptide conjugates and fluorescence detection methods for intracellular caspase assay

Figure 4.15

Compare Figures 4.13 and 4.15 and you can see that the number of hits has been reduced from 5,174 to 814.

TIP

You can apply the ISD field code to a range of dates by using the -> operator (for example: ISD/1/1/2003->12/31/2005).

Navigating the Search Results

Dr. Robert L. Forward has a Ph.D. in gravity physics (for his doctoral thesis, Dr. Forward built the world's first bar gravitational radiation detector—now on display at the Smithsonian) and worked at Hughes Research Labs for more than 30 years. During his time at Hughes and since retiring, Dr. Forward has been granted several patents. To search for all of the patents issued to Dr. Forward since 1976, we compose the following query: IN/Forward-Robert-L.

Here we have used the inventor name field code, IN, followed by the name of the inventor, last name first. Also note the placement of a dash (-) between the last and first name and between the first name and the middle initial. This search command is shown in Figure 4.16.

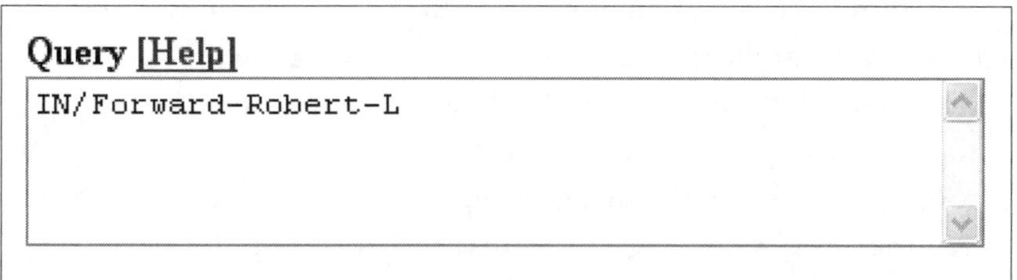

Figure 4.16

The results of our search are shown in Figure 4.17. Here we see a list of patents issued to Dr. Forward since 1976. To see the text of the first patent, just click on it with the mouse. This is shown in Figure 4.18.

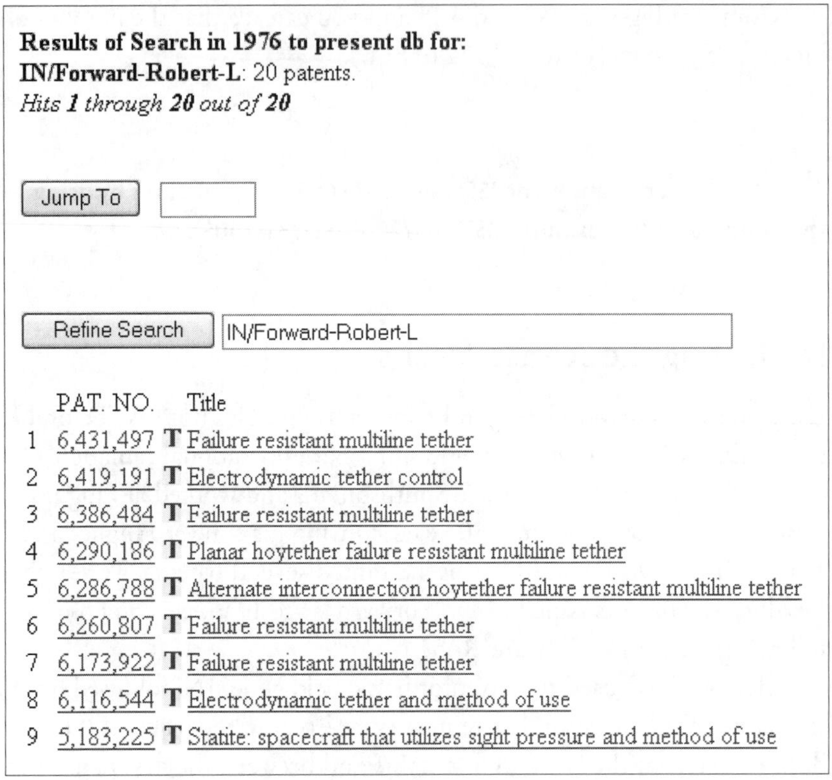

Results of Search in 1976 to present db for:
IN/Forward-Robert-L: 20 patents.
*Hits **1** through **20** out of **20***

Jump To

Refine Search IN/Forward-Robert-L

	PAT. NO.		Title
1	6,431,497	**T**	Failure resistant multiline tether
2	6,419,191	**T**	Electrodynamic tether control
3	6,386,484	**T**	Failure resistant multiline tether
4	6,290,186	**T**	Planar hoytether failure resistant multiline tether
5	6,286,788	**T**	Alternate interconnection hoytether failure resistant multiline tether
6	6,260,807	**T**	Failure resistant multiline tether
7	6,173,922	**T**	Failure resistant multiline tether
8	6,116,544	**T**	Electrodynamic tether and method of use
9	5,183,225	**T**	Statite: spacecraft that utilizes sight pressure and method of use

Figure 4.17

Within the top portion of Figure 4.18 is a series of links. On the second row from the top, you will see three links labeled "Hit List," "Next," and "Bottom." These links allow you to quickly navigate through a list of patents. After you have finished reading the text of Pat. No. 6,431,497, you can immediately jump to the next patent on the list of returned hits by clicking on the link labeled "Next." This saves you the extra step involved in going back to the patent list, then selecting the next patent title. The patent search results are listed chronologically, from the most recent to the oldest patent on the list.

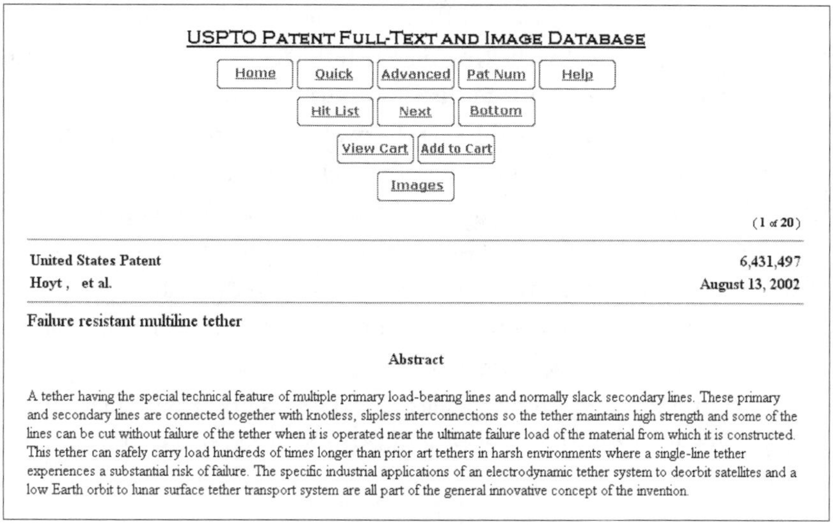

USPTO PATENT FULL-TEXT AND IMAGE DATABASE

Home | Quick | Advanced | Pat Num | Help

Hit List | Next | Bottom

View Cart | Add to Cart

Images

(1 of 20)

United States Patent 6,431,497
Hoyt , et al. August 13, 2002

Failure resistant multiline tether

Abstract

A tether having the special technical feature of multiple primary load-bearing lines and normally slack secondary lines. These primary and secondary lines are connected together with knotless, slipless interconnections so the tether maintains high strength and some of the lines can be cut without failure of the tether when it is operated near the ultimate failure load of the material from which it is constructed. This tether can safely carry load hundreds of times longer than prior art tethers in harsh environments where a single-line tether experiences a substantial risk of failure. The specific industrial applications of an electrodynamic tether system to deorbit satellites and a low Earth orbit to lunar surface tether transport system are all part of the general innovative concept of the invention.

Figure 4.18

After clicking on the Next button, you are presented with Pat. No. 6,419,191 as shown in Figure 4.19. Now, an extra directional link (labeled "Previous") has appeared in the second row of links at the top of Figure 4.19. As you might guess, clicking on this link allows you to immediately jump to the previous patent on the list. The Next and Previous links can save you a lot of time when reading through long lists of patent results.

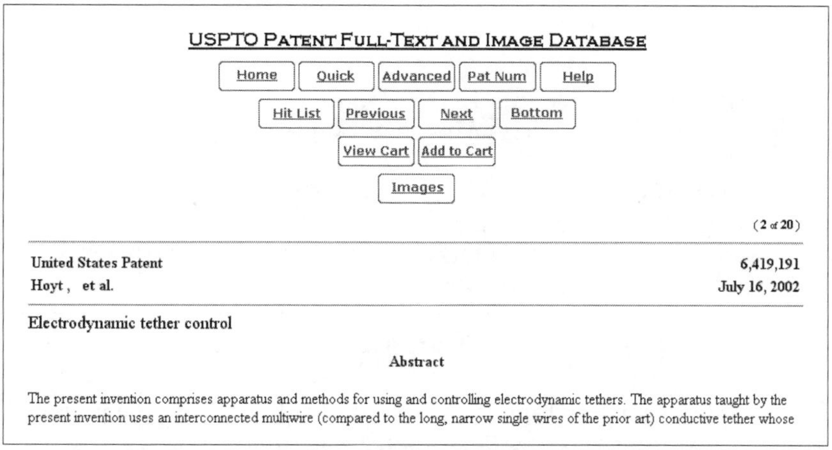

USPTO PATENT FULL-TEXT AND IMAGE DATABASE

Home | Quick | Advanced | Pat Num | Help

Hit List | Previous | Next | Bottom

View Cart | Add to Cart

Images

(2 of 20)

United States Patent 6,419,191
Hoyt , et al. July 16, 2002

Electrodynamic tether control

Abstract

The present invention comprises apparatus and methods for using and controlling electrodynamic tethers. The apparatus taught by the present invention uses an interconnected multiwire (compared to the long, narrow single wires of the prior art) conductive tether whose

Figure 4.19

By selecting the link labeled Bottom, you will be presented with the last patent on the list. By clicking on the link labeled "Hit List," you are immediately returned to our hit list summary of patent titles.

Pat. No. 5,183,225 issued to Dr. Forward (the ninth in our list) illustrates another truism of the PTO's patent search database: typos. The title of the patent reads: "Statite: spacecraft that utilizes sight pressure and method of use." However, a quick read of the patent abstract reveals that the invention actually uses *light* pressure.

This is another reason why a thorough patent search should include a search of the *Manual of Classification* with subsequent review of all patents found in the appropriate class/subclass. While a typo may rob you of a keyword hit, the patent should still be listed in the appropriate classification.

Using Wildcards

Wildcards can also be used for advanced patent searches. Let's suppose that you constructed the query: ISD/1/1/1991->12/31/1995 AND ABST/((fireproof OR firestop) AND building).

Results of Search in 1976 to present db for:
(ISD/19910101->19951231 AND ABST/((Fireproof OR Firestop) AND building)): 10 patents.
*Hits **1** through **10** out of **10***

Jump To

Refine Search ISD/1/1/1991->12/31/1995 AND ABST/((Fireproof OR F

	PAT. NO.		Title
1	5,426,908	T	Method of construction using corrugated material
2	5,425,207	T	Method of constructing buildings and other structures using corrugated material
3	5,417,019	T	Passthrough device with firestop

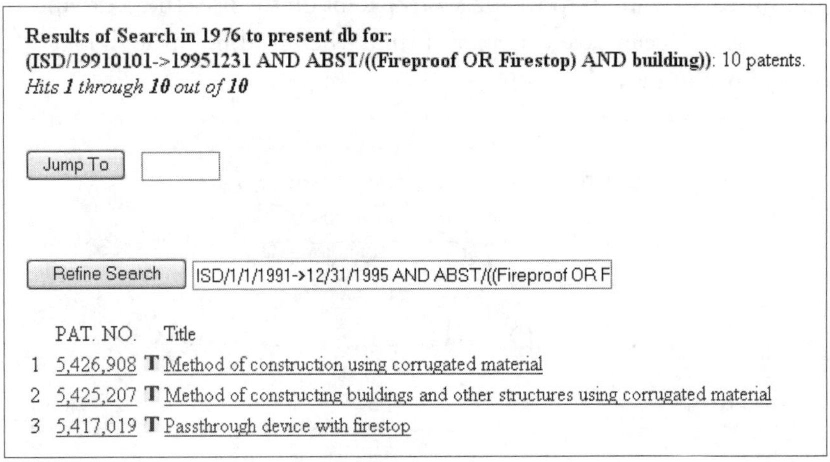

Figure 4.20

The results for searching the abstracts of patents, from the years 1991 through 1995, are shown in Figure 4.20. As you can see, there were 10 hits, or occurrences, of our search query. To widen the scope of our search to include words like fireplace, firewall, and firetrap we could use a series of OR statements such as: ISD/1/1/1991->12/31/1995 AND ABST/((fireproof OR firestop OR fireplace OR firewall OR firetrap) AND building).

A more through and efficient approach would be to use the wildcard $ to substitute for any characters occurring after the word fire. Now our search command looks as follows: ISD/1/1/1991->12/31/1995 AND ABST/(fire$ AND building).

The results of this query are shown in Figure 4.21. As you can see, there are now 111 hits, as opposed to 10 hits for our previous search.

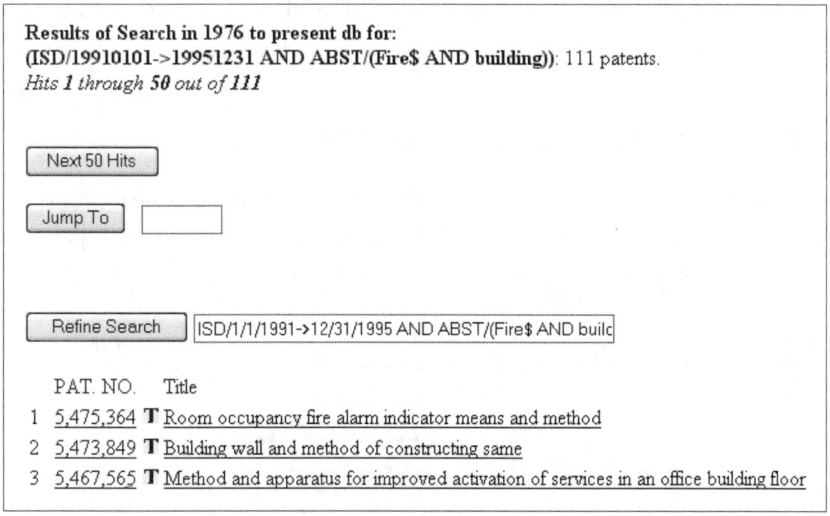

Results of Search in 1976 to present db for:
(ISD/19910101->19951231 AND ABST/(Fire$ AND building)): 111 patents.
*Hits **1** through **50** out of **111***

Next 50 Hits

Jump To

Refine Search ISD/1/1/1991->12/31/1995 AND ABST/(Fire$ AND builc

	PAT. NO.		Title
1	5,475,364	**T**	Room occupancy fire alarm indicator means and method
2	5,473,849	**T**	Building wall and method of constructing same
3	5,467,565	**T**	Method and apparatus for improved activation of services in an office building floor

Figure 4.21

In Figure 4.21 we have actually skipped a step. Here we have taken advantage of the "Refine Search" box. (This is the entry box shown in Figure 4.20.) For each list of search results, the PTO patent server program copies your input query into this entry box. If you want to make a slight change to the query and resubmit it, you can do it right from the results page. Instead of using the back arrow to return to the Advanced Search page, just type your changes into this box and click on Refine Search.

TIP

Use the Refine Search box to save time when making minor changes to search queries.

Searching Published Patent Applications at the PTO's Website

In addition to the full text and drawings of all patents issued since 1976, the PTO's website also allows you to search patent applications published since March 15, 2001. The techniques for searching the Published Applications full-text database (AppFT) are nearly identical to those used with the Issued Patents (PatFT) database.

Patent Applications Quick Search

The main search page for the Published Applications database (Figure 4.22) is accessed from the same Web address as the main search page for the Issued Patents database (www.uspto.gov/patft).

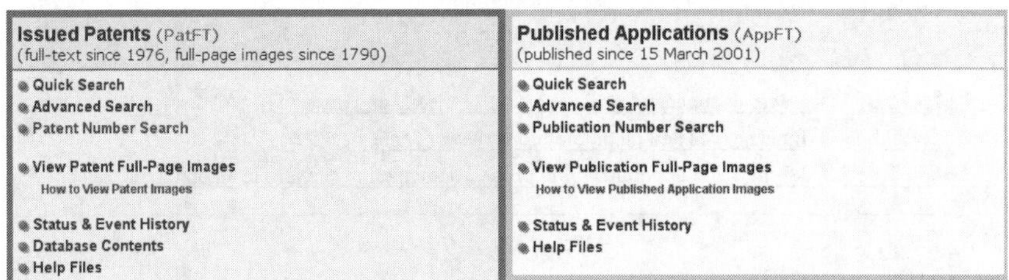

Figure 4.22

To perform a Quick Search of the AppFT database, click on the Quick Search link illustrated in Figure 4.22. Note that now we are using the links on the right-hand column. You will then be presented with the Web page shown in Figure 4.23.

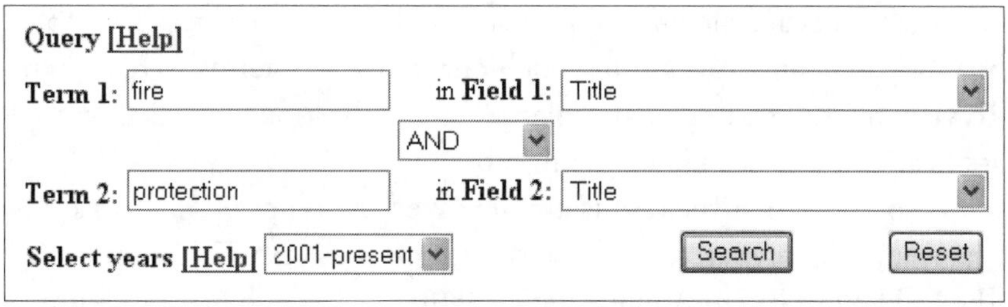

Query [Help]

Term 1: fire in **Field 1:** Title

AND

Term 2: protection in **Field 2:** Title

Select years [Help] 2001-present Search Reset

Figure 4.23

You can see from Figure 4.23 that the Quick Search pages for the issued patents and published patent applications databases are almost identical. One major difference of note is that there is only one selection in the "Select years" dropdown menu for the Published Applications database: 2001-present.

To compose a Quick Search query of published patent applications, use the same methods previously covered for a Quick Search of issued patents discussed in Chapter 3. For example, to search the title fields of published patent applications since 2001 for the words "fire" and "protection," we would fill in the Quick Search fields as shown in Figure 4.23. To perform the search, just click on the Search button.

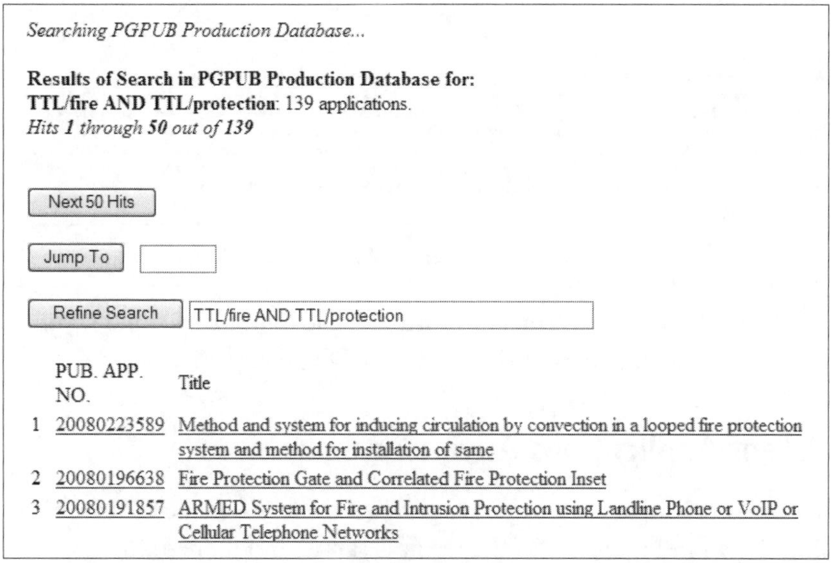

Searching PGPUB Production Database...

Results of Search in PGPUB Production Database for:
TTL/fire AND TTL/protection: 139 applications.
*Hits **1** through **50** out of **139***

Next 50 Hits

Jump To

Refine Search TTL/fire AND TTL/protection

	PUB. APP. NO.	Title
1	20080223589	Method and system for inducing circulation by convection in a looped fire protection system and method for installation of same
2	20080196638	Fire Protection Gate and Correlated Fire Protection Inset
3	20080191857	ARMED System for Fire and Intrusion Protection using Landline Phone or VoIP or Cellular Telephone Networks

Figure 4.24

The results are shown in Figure 4.24. The system has reported 139 hits, or patent applications, in which our two search terms were found. To view the full text of a particular patent application, just click on the application's title or publication number.

Also notice that the results are displayed in groups of 50. To see the next group of search results, just click on the Next 50 Hits button. The full text of Patent Application 200800223589 is shown in Figure 4.25. Here, you can review the inventor's name and patent abstract. By scrolling down the page, you can see the current classification, claims, and description.

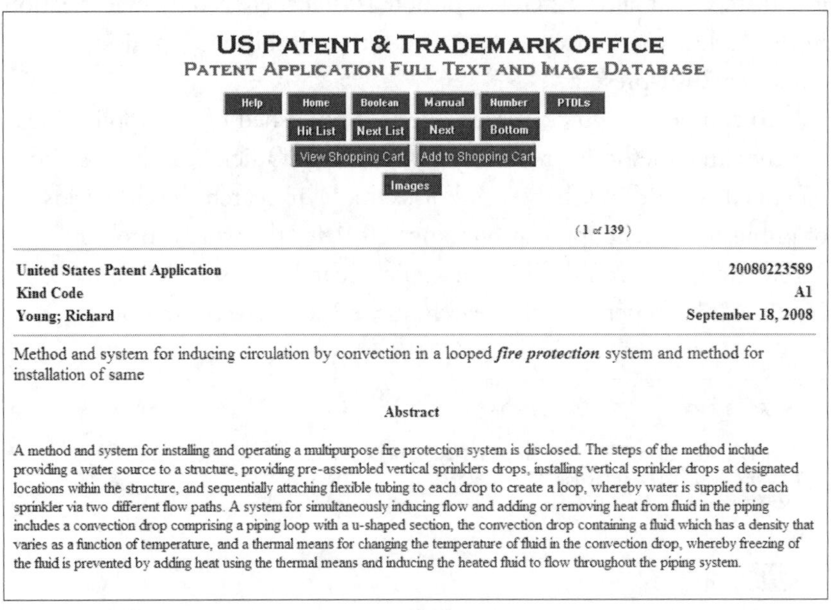

Figure 4.25

By clicking on the "Images" button at the top of Figure 4.25, you can review the drawings of the patent application.

Patent Applications Advanced Search

To get to the Advanced Search page, click on the "Advanced Search" link shown in Figure 4.22. The result is shown in Figure 4.26.

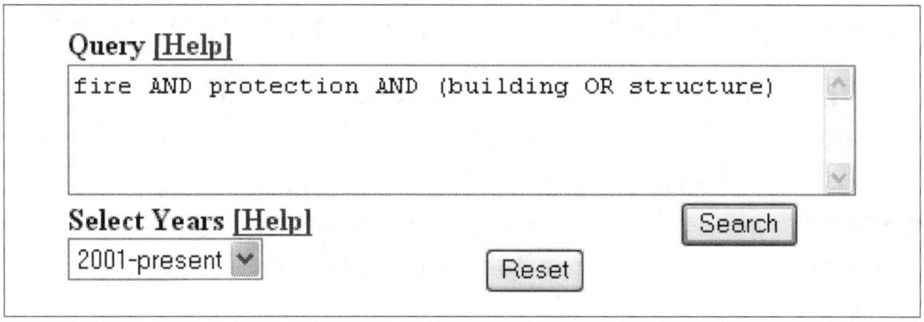

Query [Help]

fire AND protection AND (building OR structure)

Select Years [Help]

2001-present

Search

Reset

Figure 4.26

From Figure 4.26, we see that the Advanced Search pages for the issued patents and published patent applications databases are also almost identical. Again, the major difference is that the "Select Years" dropdown menu for Published Applications is limited to "2001-present."

In Figure 4.26, we have composed the query "fire AND protection AND (building OR structure)." These results are displayed in Figure 4.27.

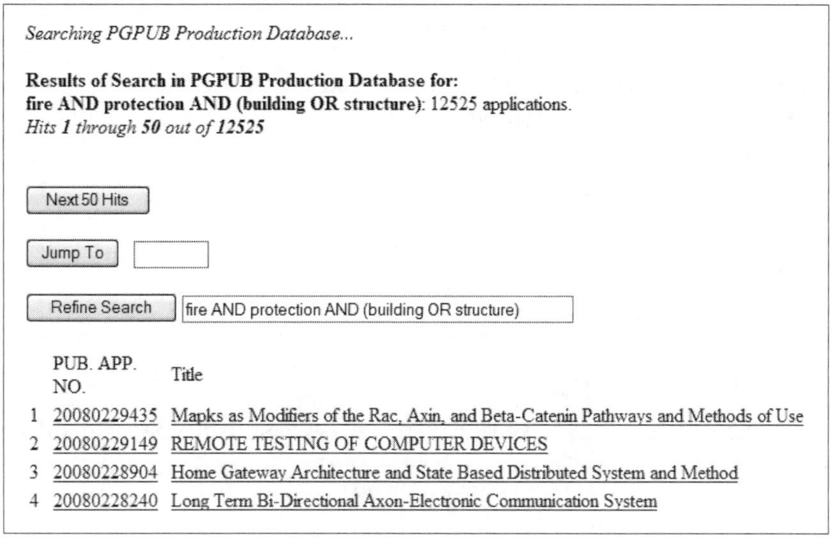

Searching PGPUB Production Database...

Results of Search in PGPUB Production Database for:
fire AND protection AND (building OR structure): 12525 applications.
*Hits **1** through **50** out of **12525***

Next 50 Hits

Jump To

Refine Search fire AND protection AND (building OR structure)

	PUB. APP. NO.	Title
1	20080229435	Mapks as Modifiers of the Rac, Axin, and Beta-Catenin Pathways and Methods of Use
2	20080229149	REMOTE TESTING OF COMPUTER DEVICES
3	20080228904	Home Gateway Architecture and State Based Distributed System and Method
4	20080228240	Long Term Bi-Directional Axon-Electronic Communication System

Figure 4.27

Patent Applications Search by Application Number

To search by patent application number, select the "Publication Number Search" link in Figure 4.22. You will then be presented with the Web page shown in Figure 4.28. To review a particular patent application, just enter the application number into the Query box. In the figure, we have entered Patent Application 20070066165. The results are shown in Figure 4.29.

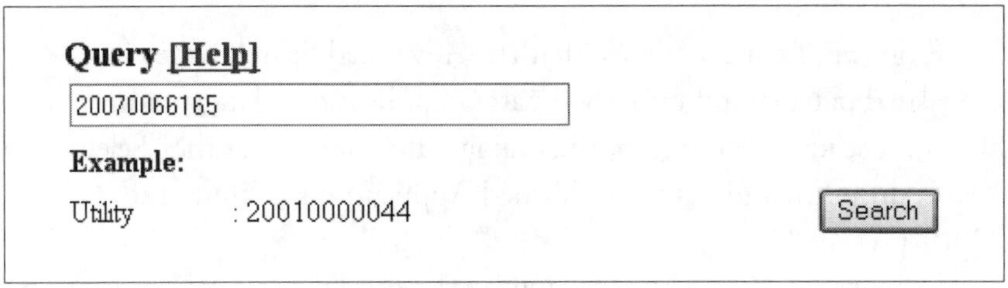

Query [Help]

20070066165

Example:

Utility : 20010000044

Search

Figure 4.28

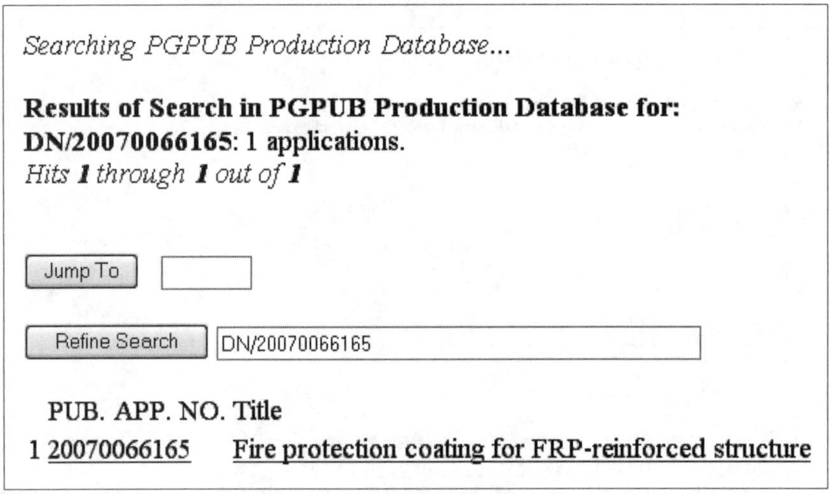

Searching PGPUB Production Database...

Results of Search in PGPUB Production Database for:
DN/20070066165: 1 applications.
*Hits **1** through **1** out of **1***

Jump To

Refine Search DN/20070066165

	PUB. APP. NO.	Title
1	20070066165	Fire protection coating for FRP-reinforced structure

Figure 4.29

One difference between the Published Applications number search and the Issued Patents number search is that when an issued patent number is entered, the results page displays the patent immediately. In the case of the Published Applications number search, an extra step is required. In Figure 4.29, you will see a hit summary consisting of the single patent application we were searching for. To actually review this patent application, it is necessary to click on the patent application number or title. The results are similar to the patent application as displayed in Figure 4.25.

CHAPTER

5

Patent Searching at the EPO Website

So far, we have limited our Internet patent searches to the databases provided by the PTO. However, it is important to look beyond the United States when making a thorough prior art search. As we have explained, just because you are registering your patent within the United States does not mean that prior art is limited to American inventions. Patents issued in other countries are considered valid prior art to be used in the prosecution (patent lingo for the application process) of U.S. applications. This chapter introduces you to the patent search resources available at the European Patent Office (EPO) website.

TIP

To reach the EPO's nonsearch homepage—a source for many helpful patent resources—go to www.epo.org.

Patent Searching at the EPO

A portion of the EPO's patent database homepage (http://ep.espacenet.com) is shown in Figure 5.1. You can see that there are four types of searches that can be performed: quick, advanced, number, and classification. Below, we examine each of these search capabilities.

SmartSearch: A New EPO Search Feature

At the time of publication of this edition, the EPO had launched a beta (test) version of a new search feature known as SmartSearch. SmartSearch uses artificial intelligence to "guess" the patent field in which to search. For example, if you type "General Motors 2008" into the search box, SmartSearch would first look for General Motors as being the inventor/applicant (because the first letters are in uppercase) and would next look for all patents published in 2008 (because your search included a number with four digits, which Smart Search recognizes as being relevant for the year of publication). We expect that the EPO will tweak this new and exciting feature within the coming years.

Quick Search

To perform a quick search at the EPO website click on the "Quick Search" link shown in Figure 5.1. You will then be presented with the Web page shown in Figure 5.2.

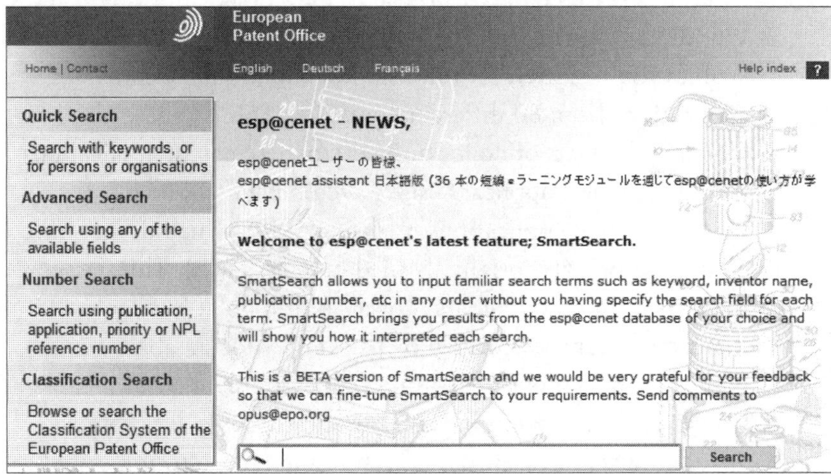

Figure 5.1

Quick Search

1. Database

Select patent database: Worldwide
EP - esp@cenet
Worldwide
WIPO - esp@cenet

2. Type of search

Select whether you wish to search with simple words in the titles or abstracts (where available) or with the name of an individual or organisation:

Select what to search: ⊙ Words in the title or abstract ○ Persons or organisations

3. Search terms

Enter search terms (not case sensitive):

Search term(s): fire AND protection plastic and bicycle

SEARCH CLEAR

Figure 5.2

As you can see, there are three steps to performing a quick search at the EPO website: (1) Select a search database; (2) choose the type of search; and (3) enter your search terms.

Step 1: Selecting a Database

When selecting a search database, the available choices are:

- **Worldwide.** This is the default selection. The worldwide database enables you to search for information about published patent applications from 80 different countries. This database also contains abstracts of nonexamined Japanese patent applications filed by Japanese applicants since October 1976, and all Japanese patent applications filed since 1998 which do not have a Japanese priority (originally filed outside Japan). This database includes millions of patents—over 56 million at last count. The list of countries covered by the worldwide database along with their corresponding country codes are shown in the table below. The importance of these country codes will become apparent when we view our search results. It is also important to note that the content of the worldwide database varies from country to country. Some country collections have abstracts and international classification codes, while others may not even have titles.

TIP

You can obtain detailed coverage of the worldwide database at: http://patentinfo.european-patent-office.org/_resources/data/pdf/global_patent_data_coverage.pdf.

- **EP.** The European Patent (EP) applications database selection enables you to search the patent applications published by the EPO over the last 24 months. In both the WIPO (discussed below) and EP databases, it is not possible to perform searches either in the abstract field or using a European classification symbol.

Country Codes Used by the EPO	
Country Code	**Name of Country**
AP	African Regional Industrial Property Organization
AR	Argentina
AT	Austria
AU	Australia
BA	Bosnia and Herzegovina
BE	Belgium
BG	Bulgaria
BR	Brazil
CA	Canada
CH	Switzerland
CN	China
CS	Czechoslovakia (up to 1993)
CU	Cuba
CY	Cyprus
CZ	Czech Republic
DD	Germany, excluding the territory that, prior to October 3, 1990, constituted the Federal Republic of Germany
DE	Germany
DK	Denmark
DZ	Algeria
EA	Eurasian Patent Organization
EE	Estonia
EG	Egypt
EP	European Patent Office
ES	Spain
FI	Finland
FR	France
GB	United Kingdom
GR	Greece
HK	Hong Kong
HR	Croatia
HU	Hungary
IE	Ireland
IL	Israel
IN	India
IT	Italy
JP	Japan
KE	Kenya

Country Codes Used by the EPO (cont'd)	
Country Code	**Name of Country**
KR	Republic of Korea
LT	Lithuania
LU	Luxembourg
LV	Latvia
MC	Monaco
MD	Republic of Moldova
MN	Mongolia
MT	Malta
MW	Malawi
MX	Mexico
MY	Malaysia
NC	New Caledonia
NL	Netherlands
NO	Norway
NZ	New Zealand
OA	African Intellectual Property Organization
PH	Philippines
PL	Poland
PT	Portugal
RO	Romania
RU	Russian Federation
SE	Sweden
SG	Singapore
SI	Slovenia
SK	Slovakia
SU	Union of Soviet Socialist Republics (USSR)
TJ	Tajikistan
TR	Turkey
TT	Trinidad and Tobago
TW	Taiwan
UA	Ukraine
US	United States of America
VN	Vietnam
WO	World Intellectual Property Organization (WIPO)
YU	Yugoslavia
ZA	South Africa
ZM	Zambia
ZW	Zimbabwe

- **WIPO.** The World Intellectual Property Organization (WIPO) is a United Nations agency that administers many international treaties dealing with different aspects of intellectual property protection. This database selection enables you to search in the patent applications published by the WIPO (WO publications) in the last 24 months. Only the bibliographic data of WO patent documents can be searched and displayed.

Step 2: Type of Search

Next, you must select a type of search. There are two radio box selections available: (Figure 5.2) Words in the title or abstract, or Persons and organizations.

Step 3: Search Terms

The third and final step is to enter one or more search terms. Multiple terms may be connected by Boolean operators.

In Figure 5.2 we have selected the worldwide database, elected to search for words in the title or abstract, and entered the query "fire AND protection." The results are shown in Figure 5.3.

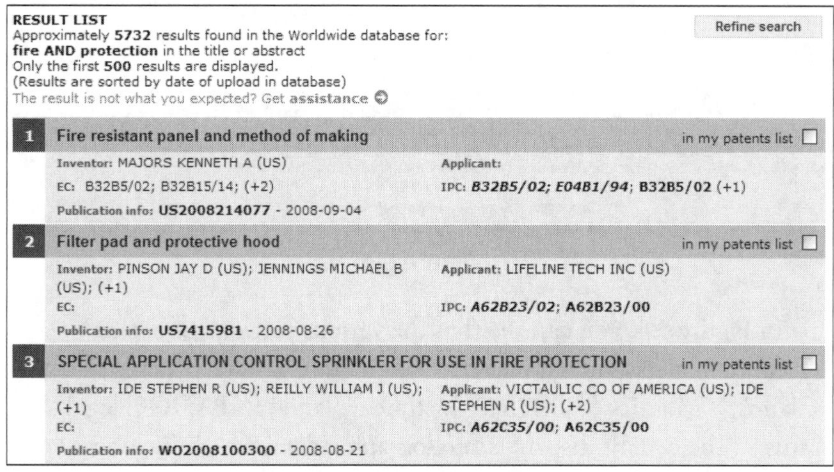

Figure 5.3

From the summary at the top of the figure we see that there were 5,732 hits returned from the worldwide database. The first three hits are shown in Figure 5.3. Each hit displays the title of the document (a link which will take you to a further description of the patent), the inventor's name, the applicant (not necessarily the same as the inventor), the European classification symbols (EC—a link to a classification description), the International Patent Classification symbols (IPC) and the publication information (publication number and date).

If you click on the patent title from Hit 1 in Figure 5.3 (Fire/smoke protection zone formation system) you will see a further description of the patent as shown in Figure 5.4.

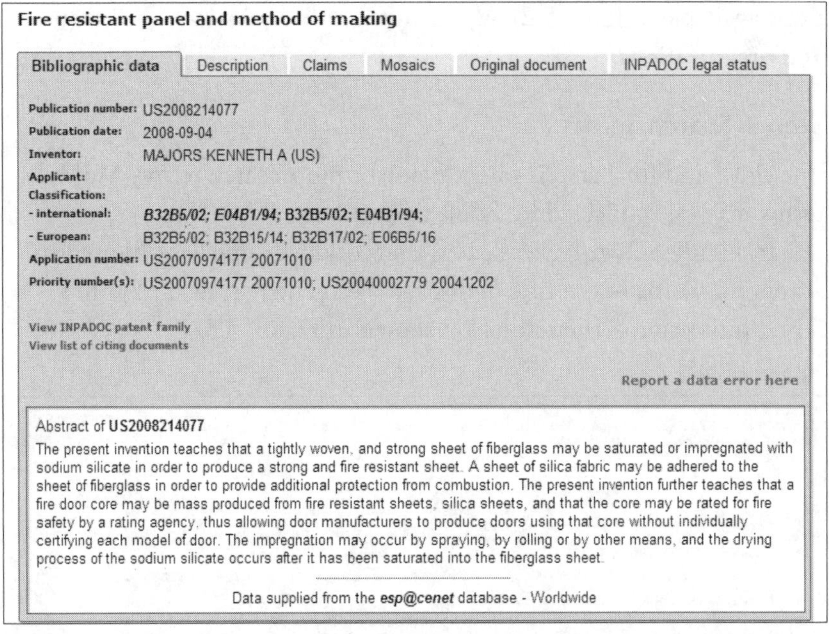

Figure 5.4

In Figure 5.4, you can see that the various sections of patent information are separated by tabs: "Bibliographic data," "description," "Claims," "Mosaics," "Original document," and "INPADOC legal status." (The default display is Bibliographic data, which includes the patent abstract.) In the example in Figure 5.4, certain tabs are grayed out because the information is not available. You can see an example of a mosaic of the patent drawings from another patent in Figure 5.5. You will need Adobe Reader installed to view the images.

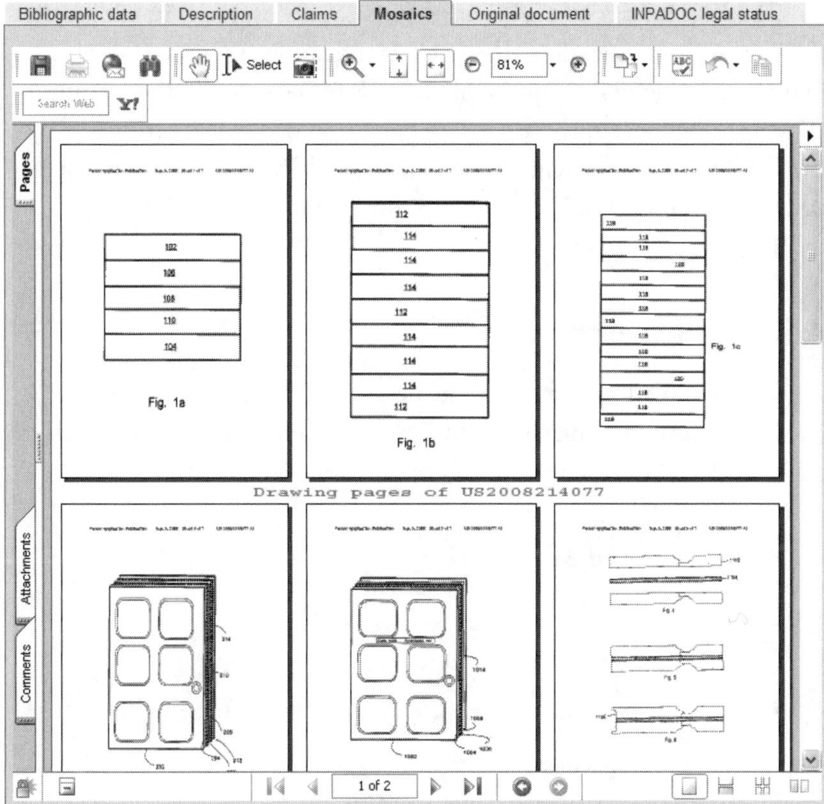

Figure 5.5

Before moving on to advanced and classification searching, a further discussion of classification symbols is in order. The IPC has a hierarchical structure as shown below.

The International Patent Classification Structure	
Sections	e.g., A
Classes	e.g., A47
Subclasses	e.g., A47J
Groups	e.g., A47J37
Subgroups	e.g., A47J37/06

The IPC is used by PTOs of various countries, often in addition to a national classification. The IPC classification system currently divides technology into approximately 68,000 subareas. The European Classification System (ECLA) is an extension of the IPC. It is used by the EPO to classify patent applications. The EPO classification system adds subgroups to the IPC symbol—for example, A47J37/06C or A47J37/06C3.

Advanced Search

To perform an advanced search at the EPO website, click on the "Advanced Search" link shown in Figure 5.1 and you will see a Web page similar to that shown in Figure 5.6.

Advanced Search

1. Database

Select patent database:	Worldwide

2. Search terms

Enter keywords in English

Field	Entry	Example
Keyword(s) in title:		plastic and bicycle
Keyword(s) in title or abstract:	Fire AND Protection	hair
Publication number:		WO03075629
Application number:		DE19971031696
Priority number:		WO1995US15925
Publication date:	2006 2007	yyyymmdd
Applicant(s):		Institut Pasteur
Inventor(s):		Smith
European Classification (ECLA):		F03G7/10
International Patent Classification (IPC):		H03M1/12

SEARCH CLEAR

Figure 5.6

As you can see in Figure 5.6, there are now several fields available to narrow your search results. For example, in Figure 5.6 we have entered the years 2006 and 2007 to limit our returned search matches to those years. In the "Keyword(s) in the title or abstract" field we have repeated the search query "Fire AND Protection." You are limited to a maximum of four search terms in each search field. The results of the search are shown in Figure 5.7, where the number of hits has been reduced from 5,732 to 745 just by limiting the years to be searched.

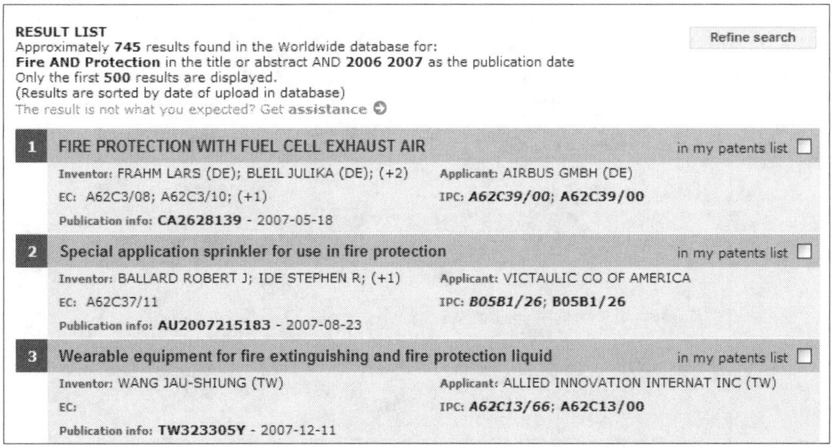

RESULT LIST
Approximately **745** results found in the Worldwide database for:
Fire AND Protection in the title or abstract AND **2006 2007** as the publication date
Only the first **500** results are displayed.
(Results are sorted by date of upload in database)
The result is not what you expected? Get **assistance**

Refine search

1 FIRE PROTECTION WITH FUEL CELL EXHAUST AIR — in my patents list
Inventor: FRAHM LARS (DE); BLEIL JULIKA (DE); (+2) — Applicant: AIRBUS GMBH (DE)
EC: A62C3/08; A62C3/10; (+1) — IPC: ***A62C39/00***; **A62C39/00**
Publication info: **CA2628139** - 2007-05-18

2 Special application sprinkler for use in fire protection — in my patents list
Inventor: BALLARD ROBERT J; IDE STEPHEN R; (+1) — Applicant: VICTAULIC CO OF AMERICA
EC: A62C37/11 — IPC: ***B05B1/26***; **B05B1/26**
Publication info: **AU2007215183** - 2007-08-23

3 Wearable equipment for fire extinguishing and fire protection liquid — in my patents list
Inventor: WANG JAU-SHIUNG (TW) — Applicant: ALLIED INNOVATION INTERNAT INC (TW)
EC: — IPC: ***A62C13/66***; **A62C13/00**
Publication info: **TW323305Y** - 2007-12-11

Figure 5.7

Of particular significance is the patent classification. For the first patent shown in Figure 5.7 (Fire protection with fuel cell exhaust air), there are two EC symbols: A62C3/08 and A62C3/10. Note that a maximum of three IPC or ECLA classifications will be displayed in the results. If a patent is allocated to more than three classes, this is shown by a plus sign (+) followed by the number of additional classes. In this case, there is one additional class denoted by "(+1)." From the classification discussion in the previous section, we know that the first three IPC characters (A62) signify Section A, Class 62 in the IPC Classification hierarchy.

To use the IPC classification to further limit the search results, we enter A62 in the IPC field as shown in Figure 5.8. The results are shown in Figure 5.9.

Advanced Search

1. Database

Select patent database:	Worldwide	

2. Search terms

Enter keywords in English

Field	Entry	Example
Keyword(s) in title:		plastic and bicycle
Keyword(s) in title or abstract:	Fire AND Protection	hair
Publication number:		WO03075629
Application number:		DE19971031696
Priority number:		WO1995US15925
Publication date:	2006 2007	yyyymmdd
Applicant(s):		Institut Pasteur
Inventor(s):		Smith
European Classification (ECLA):		F03G7/10
International Patent Classification (IPC):	A62	H03M1/12

SEARCH CLEAR

Figure 5.8

RESULT LIST
Approximately **200** results found in the Worldwide database for:
Fire AND Protection in the title or abstract AND **2006 2007** as the publication date AND **A62** as the IPC classification
(Results are sorted by date of upload in database)
The result is not what you expected? Get **assistance**

Refine search

1 FIRE PROTECTION WITH FUEL CELL EXHAUST AIR in my patents list
Inventor: FRAHM LARS (DE); BLEIL JULIKA (DE); (+2) Applicant: AIRBUS GMBH (DE)
EC: A62C3/08; A62C3/10; (+1) IPC: ***A62C39/00***; **A62C39/00**
Publication info: **CA2628139** - 2007-05-18

2 Wearable equipment for fire extinguishing and fire protection liquid in my patents list
Inventor: WANG JAU-SHIUNG (TW) Applicant: ALLIED INNOVATION INTERNAT INC (TW)
EC: IPC: ***A62C13/66***; **A62C13/00**
Publication info: **TW323305Y** - 2007-12-11

3 GARMENT COMPRISING FIRE RESISTANT MESH in my patents list
Inventor: SILVER JAMES BARRY (CA) Applicant: SAFETY SHORT WORKWAIR INC (CA)
EC: A41D13/02; A41D13/05B; (+2) IPC: ***A41D13/00; A62B17/00***; **A41D13/00** (+1)
Publication info: **CA2510827** - 2006-12-22

Figure 5.9

Classification Search

To perform a classification search at the EPO website, click on the "Classification Search" link shown in Figure 5.1, after which you will see the Web page shown in Figure 5.10. In the figure, the main European Classification Sections A through H are displayed. Across the top of the display are two search boxes. The center search box allows you to search the European classification index by keyword. The box on the right allows you to retrieve the class description for a specific class/subclass.

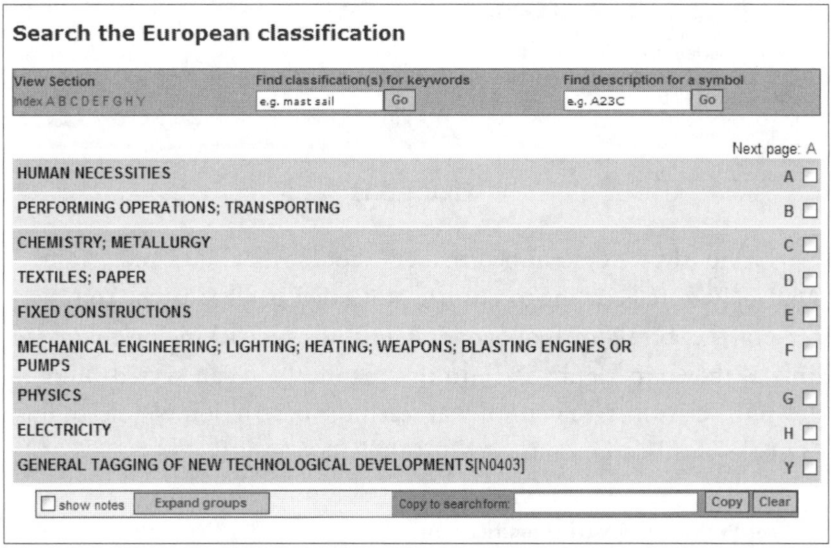

Figure 5.10

The class section letters are actually hypertext links that will direct you to a breakdown of the classes contained within that section. Figure 5.11 shows this breakdown for Section A—Human Necessities.

Search the European classification

View Section	Find classification(s) for keywords	Find description for a symbol
Index A B C D E F G H Y	syringe injection [Go]	e.g. A21D10 [Go]

Next page: A01

HUMAN NECESSITIES	A
AGRICULTURE; FORESTRY; ANIMAL HUSBANDRY; HUNTING; TRAPPING; FISHING	A01
BAKING; EDIBLE DOUGHS	A21
BUTCHERING; MEAT TREATMENT; PROCESSING POULTRY OR FISH	A22
FOODS OR FOODSTUFFS; THEIR TREATMENT, NOT COVERED BY OTHER CLASSES	A23
TOBACCO; CIGARS; CIGARETTES; SMOKERS' REQUISITES	A24
WEARING APPAREL	A41
HEADWEAR	A42
FOOTWEAR	A43
HABERDASHERY; JEWELLERY	A44
HAND OR TRAVELLING ARTICLES	A45
BRUSHWARE	A46
FURNITURE (arrangements of seats for, or adaptations of seats to, vehicles B60N); DOMESTIC ARTICLES OR APPLIANCES; COFFEE MILLS; SPICE MILLS; SUCTION CLEANERS IN GENERAL (ladders E06C)	A47
MEDICAL OR VETERINARY SCIENCE; HYGIENE	A61
LIFE-SAVING; FIRE-FIGHTING (ladders E06C)	A62
SPORTS; GAMES; AMUSEMENTS	A63

show notes [Expand groups] Copy to searchform: [Copy] [Clear]

Figure 5.11

Previously, we determined that IPC codes A62C3/08 and A62C3/10 were germane to our fire protection patent search. You can get a further breakdown of Section/Class A62 by clicking on that link (as shown in Figure 5.11). In this manner, you can keep drilling down the class hierarchy until you reach the description you need. For example, the description for A62C3/00 is shown in Figure 5.12.

Search the European classification

View Section	Find classification(s) for keywords	Find description for a symbol
Index A B C D E F G H Y	syringe injection [Go]	e.g. A21D10 [Go]

Previous page: A61Q99/00 Next page: A62B

HUMAN NECESSITIES	A
LIFE-SAVING; FIRE-FIGHTING (ladders E06C)	A62
DEVICES, APPARATUS OR METHODS FOR LIFE-SAVING (valves specially adapted for medical use A61M39/00; life-saving devices, apparatus or methods specially adapted for use in water B63C9/00; divers' equipment B63C11/00; specially adopted for use with aircraft, e.g. parachutes, ejector seats, B64D; rescue devices peculiar to mining E21F11/00)	A62B
FIRE-FIGHTING (fire-extinguishing compositions, use of chemical substances in extinguishing fires A62D1/00; spraying, applying liquids or other fluent materials to surfaces in general B05; alarm arrangements G08B, e.g. fire alarms actuated by smoke or gases G08B17/10)	A62C
CHEMICAL MEANS FOR EXTINGUISHING FIRES OR FOR COMBATING OR PROTECTING AGAINST HARMFUL CHEMICAL AGENTS; CHEMICAL MATERIALS FOR USE IN BREATHING APPARATUS	A62D

show notes [Expand groups] Copy to searchform: [Copy] [Clear]

Figure 5.12

If you would like a shortcut to produce a list of every issued patent within a certain class, click inside the check box next to the class designation. For example, we have checked the box for A62C39 shown in Figure 5.12.

Next, you would click the "Copy" button next to the "Copy to searchform" entry box shown at the bottom of Figures 5.11 and 5.12. That causes the Advanced Search panel to pop up with the appropriate ECLA classification already filled in. This result is shown in Figure 5.13.

Advanced Search

1. Database

Select patent database:	Worldwide

2. Search terms

Enter keywords in English

Field	Entry	Example
Keyword(s) in title:		plastic and bicycle
Keyword(s) in title or abstract:		hair
Publication number:		WO03075629
Application number:		DE19971031696
Priority number:		WO1995US15925
Publication date:		yyyymmdd
Applicant(s):		Institut Pasteur
Inventor(s):		Smith
European Classification (ECLA):	A62C39	F03G7/10
International Patent Classification (IPC):		H03M1/12

SEARCH CLEAR

Figure 5.13

To produce a list of all the patents within the ECLA class A62C39, click the "Search" button shown at the bottom of Figure 5.13. The result is shown in Figure 5.14.

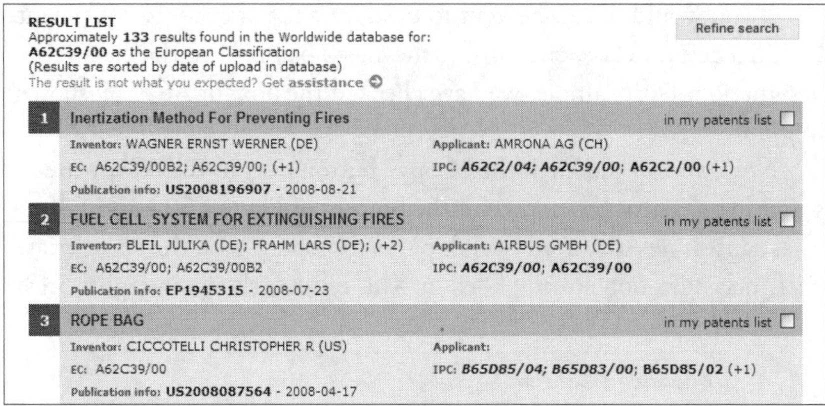

Figure 5.14

If you already know the class symbols, you can go directly to a description of that class by entering those symbols into the description box shown at the right of Figure 5.15.

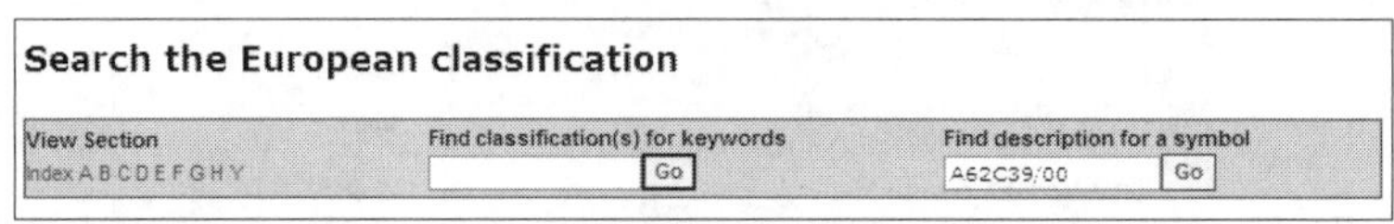

Figure 5.15

You can also search the European classification hierarchy by entering keywords into the search box shown in the center of Figure 5.15.

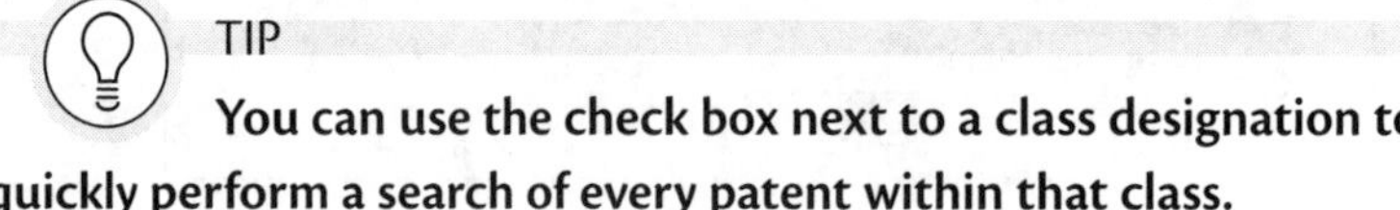

TIP

You can use the check box next to a class designation to quickly perform a search of every patent within that class.

Number Search

To perform a patent number search at the EPO website, click on the "Number Search" link shown in Figure 5.1. You will then see a Number Search Web page as presented in Figure 5.16.

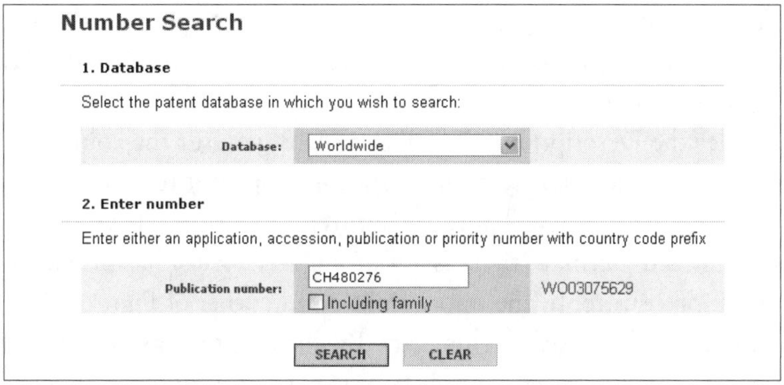

Number Search

1. Database

Select the patent database in which you wish to search:

Database: Worldwide

2. Enter number

Enter either an application, accession, publication or priority number with country code prefix

Publication number: CH480276 WO03075629

Including family

SEARCH CLEAR

Figure 5.16

In Figure 5.16, we selected the Worldwide database and entered CH480276. This patent was one of the foreign patents referenced in our search in Chapter 3 (Figure 3.15). The results are shown in Figure 5.17.

RESULT LIST
1 result found in the Worldwide database for:
CH480276 as the publication, application, priority or NPL reference number
(Results are sorted by date of upload in database)
The result is not what you expected? Get **assistance**

Refine search

1 **Verbundsicherheitsscheibe** in my patents list

Inventor: PEILSTOECKER GUENTER DR (DE); DIETZEL KARL DR (DE)
Applicant: BAYER AG (DE)
EC: B32B17/10C4; B32B27/00
IPC: ***B32B17/10; B32B27/00; C03C27/12*** (+5)
Publication info: **CH480276** - 1969-10-31

Figure 5.17

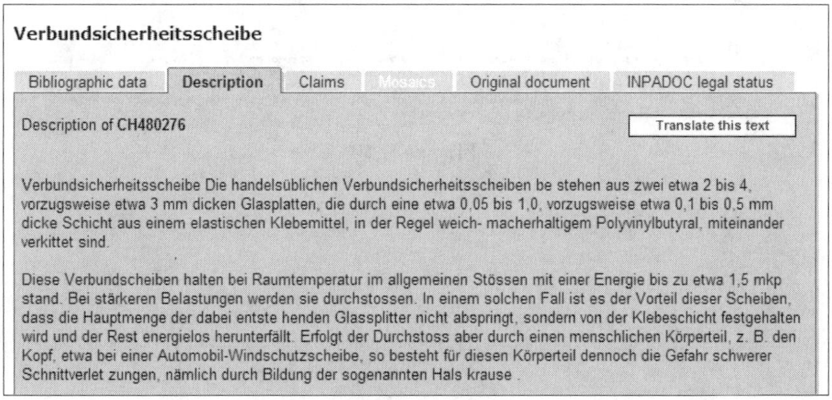

Verbundsicherheitsscheibe

Bibliographic data | **Description** | Claims | Mosaics | Original document | INPADOC legal status

Description of CH480276

Translate this text

Verbundsicherheitsscheibe Die handelsüblichen Verbundsicherheitsscheiben be stehen aus zwei etwa 2 bis 4, vorzugsweise etwa 3 mm dicken Glasplatten, die durch eine etwa 0,05 bis 1,0, vorzugsweise etwa 0,1 bis 0,5 mm dicke Schicht aus einem elastischen Klebemittel, in der Regel weich- macherhaltigem Polyvinylbutyral, miteinander verkittet sind.

Diese Verbundscheiben halten bei Raumtemperatur im allgemeinen Stössen mit einer Energie bis zu etwa 1,5 mkp stand. Bei stärkeren Belastungen werden sie durchstossen. In einem solchen Fall ist es der Vorteil dieser Scheiben, dass die Hauptmenge der dabei entste henden Glassplitter nicht abspringt, sondern von der Klebeschicht festgehalten wird und der Rest energielos herunterfällt. Erfolgt der Durchstoss aber durch einen menschlichen Körperteil, z. B. den Kopf, etwa bei einer Automobil-Windschutzscheibe, so besteht für diesen Körperteil dennoch die Gefahr schwerer Schnittverlet zungen, nämlich durch Bildung der sogenannten Hals krause .

Figure 5.18

To read a description of this patent, click on the patent title and you will see the result as shown in Figure 5.18 where we have displayed the Description tab.

Under the Description tab in Figure 5.18, you see the country code "CH," which refers to Switzerland. It's apparent from the text of the patent description that it was written in German. If you don't happen to read German, there is a solution—the EPO has provided a translation feature. In the upper right-hand corner of Figure 5.18 is a button labeled "Translate this text." By clicking on this button you will be presented with an English-language translation of the German-language Description for this patent. The result of this action is shown in Figure 5.19.

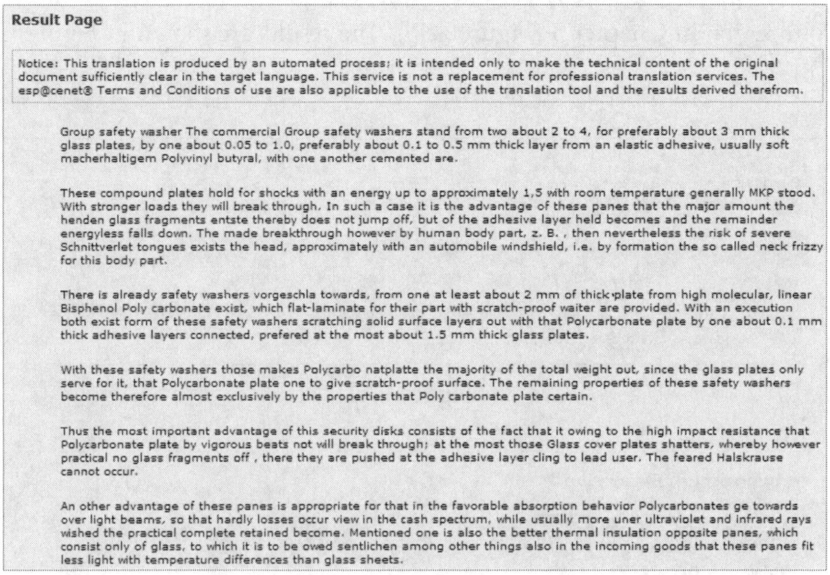

Result Page

Notice: This translation is produced by an automated process; it is intended only to make the technical content of the original document sufficiently clear in the target language. This service is not a replacement for professional translation services. The esp@cenet® Terms and Conditions of use are also applicable to the use of the translation tool and the results derived therefrom.

Group safety washer The commercial Group safety washers stand from two about 2 to 4, for preferably about 3 mm thick glass plates, by one about 0.05 to 1.0, preferably about 0.1 to 0.5 mm thick layer from an elastic adhesive, usually soft macherhaltigem Polyvinyl butyral, with one another cemented are.

These compound plates hold for shocks with an energy up to approximately 1,5 with room temperature generally MKP stood. With stronger loads they will break through. In such a case it is the advantage of these panes that the major amount the henden glass fragments entste thereby does not jump off, but of the adhesive layer held becomes and the remainder energyless falls down. The made breakthrough however by human body part, z. B. , then nevertheless the risk of severe Schnittverlet tongues exists the head, approximately with an automobile windshield, i.e. by formation the so called neck frizzy for this body part.

There is already safety washers vorgeschla towards, from one at least about 2 mm of thick plate from high molecular, linear Bisphenol Poly carbonate exist, which flat-laminate for their part with scratch-proof waiter are provided. With an execution both exist form of these safety washers scratching solid surface layers out with that Polycarbonate plate by one about 0.1 mm thick adhesive layers connected, prefered at the most about 1.5 mm thick glass plates.

With these safety washers those makes Polycarbo natplatte the majority of the total weight out, since the glass plates only serve for it, that Polycarbonate plate one to give scratch-proof surface. The remaining properties of these safety washers become therefore almost exclusively by the properties that Poly carbonate plate certain.

Thus the most important advantage of this security disks consists of the fact that it owing to the high impact resistance that Polycarbonate plate by vigorous beats not will break through; at the most those Glass cover plates shatters, whereby however practical no glass fragments off , there they are pushed at the adhesive layer cling to lead user. The feared Halskrause cannot occur.

An other advantage of these panes is appropriate for that in the favorable absorption behavior Polycarbonates ge towards over light beams, so that hardly losses occur view in the cash spectrum, while usually more uner ultraviolet and infrared rays wished the practical complete retained become. Mentioned one is also the better thermal insulation opposite panes, which consist only of glass, to which it is to be owed sentlichen among other things also in the incoming goods that these panes fit less light with temperature differences than glass sheets.

Figure 5.19

CHAPTER

6

Other Patent Search Websites

There are numerous patent databases besides the PTO and the EPO. Some offer free searching; others involve a fee. In this chapter we will review a few of these resources.

SurfIP

SurfIP (www.surfIP.com) is a powerful search engine that allows users to retrieve patent information, discover invention commercialization opportunities, and search for patent professionals. The site is an initiative of the Intellectual Property Office of Singapore.

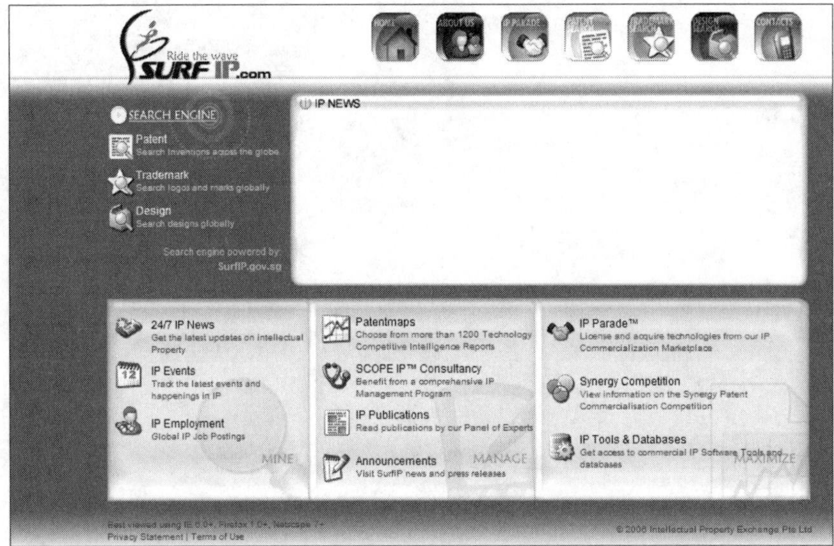

Figure 6.1

Database Coverage

The data sources covered in SurfIP patent searches are shown in the table below.

SurfIP Patent Search Database Coverage	
USPTO	Patents from the U.S. Patent and Trademark Office
EPO	Patent applications published in the last 24 months, from the EPO
IPOS	Patent documents from the Intellectual Property Office of Singapore
SIPO	Patent documents from the State Intellectual Property Office of the P.R.C.
CIPO	Granted patents from the Canadian Intellectual Property Office
WIPO	Patent Cooperation Treaty publications from the World Intellectual Property Organization
TIPO	Patent bibliographic data provided by Chinese Taipei Patent Index
UKPO	Patent applications published in the last 24 months, from the UK PTO
KIPO	Patent documents from the Korean Intellectual Property PTO
TIPIC	Patent documents from the Thailand Industrial Property Information Center
PM	Descriptions of patent mapping and analysis reports from Patentmaps.com

You can use SurfIP to search patents across multiple databases and then sort, aggregate, and integrate the results. When you enter a search query, that query is performed at the various sites using the search engines on those sites. Selection boxes are used instead of command line interfaces that require users to remember syntax and filenames.

To perform a patent search at the SurfIP website, click on the "Patent—Search Inventions across the globe" link shown at the upper left of Figure 6.1. Next you will see the Web page shown in Figure 6.2.

There are five types of searches that can be performed: a quick search, simple search, IPC Search, patent number search, and structured search. The Quick Search screen in Figure 6.2 provides results with minimal user configuration and searches all available patent data sources. The user can simply enter the search criteria and start the search.

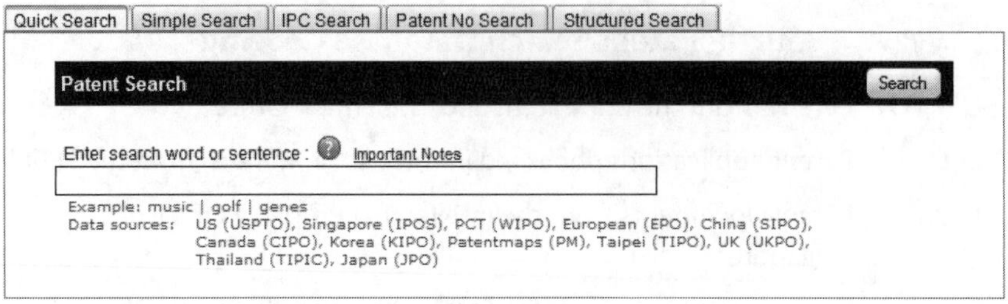

Quick Search | Simple Search | IPC Search | Patent No Search | Structured Search

Patent Search — Search

Enter search word or sentence : Important Notes

Example: music | golf | genes
Data sources: US (USPTO), Singapore (IPOS), PCT (WIPO), European (EPO), China (SIPO), Canada (CIPO), Korea (KIPO), Patentmaps (PM), Taipei (TIPO), UK (UKPO), Thailand (TIPIC), Japan (JPO)

Figure 6.2

In Simple Search, the user can search in one or more patent data sources. These data sources are selected by clicking on the appropriate box as shown in Figure 6.3. Clicking the ALL option (seen on the right side of the box) selects all available patent sources.

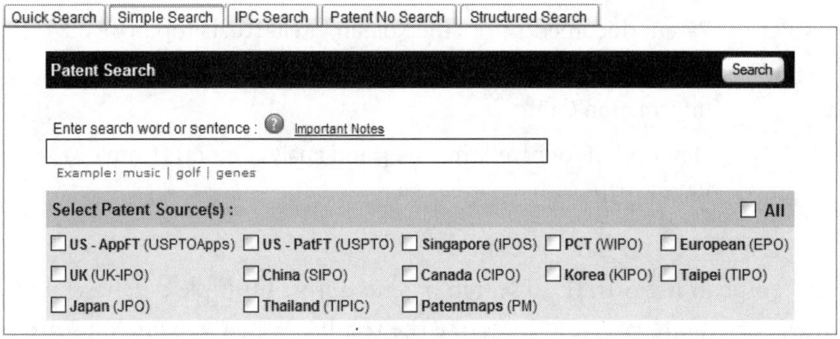

Quick Search | Simple Search | IPC Search | Patent No Search | Structured Search

Patent Search — Search

Enter search word or sentence : Important Notes

Example: music | golf | genes

Select Patent Source(s) : All

US - AppFT (USPTOApps) | US - PatFT (USPTO) | Singapore (IPOS) | PCT (WIPO) | European (EPO)
UK (UK-IPO) | China (SIPO) | Canada (CIPO) | Korea (KIPO) | Taipei (TIPO)
Japan (JPO) | Thailand (TIPIC) | Patentmaps (PM)

Figure 6.3

Figure 6.4 shows the IPC Search tab. In IPC Search the user can search by IPC codes. The results display all patent documents classified under the queried subclass, group, or subgroup. For information on IPC listings, please refer to the WIPO website (www.wipo.int) and see International Classifications (www.wipo.int/ classifications/fulltext/ new_ipc/ipcen.html).

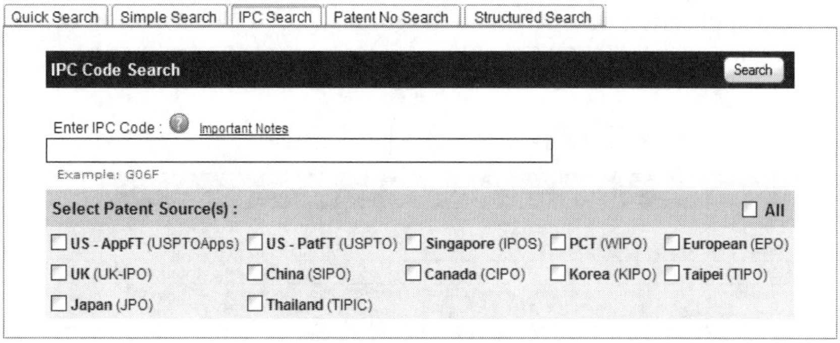

Figure 6.4

The table below shows the entry format for an IPC search for different sources. Truncation searching is supported by some sources.

IPC Entry Format		
Data Source	**Subclass Format**	**Group and Subgroup Format**
USPTO	G06F*	G06F 19/00
WIPO	G06F	G06F-19/00
EPO	G06F	G06F 19/00
IPOS	G06F	G06F 19/00; G06F 19*
SIPO	G06F*	G06F19/00, G06F19*
CIPO	G06F	G06F 19/00
TIPO	G06F	G06F19/00
UKPO	G06F	G06F19/00
KIPO	G06F	G06F 19/00
TIPIC	G06F	G06F19

Figure 6.5 shows the Patent Search tab. In patent number search, the user can search for published patent applications and granted patents, where available, by entering the appropriate patent number. Please note that searching the Application Number in the USPTO currently returns the application serial number of U.S. granted patents.

Actual application numbers searches from the USPTO will only be available when the U.S. Patent Applications database (AppFT) is added.

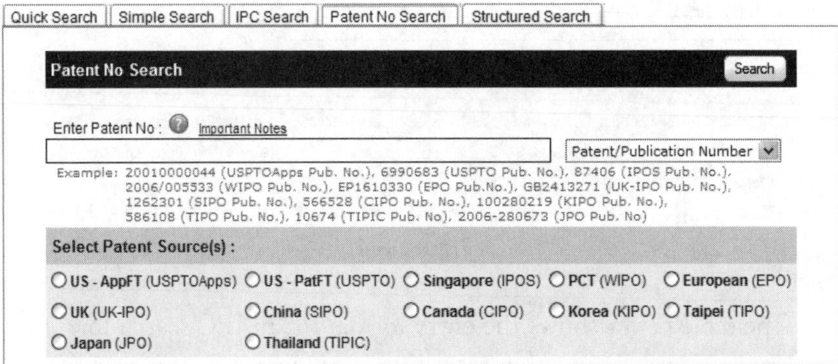

Figure 6.5

The entry format for application number and publication number searches differ from source to source. The table below illustrates the correct format that should be entered in the various data sources. Entering the number in other formats may lead to inaccurate results.

Patent Number Search Formats		
Data Source	**Application Number Format**	**Publication Number Format**
USPTO	845948	6990683
WIPO	EP/2004/008531	2005/098230
EPO	EP20020762866	EP1333613
IPOS	200507268-1	117045
SIPO	100762	1309841
CIPO	2172863	566528
TIPO	90121515	595092
UKPO	GB20040008721	GB2413271A
KIPO	1019980006278	100280219
TIPIC	13884	10674

Boolean and truncation searches are not supported for application number and publication number fields.

Quick Search | Simple Search | IPC Search | Patent No Search | Structured Search

Patent Structured Search Search

Structured Search : Important Notes

Select a Field

AND Select a Field

AND Select a Field

AND Select a Field

Reset

Select Patent Source(s) : All

US - AppFT (USPTOApps) **US - PatFT** (USPTO) **Singapore** (IPOS) **PCT** (WIPO) **European** (EPO)

UK (UK-IPO) **China** (SIPO) **Canada** (CIPO) **Korea** (KIPO) **Taipei** (TIPO)

Thailand (TIPIC)

Figure 6.6

Figure 6.6 shows the Structured Search tab. In Structured Search, you can search within individual fields of patent documents. Structured Search also provides for searching combinations of fields with the AND operator provided.

The same field should not be selected in more than one dropdown box. Patent Structured Search does support Boolean searching within a field. For instance, to search for "radio AND signal" in the "Title" field, the user should select the "Title" field once and enter the entire Boolean query in the corresponding text box—that is, instead of selecting the "Title" field in two separate dropdown boxes, keying "radio" and "signal" separately, and then connecting them with an AND operator.

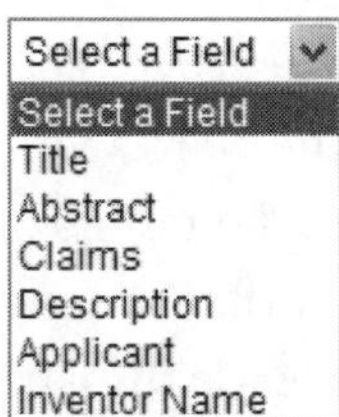

Figure 6.7

(Figure 6.7, shows the various fields available from the "Select a Field" dropdown menu.) The table below shows the fields supported in Structured Search for available patent data sources.

Supported Fields in Structured Search						
Database	**Title**	**Abstract**	**Claims**	**Description**	**Applicant**	**Inventor**
USPTO	✓	✓	✓	✓	✓	✓
WIPO	✓	✓	✓	✓	✓	✓
EPO	✓				✓	✓
IPOS	✓	✓			✓	✓
SIPO	✓	✓			✓	✓
CIPO	✓	✓	✓		✓	✓
TIPO	✓	✓			✓	✓
UKPO	✓				✓	✓
KIPO	✓	✓			✓	✓
TIPIC	✓	✓	✓		✓	✓

The Boolean operators available for searching include AND, OR, and NOT. The right truncation operator "*" and the single truncation operator "?" can also be used where supported—for example, a search for "car*" will return patents containing the words carbon, cartel, and so on, while a search for "car?" will return patents containing the words card, cars, and others. A search for a phrase or a combination of words, such as "motor vehicle," will return all patents containing the phrase, not the individual words. Phrases can also be searched in combination with Boolean searches—for example, a search for ""motor vehicle," NOT car" will return all patents that contain the phrase "motor vehicle" and do not contain the word "car."

In Figure 6.8, you can see the results of a structured search for " "motor vehicle" NOT car" in the Abstract field of all available databases. Results from each source are displayed in separate tabs. (In Figure 6.8, the Combined Result tab has been selected.)

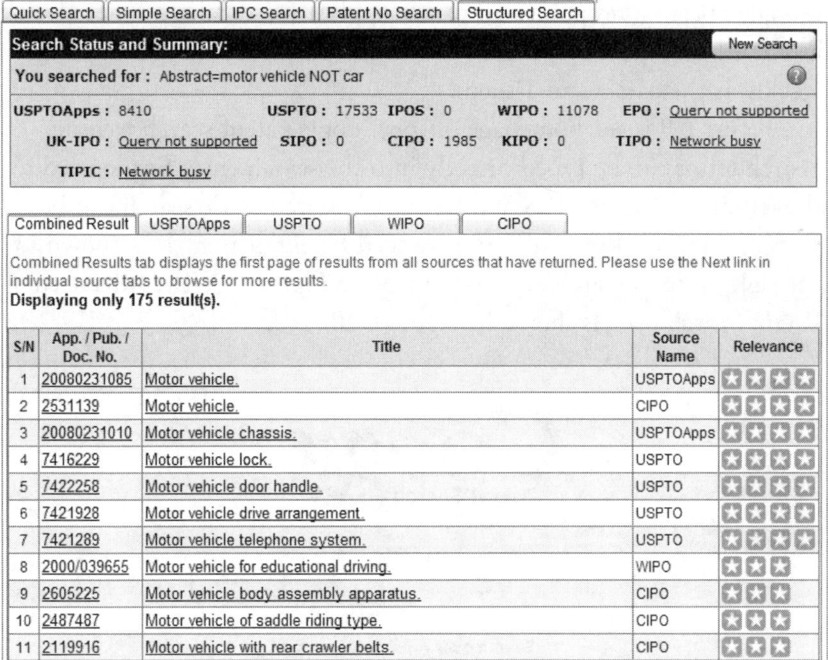

Quick Search | Simple Search | IPC Search | Patent No Search | Structured Search

Search Status and Summary: New Search

You searched for : Abstract=motor vehicle NOT car

USPTOApps : 8410 **USPTO :** 17533 **IPOS :** 0 **WIPO :** 11078 **EPO :** Query not supported
UK-IPO : Query not supported **SIPO :** 0 **CIPO :** 1985 **KIPO :** 0 **TIPO :** Network busy
TIPIC : Network busy

Combined Result | USPTOApps | USPTO | WIPO | CIPO

Combined Results tab displays the first page of results from all sources that have returned. Please use the Next link in individual source tabs to browse for more results.
Displaying only 175 result(s).

S/N	App. / Pub. / Doc. No.	Title	Source Name	Relevance
1	20080231085	Motor vehicle.	USPTOApps	
2	2531139	Motor vehicle.	CIPO	
3	20080231010	Motor vehicle chassis.	USPTOApps	
4	7416229	Motor vehicle lock.	USPTO	
5	7422258	Motor vehicle door handle.	USPTO	
6	7421928	Motor vehicle drive arrangement.	USPTO	
7	7421289	Motor vehicle telephone system.	USPTO	
8	2000/039655	Motor vehicle for educational driving.	WIPO	
9	2605225	Motor vehicle body assembly apparatus.	CIPO	
10	2487487	Motor vehicle of saddle riding type.	CIPO	
11	2119916	Motor vehicle with rear crawler belts.	CIPO	

Figure 6.8

Results displayed from each source are presented according to relevance to the search term. At a higher level, results from all sources that have returned are combined and sorted in the Combined Results tab to allow the user a quick glance through the documents that best match the search terms among the list of documents displayed.

By the way, if you register with SurfIP you can access patent search management tools that allow you to save, monitor, and track your search results.

Google Patent Search

One advantage that Google's patent database and search feature (www.google.com/patents) has over the PTO's patent website is the ability to search older patents. Google includes the full searchable text of these patents. Another advantage is that you can download an Adobe Acrobat PDF document of the entire issued patent, including drawings.

Google's patent and published patent application database is not always as current as the PTO's; the PTO's online patent database is updated weekly as the patents are issued.

Figure 6.9 is the homepage of the Google patent search website. Search terms can be typed directly into the search entry box located to the left of the "Search Patents" button. A more precise search can be performed by clicking on the "Advanced Patent Search" link shown to the right of the "Search Patents" button in Figure 6.9. The Advanced Patent Search page is shown in Figure 6.10.

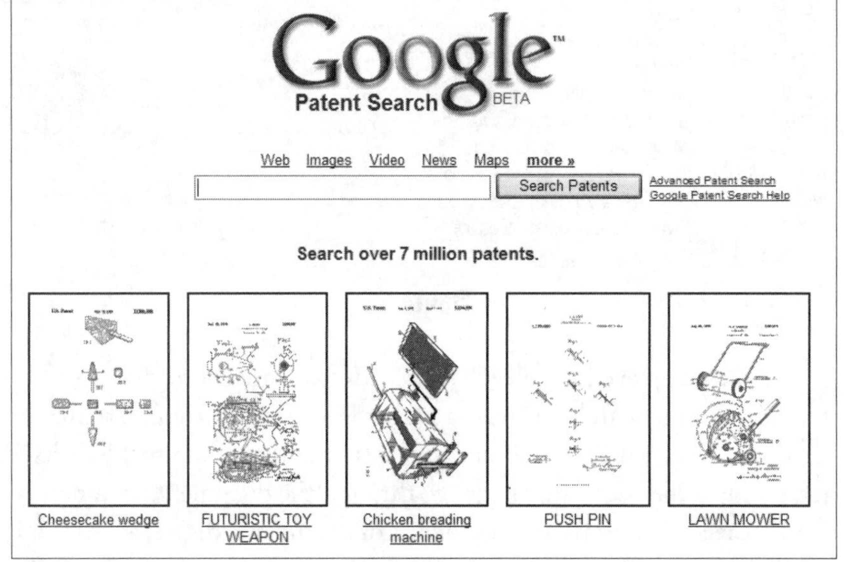

Figure 6.9

On the Advanced Patent Search Web page, search results can be gathered in many ways. The first entry box shown in Figure 6.10 is labeled "with all of the words," which corresponds to the Boolean AND function. Search terms placed in this entry box are AND-ed together.

The second entry box is labeled "with the exact phrase." This box allows multiple word phrases to be entered. Quotation marks are optional in this entry box. The third entry box, "with at least one of the words," corresponds to the Boolean OR function. Finally, the fourth entry box, "without the words," corresponds to the Boolean NOT function and allows the user to exclude certain words from the search results.

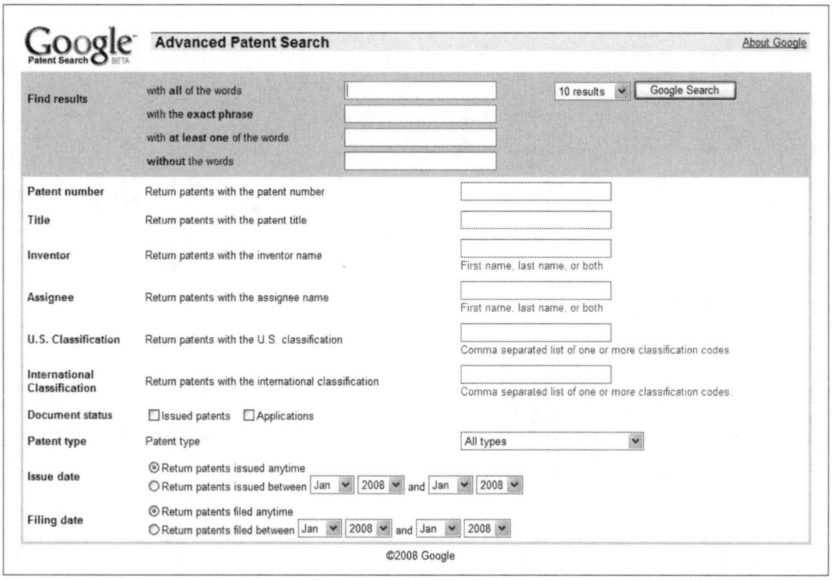

Figure 6.10

Additionally, on the Advanced Patent Search Web page you can search by patent number, patent title, inventor name, assignee name, U.S. classification, and international classification. You can also restrict your search results to a range of patent issue and filing dates.

To illustrate some of the differences between patent searching on Google versus on the PTO website, consider a simple query consisting of a single patent number (3,000,000) shown in Figure 6.11.

Figure 6.11 presents a listing for an Automatic Reading System by K.R. Eldredge. The issue date on this patent is September 12, 1961. This issue date precedes the 1976 cutoff date for full-text patent searching on the PTO website. If you clicked on the title of the patent, you would see the information presented in Figure 6.12.

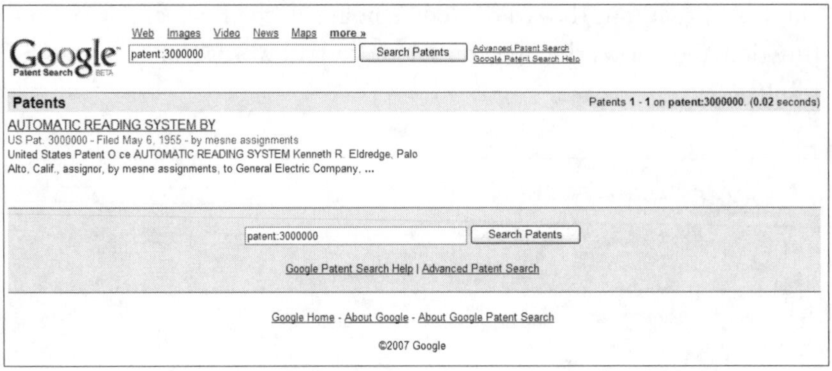

Google Patent Search BETA
Web Images Video News Maps more »
patent:3000000 | Search Patents | Advanced Patent Search | Google Patent Search Help

Patents Patents **1** - **1** on **patent:3000000**. (**0.02** seconds)

AUTOMATIC READING SYSTEM BY
US Pat. 3000000 - Filed May 6, 1955 - by mesne assignments
United States Patent O ce AUTOMATIC READING SYSTEM Kenneth R. Eldredge, Palo Alto, Calif., assignor, by mesne assignments, to General Electric Company, ...

patent:3000000 | Search Patents
Google Patent Search Help | Advanced Patent Search

Google Home - About Google - About Google Patent Search
©2007 Google

Figure 6.11

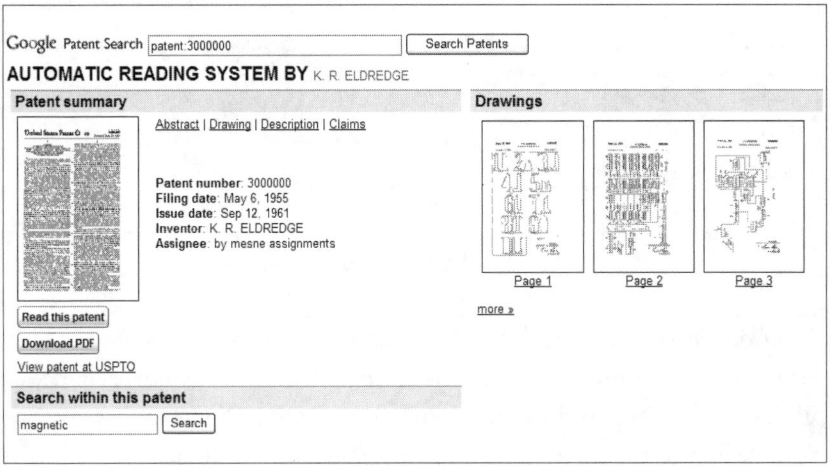

Google Patent Search patent:3000000 | Search Patents

AUTOMATIC READING SYSTEM BY K. R. ELDREDGE

Patent summary

Abstract | Drawing | Description | Claims

Patent number: 3000000
Filing date: May 6, 1955
Issue date: Sep 12, 1961
Inventor: K. R. ELDREDGE
Assignee: by mesne assignments

Read this patent
Download PDF
View patent at USPTO

Drawings

Page 1 Page 2 Page 3
more »

Search within this patent
magnetic | Search

Figure 6.12

Figure 6.12 displays several links to the various sections of this 1961 patent. These links include the patent abstract, drawings, description, and claims. Thumbnail sketches of the patent drawings are also displayed. Scanned images of the patent can be viewed by clicking on the patent front page image shown on the left-hand side of Figure 6.12. You will also note a button labeled "Read this patent" that enables you to view scanned images of the patent with arrow controls right in your Web browser. You can also click "Download PDF" and download a copy of the complete patent.

As shown in Figure 6.13, the popup window permits you to save a copy of the PDF on your computer's hard disk.

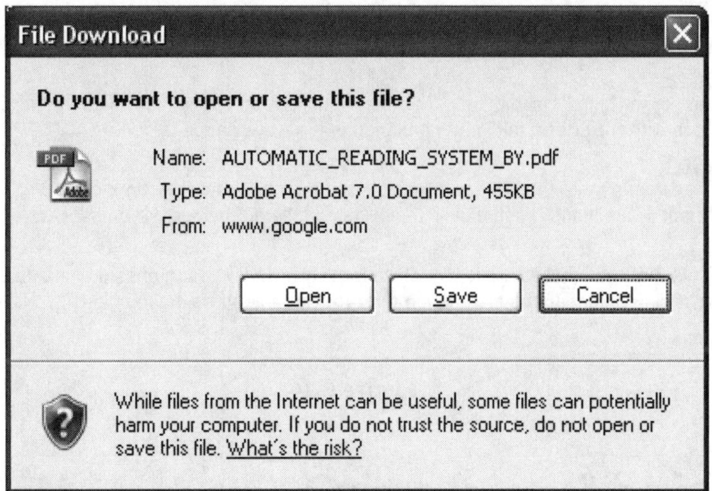

Figure 6.13

A significant feature of the Google patent search website is the ability to search within these older patents. At the bottom of Figure 6.12 is an entry box labeled "Search within this patent." For our example, the word "magnetic" has been entered into the search box. To perform this search, click on the adjacent button labeled "Search." The results are shown in Figure 6.14.

Figure 6.14 displays links to various occurrences of the search word within the patent document. To view a particular page of interest, click on the appropriate link. Figure 6.15 shows a typical page of the patent with the search term highlighted (also underlined for clarity) so that it can be read in the context of the rest of the patent. Google is able to accomplish this by using OCR software to search the scanned images of older patents and highlight the positions of our search words.

Search within this patent

magnetic | Search

Page 5

Such a writing material may be a **magnetic** ink, which is described and claimed in an application by Charles B. Clark for **Magnetic** Ink, filed 5 February, ...

Page 6

3000000 the numerals 0 through and the associated characteristic wave shapes obtained when these numerals are printed with **magnetic**-writing material, ...

Page 7

In any event, this embodiment of the invention illustrates how, from a character written with **magnetic** ink in human language, a wave shape is derived, ...

Page 8

For example, more than one **magnetic** head may be used to scan a character from different 5 directions, each of which provides a different unique wave shape ...

Page 9

3000000 of said characters is written with **magnetic** ink, each of said characters comprising a continuous distribution of **magnetic** ink on said document, ...

more »

Figure 6.14

United States Patent O ce — 3,000,000 — Patented Sept. 12, 1961

1

3,000,000
AUTOMATIC READING SYSTEM
Kenneth R. Eldredge, Palo Alto, Calif., assignor, by mesne assignments, to General Electric Company, New York, N.Y., a corporation of New York
Filed May 6, 1955, Ser. No. 506,598
21 Claims. (Cl. 340—149)

This invention relates to apparatus for reading characters in human language and providing therefrom signals representative thereof in machine language.

One of the difficulties blocking the extensive utilization of automatic data-processing machines, is that of providing the information on which such machine is to operate in a form wherein it can be rapidly transferred into the machine from the original documents on which the information exists in human language. By "human language" is meant the well-known printed or written characters by which human beings communicate with one another on paper. Specifically, the term "human language character" means a figure that conveys information, or is recognizable, from its shape and orientation; such as figures having the shapes of letters of the alphabet, numerals, punctuation marks, etc. Figures classed as human language characters are to be distinguished from permutations and combinations of groups of key elements employed to convey information; such as Morse codes, punched paper tape codes, etc. Presently known techniques for transferring the data contained on bills or inventory sheets, for example, requires that this information be either punched as holes in cards, or as holes in paper tape, or be written magnetically in coded form on magnetic tape. Any one of these can then be fed by means of suitable input devices to an automatic data-

2

verted into machine language with a writing material having magnetic properties. Such a writing material may be a magnetic ink, which is described and claimed in an application by Charles B. Clark for Magnetic Ink, filed February 8, 1955, Serial Number 486,985, or a Magnetic Transfer Paper, by Maurice Adler, filed March 7, 1955, Serial Number 492,787, both applications being assigned to a common assignee. Both of these applications are now abandoned. When characters written with a magnetic writing material are magnetized and then passed in sequence under a magnetic reading head, it can be shown that the output obtained from the reading head for each character is a signal having a wave shape or envelope which is characteristic of the character being scanned by the head. Suitable recognition apparatus is employed which senses a characteristic wave shape and converts it into a code number which is suitable for subsequent utilization by automatic data-processing machinery. There are two embodiments of the recognition apparatus described herein, although it will be readily realized that these are illustrative and not to be taken as limiting.

In one embodiment, the output of the reading head is passed through a delay line. When the entire signal is within the delay line, the amplitude of the signal at various significant (from the standpoint of distinguishing between wave shapes) positions are sampled. The maximum one of these amplitudes is determined. A portion of this maximum amplitude is employed in such a manner so that further amplification is made only of those sampled amplitudes which exceed this portion of the maximum amplitude. Since each one of the sampled portions is preserved in what may be considered as its own channel, the last step provides a voltage pattern akin to an

Figure 6.15

Performing the same patent number search on the PTO website produces the Web page shown in Figure 6.16. Figure 6.16 informs us that full-text searching for Pat. No. 3,000,000 is not available.

USPTO PATENT FULL-TEXT AND IMAGE DATABASE

Home | Quick | Advanced | Pat Num | Help

Bottom

View Cart | Add to Cart

Images

(1 of 1)

Full text is not available for this patent. Click on "Images" button above to view full patent.

United States Patent	3,000,000
Issue Date:	September 12, 1961
Current U.S. Class:	382/182 ; 235/449; 382/183; 382/320
Current International Class:	G06K 9/00 (20060101)

Figure 6.16

However, images of the patent pages can be viewed by clicking on the "Images" button. After performing this action, you will be presented with the Web page illustrated in Figure 6.17.

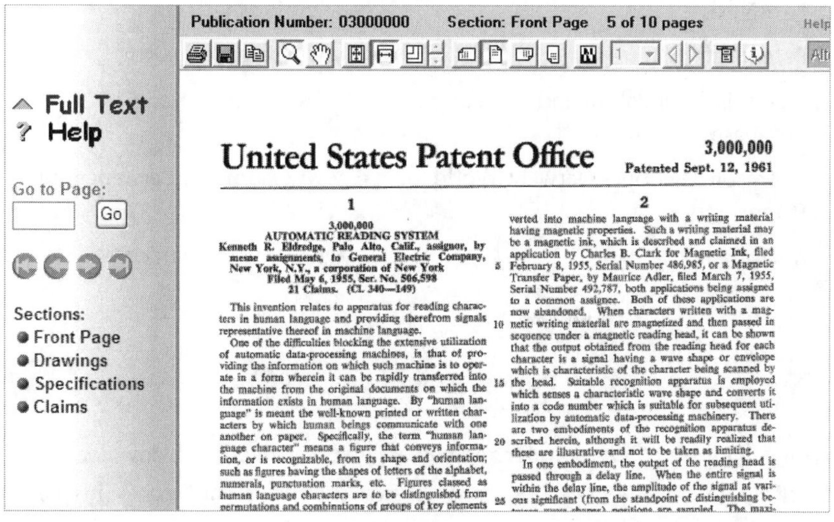

United States Patent Office

3,000,000

Patented Sept. 12, 1961

1

3,000,000

AUTOMATIC READING SYSTEM

Kenneth R. Eldredge, Palo Alto, Calif., assignor, by mesne assignments, to General Electric Company, New York, N.Y., a corporation of New York

Filed May 6, 1955, Ser. No. 506,598

21 Claims. (Cl. 340—149)

This invention relates to apparatus for reading characters in human language and providing therefrom signals representative thereof in machine language.

One of the difficulties blocking the extensive utilization of automatic data-processing machines, is that of providing the information on which such machine is to operate in a form wherein it can be rapidly transferred into the machine from the original documents on which the information exists in human language. By "human language" is meant the well-known printed or written characters by which human beings communicate with one another on paper. Specifically, the term "human language character" means a figure that conveys information, or is recognizable, from its shape and orientation; such as figures having the shapes of letters of the alphabet, numerals, punctuation marks, etc. Figures classed as human language characters are to be distinguished from permutations and combinations of groups of key elements

2

verted into machine language with a writing material having magnetic properties. Such a writing material may be a magnetic ink, which is described and claimed in an application by Charles B. Clark for Magnetic Ink, filed February 8, 1955, Serial Number 486,985, or a Magnetic Transfer Paper, by Maurice Adler, filed March 7, 1955, Serial Number 492,787, both applications being assigned to a common assignee. Both of these applications are now abandoned. When characters written with a magnetic writing material are magnetized and then passed in sequence under a magnetic reading head, it can be shown that the output obtained from the reading head for each character is a signal having a wave shape or envelope which is characteristic of the character being scanned by the head. Suitable recognition apparatus is employed which senses a characteristic wave shape and converts it into a code number which is suitable for subsequent utilization by automatic data-processing machinery. There are two embodiments of the recognition apparatus described herein, although it will be readily realized that these are illustrative and not to be taken as limiting.

In one embodiment, the output of the reading head is passed through a delay line. When the entire signal is within the delay line, the amplitude of the signal at various significant (from the standpoint of distinguishing be-

Figure 6.17

Here, you can scan the various pages of the older patent, but you cannot search within the text of the patent. You can obtain a printout of the currently displayed page of the patent by clicking on the print icon shown in the upper left of Figure 6.17. But, unlike with Google's system, you cannot get a printout of the entire patent without viewing each patent page, one at a time.

Fee-Based Patent-Searching Websites

There are a number of Internet-based patent search systems that charge a fee for certain services. Many of these firms will perform much of the patent-searching work for you, including searching foreign patent databases. Several fee-based patent search companies are listed in the table below.

Fee-Based Websites and Their URLs

Company	Web Address
Delphion	www.delphion.com
LexisNexis	www.lexisnexis.com
PatentCafe	www.patentcafe.com
Questel–Orbit Patent and Trademark Databases	www.questel.com
Thomson Scientific–Derwent World Patents Index	www.thompsonderwent.com
Micropatent	www.micropatent.com

Patent Download Sites

If you have a patent number and you are just seeking a quick download of a patent PDF, you can also consider sites such as Patent Fetcher (http://free.patentfetcher.com/Patent-Fetcher-Form.php) or Free Patents Online (http://freepatentsonline.com).

Figure 6.18

A number of smaller patent service websites are also available. These websites will often provide custom services for a fee. One such website, PlanetPatent (www.planetpatent.com), is shown in Figure 6.18.

Figure 6.19 shows a partial list of some of the services available at this website. Mr. Glen Kotapish is the founder of Planet Patent. Mr. Kotapish is also the president of the Center for Patent Policy, (www.patentpolicy.org), a Washington, D.C.-area patent policy think tank.

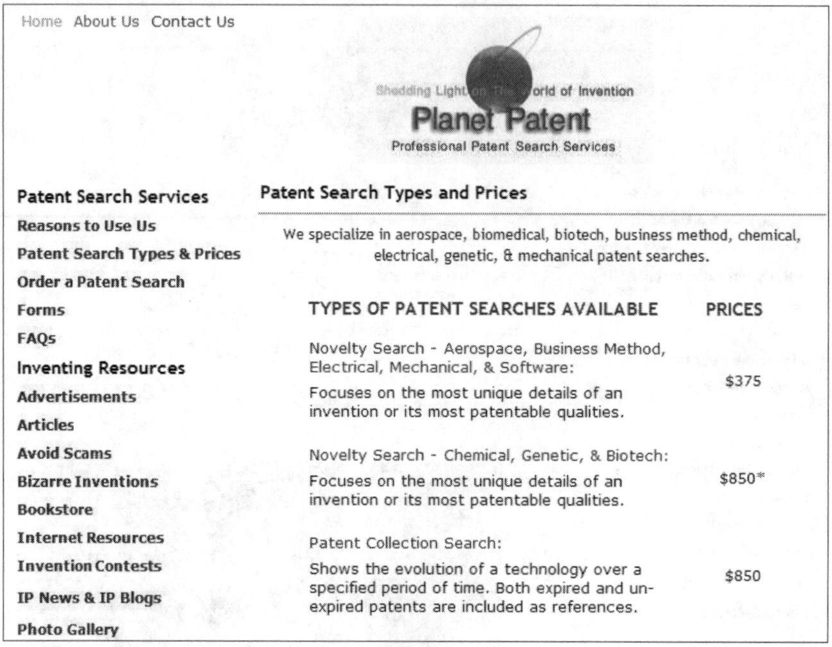

Home About Us Contact Us

Shedding Light on The World of Invention

Planet Patent

Professional Patent Search Services

Patent Search Services

- Reasons to Use Us
- Patent Search Types & Prices
- Order a Patent Search
- Forms
- FAQs

Inventing Resources

- Advertisements
- Articles
- Avoid Scams
- Bizarre Inventions
- Bookstore
- Internet Resources
- Invention Contests
- IP News & IP Blogs
- Photo Gallery

Patent Search Types and Prices

We specialize in aerospace, biomedical, biotech, business method, chemical, electrical, genetic, & mechanical patent searches.

TYPES OF PATENT SEARCHES AVAILABLE	PRICES
Novelty Search - Aerospace, Business Method, Electrical, Mechanical, & Software: Focuses on the most unique details of an invention or its most patentable qualities.	$375
Novelty Search - Chemical, Genetic, & Biotech: Focuses on the most unique details of an invention or its most patentable qualities.	$850*
Patent Collection Search: Shows the evolution of a technology over a specified period of time. Both expired and un-expired patents are included as references.	$850

Figure 6.19

CHAPTER

7

Additional Sources of Prior Art

So far in this book, we have restricted ourselves to patent-searching resources. However, prior art is not limited to patented inventions. Any published information that is relevant to the novelty or unobviousness of your invention can be considered as prior art and, in some cases, may prevent a patent from being granted on your invention. In this chapter, we will consider prior art search resources, such as Google (and related Internet search engines), government websites, and industrial product and manufacturer listings.

Google

How do you search through all of the commercial, personal, and government websites—estimated to total more than 570,000,000 sites in 2008—to see if your invention idea has already been produced as a commercial product? If you're like most people, you use the Google search engine (www.google.com).

Figure 7.1

Like many search engines, the Google search engine incorporates the Boolean operator AND within the Google search box—that is, the AND operator is automatically applied to *all* search terms that you enter in a single string.

For example, Figure 7.2 shows a few of the results if you entered a search for the word "physics" and the phrase "low temperature." As you're probably aware, you can review any of these references in detail by clicking on the reference.

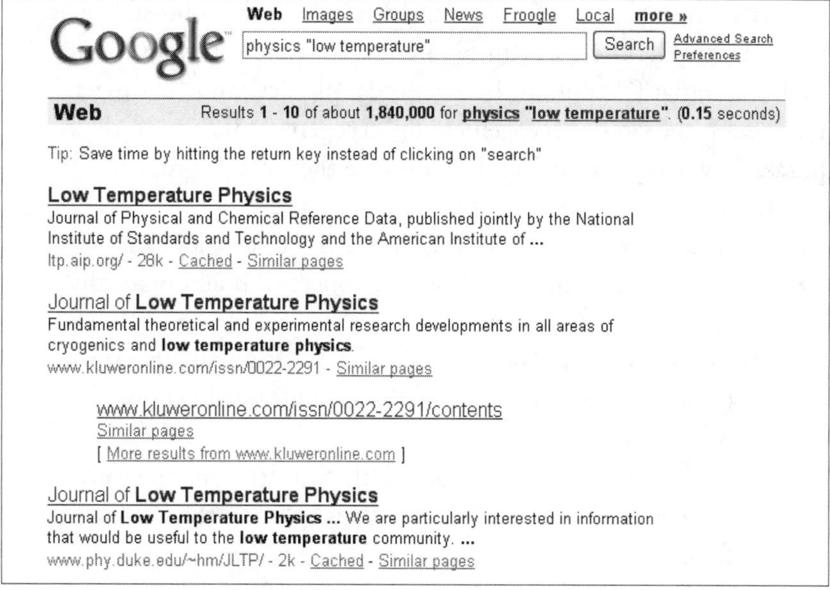

Figure 7.2

Google's Advanced Search Features

By clicking on the "Advanced Search" link at the Google site, you will see the Advanced Search page (Figure 7.3). The advanced search option gives you more options than the default setting and you may also notice that it shares similarities with the search engine used by Google's patent database, discussed in Chapter 6.

Google Advanced Search
Advanced Search Tips | Hurricane Katrina Resources - About Google

Find results — with **all** of the words: physics hydrogen — 10 results — Google Search
with the **exact phrase**: "low temperature"
with **at least one** of the words: cryogenics cryogeny
without the words: nitrogen

Language — Return pages written in — English
File Format — Only return results of the file format — any format
Date — Return web pages updated in the — anytime
Occurrences — Return results where my terms occur — anywhere in the page
Domain — Only return results from the site or domain — e.g. google.com, .org More info
SafeSearch — No filtering — Filter using SafeSearch

Figure 7.3

As an example of the sophisticated searching that's possible with Google, consider the query in Figure 7.3. Imagine you want to find all Web pages that (1) contain the keywords "physics" and "hydrogen," (2) contain the words "cryogenics" or "cryogeny," (3) contain the exact phrase "low temperature," and (4) exclude the word "nitrogen."

To do so:

1. In The box "with all of the words," type "physics" and "hydrogen." (The AND Boolean operator is automatically applied to these two words.)
2. In the box "with the exact phrase," type "low temperature." (Note that the quotation marks around the phrase are optional.)
3. In the box "with at least one of the words," type the words "cryogenics" and "cryogeny." (This replicates the Boolean OR function.)
4. In The box "without the words," type the word "nitrogen."

Other options on the Google Advanced Search page allow you to specify the language, file format, and date, as well other indicia. Set the language to English (as shown in Figure 7.3), though it's best to leave the other settings at their default values. The results of the query are shown in Figure 7.4.

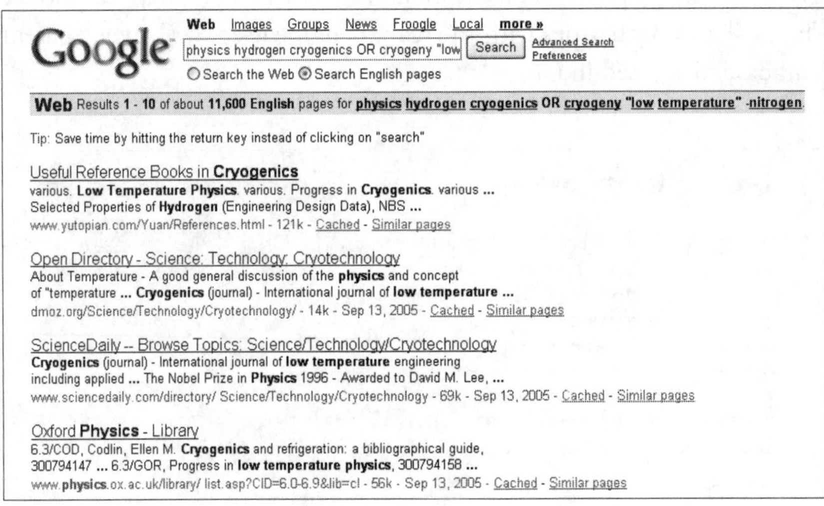

Figure 7.4

Google Scholar

Google Scholar (www.scholar.google.com) offers a method of searching solely through scholarly literature—that is, peer-reviewed papers, theses, books, abstracts, and articles from academic publishers, professional societies, preprint repositories, universities, and other scholarly organizations. The Advanced Scholar Search feature of Google Scholar operates in the same way as other Google advanced search criteria with the exception that you can limit the subject areas for searching, for example, by limiting your search solely to scholarly work in the field of physics, astronomy, and planetary science (Figure 7.5).

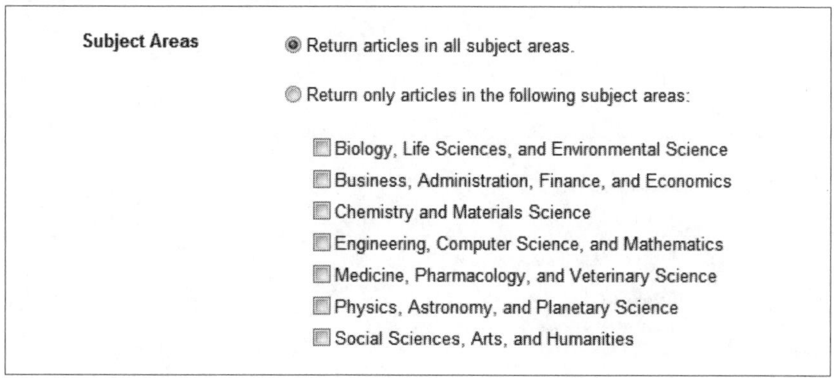

Figure 7.5

Google Book Search

In October 2008, Google made a landmark agreement with publishers and authors that will permit the digitizing of millions of books. Currently, you can search the contents of hundreds of thousands of books (including thousands of public domain and out-of-print books) at the Google Book Search site (www.books.google.com) as shown in Figure 7.6. There is also an advanced search feature (Figure 7.7) that enables you to limit your search by author, publisher, subject, date, language, and even ISBN (an identifying number used by publishers).

Google Book Search BETA
Search Books
Advanced Book Search
Google Book Search Help
Google has reached a groundbreaking agreement with authors and publishers.
Fiction
Literature
Science fiction
Fantasy
Romance
Mystery
Fairy tales
Short stories
Poetry
Non-fiction
Philosophy
Economics
Political science
Linguistics
Mathematics
Physics
Chemistry
Biology
Interesting
Mac OS X Tiger
RACE AND ETHNICITY IN MULTI-ETHNIC SCHOOLS
THE GREATER GOOD
CLAIRE GAUDIANI
the new bloomsday book
Classics
Ivanhoe
The Black Arrow
Kidnapped
The Pilgrim's Progress from this World to

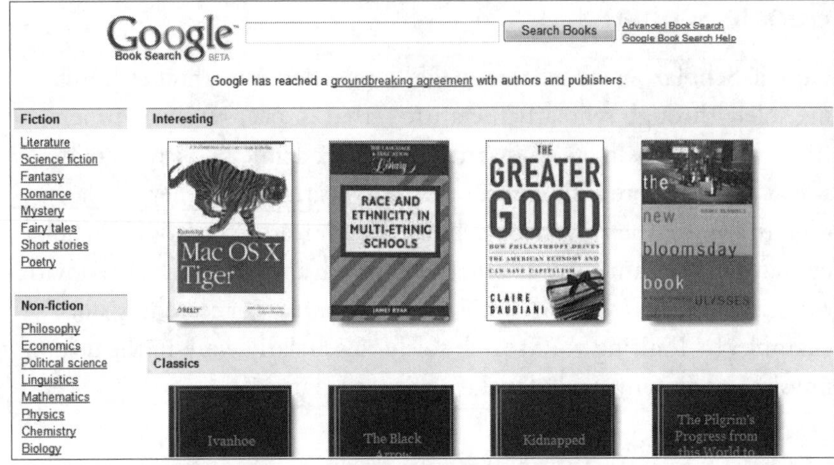

Figure 7.6

Google Book Search BETA
Advanced Book Search
Find results
with all of the words
with the exact phrase
with at least one of the words
without the words
10 results
Google Search
Search:
All books
Limited preview and full view
Full view only
Language
Return pages written in
any language
Title
Return books with the title
e.g. Books and Culture
Author
Return books written by
e.g. Hamilton Mabie or "Hamilton Wright Mabie"
Publisher
Return books published by
e.g. O'Reilly
Subject
Return books on subject
e.g. Medieval History or "Medieval History"
Publication Date
Return books published between the years of
and
e.g. 1970 and 1972
ISBN
Return books with the ISBN
e.g. 0060930314

Figure 7.7

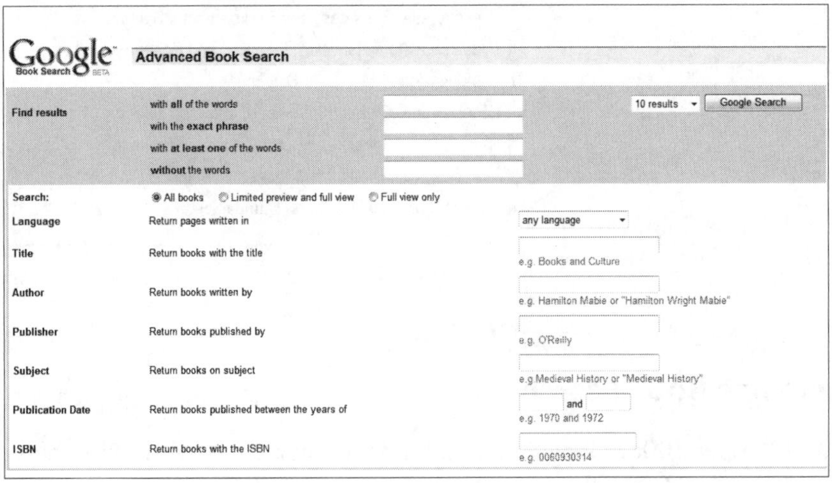

Google Tips

Here a few Google tips and tricks. You may already be familiar with some of them.

- **Image searching.** Google doesn't just search words, it also searches titles and descriptive phrases used in connection with images. This feature may prove helpful when you're curious about the appearance of an innovation or device. Enter a typical Google search and on the results page, click "Images" in the upper left corner of the screen. Using Advanced Image Search, you can even limit the photos to faces, news content, or other criteria.
- **Find related items.** The "tilde" symbol (~) may be hard to find on some keyboards, but if you type it before a search term—for example, ~automobile—Google is directed to look for related synonymous terms, such as car, auto, and vehicle.
- **Use Google as a calculator or converter.** Google will calculate any formulas you enter into the search box—for example, you can enter "440/6 + 220" and the search engine will calculate the answer. It will also provide instant conversions; for example, type in "4 pounds in kilos" to obtain a pounds-to-kilo conversion.
- **Searching for common words.** Google disregards common words and characters, such as "why," "where," and "when," as well as certain single digits and single letters, because they usually don't benefit your search and they slow down results. If you need to include a common word, place a plus sign ("+") in front of the word—for example, "fire +how."
- **Instant dictionary.** Google can provide quick definitions. Type "define:" and the word or term for which you need the meaning—for example, "define: indemnity."
- **Research timelines.** Google can provide you with instant chronologies of some events. Add the phrase "view:timeline" to your query—for example, "disk drive view:timeline."

Other Search Engines

As you're aware, Google isn't the only Internet search engine. There are many other excellent general search engines including:

- Ask.com (formerly Ask Jeeves) (www.ask.com)
- Baidu (Chinese) (www.baidu.com)
- Cuil (www.cuil.com)
- Exalead (French) (www.exalead.com)
- Live Search (formerly MSN Search) (www.live.com), and
- Yahoo! Search (www.search.yahoo.com).

There are also numerous specialized search engines—for example, that only search academic or medical sites—as well as meta search engines (search engines that combine results from general search engines). You can find them easily by—you guessed it—typing "search engines" into your search engine.

The Thomas Register

In the previous section, we looked for companies, products, and research facilities that have published information on the Internet. But what about all those companies that don't have Web pages? The Thomas Register industrial database (www.thomasnet.com) has contact information for over 100,000 American and Canadian companies. Some of these companies have websites, but many do not. When a listed company has an established website, the Register provides a link to that Internet address. When a website does not exist, the Register provides contact information such as a physical address, telephone, and fax number.

The homepage for the Thomas Register is shown in Figure 7.8. Searching is a simple three-step process.

1. Decide if you want to search for a product or service, company name, brand name, or to search the "industrial web." Select the appropriate tab as shown at the top of Figure 7.8.
2. Enter a search keyword or keywords.
3. Select the geographical area in which you wish to search.

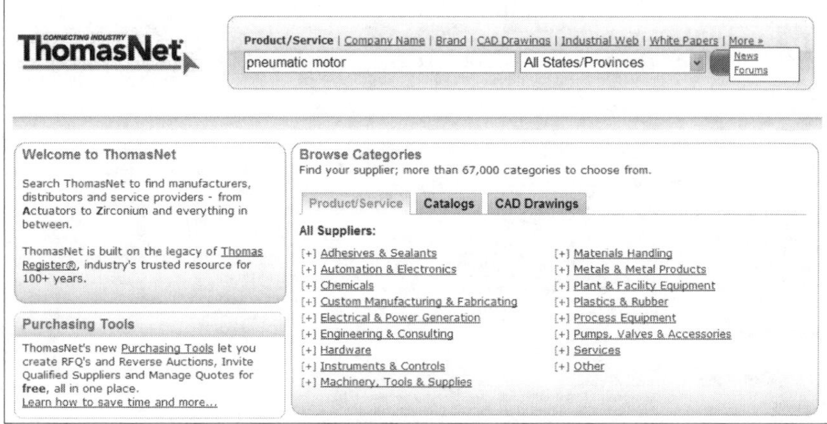

Figure 7.8

Now let's suppose that you have an invention idea for a pneumatic (air-powered) motor. To search for similar products, you enter the keywords "pneumatic" and "motor," make sure you are using the "Product/Service" tab/link, and choose the widest possible geographical coverage (All States/ Provinces) from the dropdown menu. The results are shown in Figure 7.9.

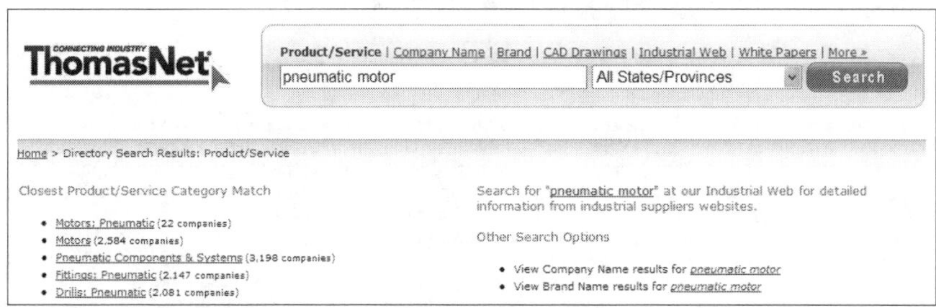

Figure 7.9

The top of Figure 7.9 displays 22 companies matching our product description (Motors: Pneumatic). Other relevant category matches are displayed below the primary listing. To get a listing of these companies, click on the "Motors: Pneumatic" link. The results are shown in Figure 7.10.

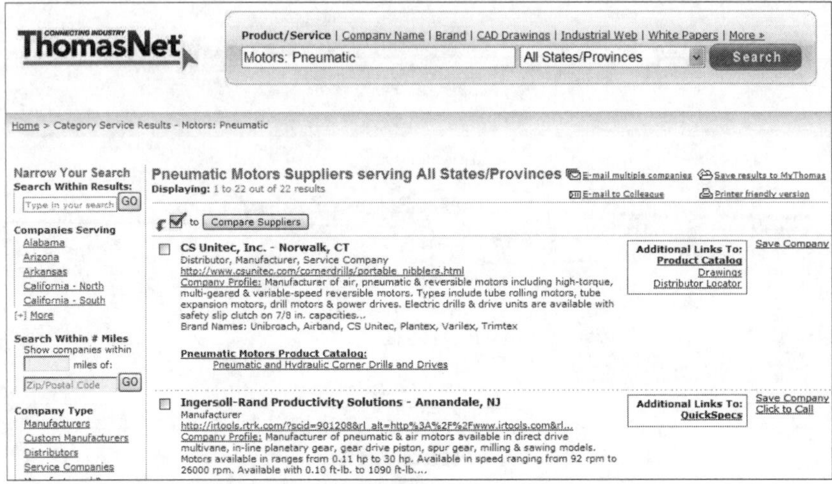

Figure 7.10

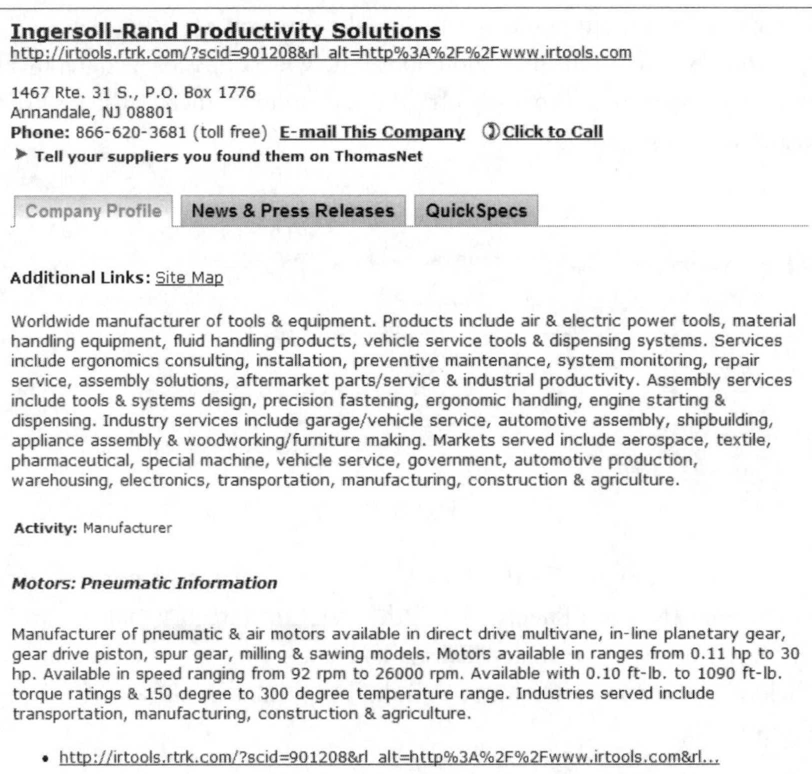

Figure 7.11

The listings displayed in Figure 7.10 give a brief company profile for each entry. To get further details, click the "Company Profile" tab/link. For example, to extract the contact information for the second listed company, Ingersoll-Rand, click the corresponding Company Profile link. The resulting page is shown in Figure 7.11.

Government Websites

The U.S. Government annually spends billions on research and it is quite possible that some of this research is directly related to your invention ideas. Most government agencies support at least one website, and much of their research information is unclassified and accessible.

DTIC

One of the most useful government websites is the Defense Technical Information Center's website (www.dtic.mil). (Note the ".mil" at the end of the website address.) DTIC contributes to the management and conduct of defense-related research, development, and acquisition efforts by providing access to, and exchange of, scientific and technical information. In turn, DTIC's Scientific and Technical Information Network (STINET) Service provides much of this scientific and technical information to the public. To search the technical reports on DTIC go to: www.dtic.mil/dtic/search/tr.

Figure 7.12 shows a section of the STINET Public Technical Reports search homepage. Let's suppose that your invention is related to recent developments in the field of nuclear rocket propulsion. To search for any related research, we enter the keywords "nuclear" and "propulsion" into the "Search for" text box. A portion of the results are shown in Figure 7.13.

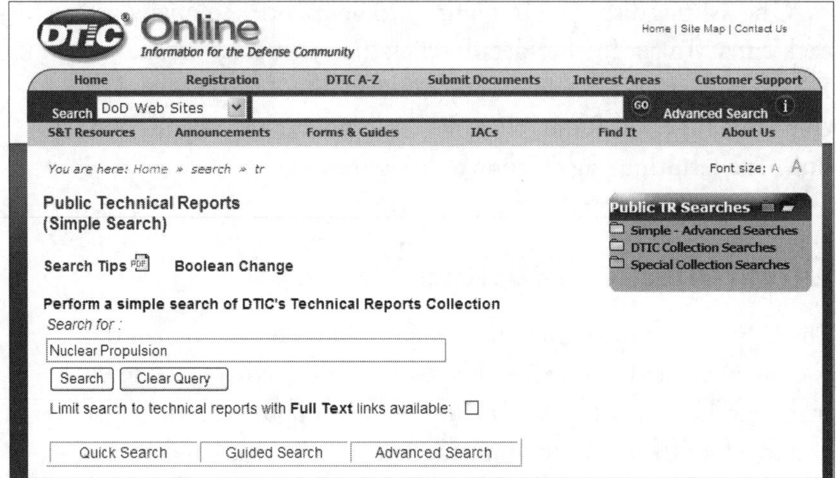

Figure 7.12

3. View TR Citation
   Title: THE APPLICATION OF MAGNETOHYDRODYNAMIC GENERATORS IN NUCLEAR ROCKET PR...
   AD Number: AD0272836
   Corporate Author: AVCO EVERETT RESEARCH LAB EVERETT MASS
   Personal Author: ROSA,R J
   Distribution Code: 01 - APPROVED FOR PUBLIC RELEASE
   Report Classification: U - Unclassified
   Source Code: 048450

4. View TR Citation | View Full Text pdf - 1 MB
   Title: Nuclear Thermal Rocket Propulsion Systems
   AD Number: ADA430931
   Corporate Author: AIR FORCE ACADEMY COLORADO SPRINGS CO DEPT OF ASTRONAUTICS
   Personal Author: Lawrence, Timothy J
   Distribution Code: 01 - APPROVED FOR PUBLIC RELEASE 26 - NOT AVAILABLE IN MICROFICHE
   Report Classification: U - Unclassified
   Source Code: 433039

Figure 7.13

To view the text of the fourth search result, click on the link labeled "View Full Text pdf -1 MB" in the listing. The result is shown in Figure 7.14, where a study is displayed comparing nuclear thermal rocket propulsion systems.

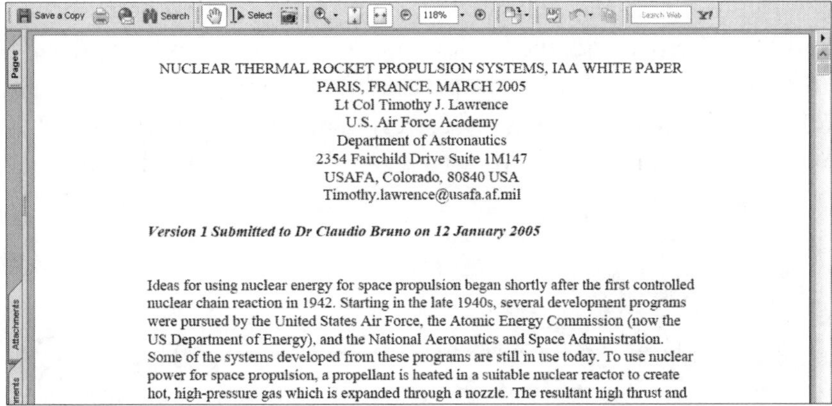

NUCLEAR THERMAL ROCKET PROPULSION SYSTEMS, IAA WHITE PAPER
PARIS, FRANCE, MARCH 2005
Lt Col Timothy J. Lawrence
U.S. Air Force Academy
Department of Astronautics
2354 Fairchild Drive Suite 1M147
USAFA, Colorado, 80840 USA
Timothy.lawrence@usafa.af.mil

Version 1 Submitted to Dr Claudio Bruno on 12 January 2005

Ideas for using nuclear energy for space propulsion began shortly after the first controlled nuclear chain reaction in 1942. Starting in the late 1940s, several development programs were pursued by the United States Air Force, the Atomic Energy Commission (now the US Department of Energy), and the National Aeronautics and Space Administration. Some of the systems developed from these programs are still in use today. To use nuclear power for space propulsion, a propellant is heated in a suitable nuclear reactor to create hot, high-pressure gas which is expanded through a nozzle. The resultant high thrust and

Figure 7.14

Advanced searching is also available at the DTIC website. To get to DTIC's Advanced Search page, click on the "Advanced Search" link shown at the center bottom of Figure 7.12. The resulting Web page is shown in Figure 7.15.

DTIC® Online
Information for the Defense Community

Home | Site Map | Contact Us

Home | Registration | DTIC A-Z | Submit Documents | Interest Areas | Customer Support

Search DoD Web Sites | GO | Advanced Search

S&T Resources | Announcements | Forms & Guides | IACs | Find It | About Us

You are here: Home » search » tr » str » advanced tr

Font size: A A

Public Technical Reports (Advanced Search)

Search Tips **Boolean Change**

Public TR Searches
Simple - Advanced Searches
DTIC Collection Searches
Special Collection Searches

Quick Search | Guided Search | **Advanced Search**
Corporate Source | Thesaurus

Limit search to only those technical reports that have **Full Text** links available:

Enter your search strategy below using FAST Query Language (FQL) and field mnemonics:

Submit Query | Clear Query

Nuclear Propulsion <and> mars

Submit Query | Clear Query

Figure 7.15

Figure 7.15 displays a limited search regarding nuclear propulsion and Mars. To that end, the Boolean operator “<and>” has been added to require all search terms to be present in the search results. The STINET site requires the use of the less-than (<) and greater than (>) syntax. The results of this advanced search are displayed in Figure 7.16.

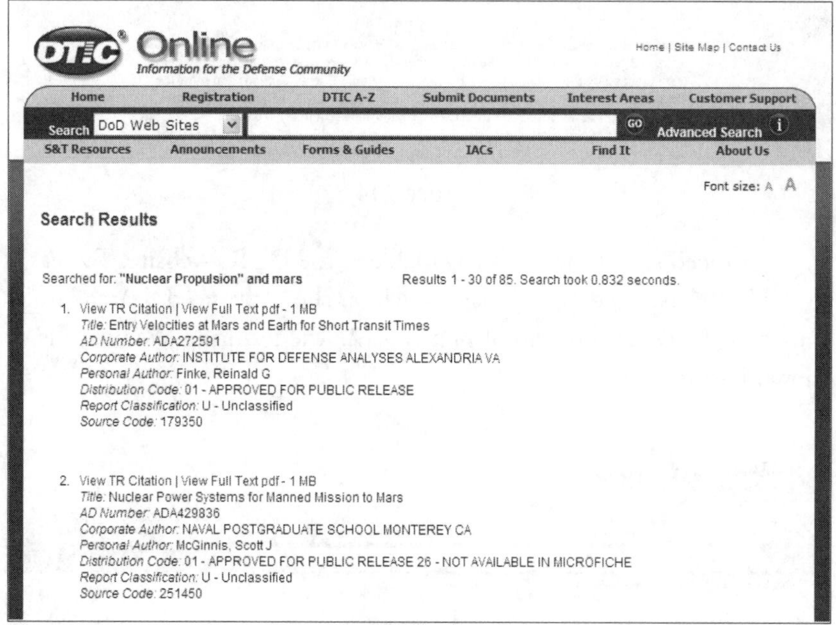

Figure 7.16

As you can see from reading the titles of the matching hits from Figure 7.16, the results have been limited to nuclear rockets that are focused on missions to Mars.

Other Government Websites

In addition to DTIC, there are a large number of other government websites which offer valuable information for prior art searches.

Websites of Selected Government Agencies	
U.S. Department of the Interior	www.doi.gov
U.S.D.A. Forest Service	www.fs.fed.us
Department of Commerce	www.commerce.gov
Department of Energy	www.doe.gov
NASA Commercial Technology Network	www.nctn.hq.nasa.gov
Department of Health and Human Services	www.os.dhhs.gov
Department of Education	www.ed.gov
National Technology Transfer Center	www.nttc.edu
Environmental Protection Agency	www.epa.gov
Department of Transportation	www.dot.gov
National Science Foundation	www.nsf.gov
U.S. Army Corps of Engineers	www.usace.army.mil

Usenet Newsgroups

Usenet is a collection of thousands of individual newsgroups devoted to a certain topic or subject. Several million people from all over the world subscribe to these newsgroups. With so many topics covered, the odds are good that one or more newsgroups will be relevant to your field of invention.

Newsgroup messages are read via a newsreader program. To access the Usenet via the email program Microsoft Outlook Express, click on the "Tools" menu and select "Newsgroups," as shown in Figure 7.17.

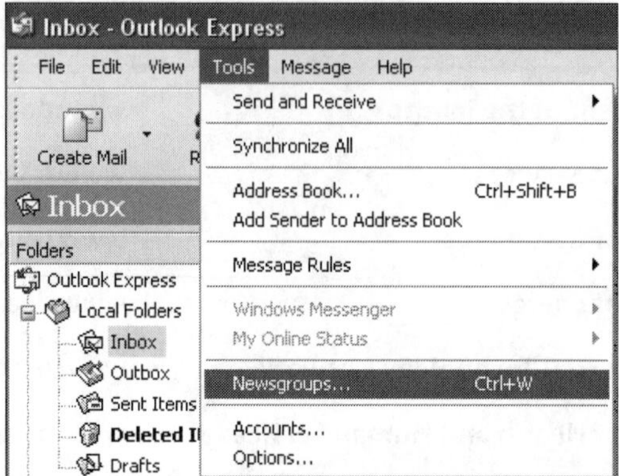

Figure 7.17

If you have not set up the newsreader service, it will be necessary to add and configure a news host. The Properties popup window will ask you for certain information. This window has tabs across the top labeled General, Server, Connection, and Advanced. Most of the fields you are likely to deal with are in the General and Server tabs.

Figure 7.18

Figure 7.18 shows some typical settings for the General tab. Here, the name "News1" has been entered in the "News Account" field. At a minimum, under "User Information," you will need to enter your user name and email address. Under the Server tab (Figure 7.19), include the news server name, account name, and password. You may have to contact your Internet Service Provider (ISP) to get the correct news server name. Typically, the news service names are something like: news.(ISP name).(com or net).

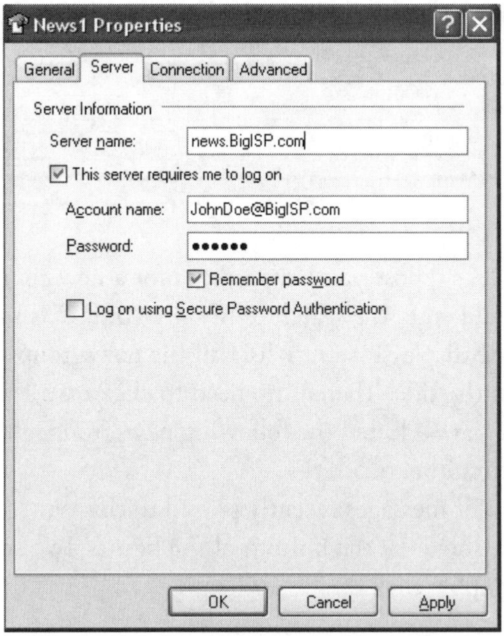

Figure 7.19

Once you have successfully connected to your ISP's newsreader service you will be prompted to download a list of current newsgroups. At last count there were more than 80,000, so this download may take a few seconds.

There are topics ranging from aviation (newsgroup name: aus. aviation) to Zenith computer systems (newsgroup name: comp.sys. zenith). There are so many newsgroups that it is helpful to search for a particular topic with the search box displayed at the top of Figure 7.20.

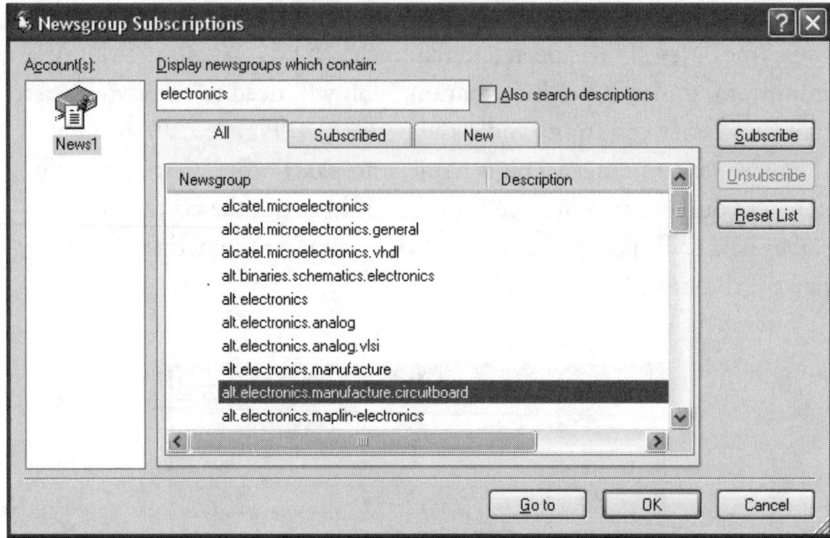

Figure 7.20

For example, suppose you have an idea for a new circuit board design. You could enter the search term "electronics" as shown in Figure 7.20. The display instantly lists all the newsgroups with the word "electronics" in the title. There is no need to click on a search button. In Figure 7.20 we have selected the following newsgroup: alt.electronics.manufacture.circuitboard.

To see a list of messages recently posted to this newsgroup, click the "Go to" button shown at the bottom of the figure. To read a particular message, just double click on it.

Figure 7.21

To post a message to the group, click on the "New Post" button in Microsoft Outlook Express shown at the upper left-hand corner of

Figure 7.21. A message window will then pop up with the newsgroup name "alt.electronics.manufacture.circuitboard" already added to the newsgroup destination line. Type in a subject line and the body of your message; to post the message to the selected newsgroup, click on the "Send" button.

The Usenet has millions of readers who like to participate in interesting discussions and answer questions. But they don't like to answer the same questions over and over again. For this reason, a "frequently asked questions" (FAQ) list of questions and answers is often posted to each group. Before you post a question to a newsgroup, please read any FAQ postings. Often you will find that your question has been anticipated and the answer already provided.

There are certain rules and conventions for posting messages to Usenet newsgroups. Some of the most important rules of are summarized below.

- Post your question or message only to the newsgroup that is the most appropriate. Sending messages to multiple newsgroups is frowned upon.
- Put a short, descriptive header into the subject line of your posting. People use these headers to select which messages to respond to.
- Keep your message short and concise.
- If you reply to a previously posted message, include the essential parts of the original message in your response, but not the entire original message.

Trade Magazines, Books, and Stores

Another good place to search for prior art is in trade magazines. Trade magazines are often very specific to one topic and provide information for inventors in that subject area. For example, let's suppose that your invention has something to do with mining equipment: The magazines *Dimensional Stone, Stone Review,* and *Stone World* may contain highly relevant information.

How do you find out what magazines are out there? Several journals list magazine titles and subjects—for example, *Writer's Market*. Other useful directories are:

- *BurrellesLuce*
- *Directory of Book, Catalog and Magazine Printers,* and
- *Directory of Small Press Magazine Editors & Publishers.*

You can also locate trade journals using the Yahoo! directory (http://dir.yahoo.com). Click on Business & Economy, Business to Business, News and Media, Magazines, and Trade Magazines.

Part III:
Resources

Part III consists of three chapters that deal with the resources available at the nationwide network of Patent and Trademark Deposit Libraries (PTDLs) and at the PTO's facility in Alexandria, Virginia. Chapter 8 explains how to use the *Index to the U.S. Patent Classification*, the *Manual of Classification,* and *Classification Definitions.* Chapter 9 offers information about the PTO's Classification and Search Support Information System (CASSIS). Finally, Chapter 10 provides background on the PTO's Examiner Assisted Search Tool (EAST) and Web-based Examiner Search Tool (WEST).

CHAPTER

8

Hitting the Books

In this chapter we leave behind the Internet and enter the world of the Patent and Trademark Depository Library (PTDL). Every PTDL has patent information available in several formats, including printed manuals, microfilm, and computerized databases. Appendix A can help you locate the PTDL nearest you.

In this chapter, we discuss three of the resources available at PTDLs: the *Index to the U.S. Patent Classification System,* the *Manual of Classification,* and *Classification Definitions.* We explain how to use these manuals to determine which classes and subclasses apply to your invention. Once you have identified the appropriate class/subclass, you can then obtain a listing of every patent that has been issued within that class by using one of several methods. As you will see, this approach to patent searching is far more efficient than randomly searching for matching keywords within issued patents. By the way, the three resources referenced above are also available online at the PTO website.

Index to the U.S. Patent Classification System

In order to explore the *Index to the U.S. Patent Classification System,* let's start by checking the patentability of a hypothetical new idea—a turn signal timer.

> **Hypothetical: Turn Signal Timer.** A common occurrence for people who drive is to see a vehicle with its turn signal stuck in the "on" position. This happens occasionally when automobiles negotiate gentle curves or during lane changes. This is a problem because other drivers can't tell if the signaling car is about to change direction or remain traveling straight ahead. While watching this happen during your drive to work one day, you come up with an idea for a turn signal timer. This device would automatically cancel the turn signal after a given period of straight-ahead travel time.

The most efficient way to start your search at a PTDL is to search the class and subclass of your invention. Then, proceed to search through the patents issued under each of the relevant classes.

Using this approach, your first task is to come up with a list of words that describe your idea. Then, use the *Index to the U.S. Patent*

Classifications System to look for those words. The *Index* contains two very useful resources:

- an alphabetical listing of all of the classes used by the PTO, and
- a cross-referenced list of all known subject areas of invention, along with the appropriate class and subclass.

Let's suppose that you have selected the following words to describe your invention: "car," "turn signal," "timer," and "electrical."

These descriptive terms are arranged in order, from the general to the specific. In other words, the term "car" describes the general product that uses our invention. The term "turn signal" refers the device upon which our invention will operate. Finally, the terms "timer" and "electrical" pertain to the type of turn signal and the timer function used to turn the signal off.

The classification system used by the PTO also flows from the general to the specific. By using this strategy you can best capture all of the classes related to your invention.

An alphabetical listing of all of the classes used by the PTO is provided at the beginning of the *Index*. Use the alphabetical listing of classes to find a class for each of the words on your list. There are approximately 430 classes and it is quite possible that you will not find a match for each of your descriptive terms. For this reason, it is helpful to come up with a few synonyms for your descriptive terms. For example, in addition to the word "car," you can add the following two descriptive terms: "automobile" and "vehicle."

Figure 8.1 shows a typical page from the alphabetical listing of classes in the *Index* (note that Class 116: Signals and Indicators, is boxed). Locate and write down the class name and number for any classes that match your descriptive words. The search results from the alphabetical list of classes are shown in Figure 8.2.

The next section of the *Index to the U.S. Patent Classification System*—making up the bulk of the *Index*—is the cross-referenced list of subject areas of invention. Here, you look up each of the classes and write down the class and subclass of any matching references. For example, searching for the term "electrical" results in a search that located Class 340 (Figure 8.2).

CLASSES ARRANGED IN ALPHABETICAL ORDER -- Continued

Class	Title of Class
271	Sheet Feeding or Delivering
413	Sheet Metal Container Making
270	Sheet-Material Associating
114	Ships
116	Signals and Indicators
117	Single-Crystal, Oriented-Crystal, and Epitaxy Growth Processes; Non-Coating Apparatus Therefor
508	Solid Anti-Friction Devices, Materials Therefor, Lubricant or Separant Compositions for Moving Solid Surfaces, and Miscellaneous Mineral Oil Compositions
241	Solid Material Comminution or Disintegration
206	Special Receptacle or Package
75	Specialized Metallurgical Processes, Compositions for Use Therein, Consolidated Metal Powder Compositions, etc.
267	Spring Devices
365	Static Information Storage and Retrieval
249	Static Molds
52	Static Structures (e.g., Buildings)
428	Stock Material or Miscellaneous Articles
125	Stone Working
126	Stoves and Furnaces
127	Sugar, Starch, and Carbohydrates
505	Superconductor Technology: Apparatus, Material, Process
248	Supports
312	Supports: Cabinet Structure
211	Supports: Racks
128	Surgery
600	Surgery
604	Surgery
606	Surgery
601	Surgery: Kinesitherapy
602	Surgery: Splint, Brace, or Bandage
607	Surgery: Light, Thermal, and Electrical Application
520	Synthetic Resins or Natural Rubbers -- Part of the Class 520 Series
521	Synthetic Resins or Natural Rubbers -- Part of the Class 520 Series
522	Synthetic Resins or Natural Rubbers -- Part of the Class 520 Series
523	Synthetic Resins or Natural Rubbers -- Part of the Class 520 Series
524	Synthetic Resins or Natural Rubbers -- Part of the Class 520 Series
525	Synthetic Resins or Natural Rubbers -- Part of the Class 520 Series
526	Synthetic Resins or Natural Rubbers -- Part of the Class 520 Series
527	Synthetic Resins or Natural Rubbers -- Part of the Class 520 Series
528	Synthetic Resins or Natural Rubbers -- Part of the Class 520 Series

A-9

Figure 8.1

Search Results From Listing of Classes

General Terms Used for Cars

Term	Class Found
Car	None
Automobile	None
Vehicle	Motor Vehicles: Class 180, Land Vehicles: Class 280

More Specific Terms Pertaining to Turn Signals

Term	Class Found
Turn Signal	None
Turn	(Turning): Class 82
Signal	Signals and Indicators: Class 116

Terms Pertaining to the Type of Turn Signal

Term	Class Found
Timer	None
Electrical	Communications: Electrical: Class 340 Electricity: Electrical Systems and Devices: Class 361

Figure 8.2

In Figure 8.3, you can see a small section of the listings under the topic Electric and Electricity. These results indicate that Class 340, subclass 425.5+ is highly relevant to vehicle-mounted electric signals. The plus sign (+) following the subclass 425.5 indicates there are subclasses that further differentiate vehicle-mounted electric signals.

Surgical	607	1+
Therapeutic application	607	115+
Trawl net fish control	43	9.6
Signaling, electric (see signal)	340	
Noise suppression in signal	128	901*
Radio	455	
Railway	246	
Telegraph	178	
Telephone	379	
Television transmission	348	469+
Vehicle mounted	340	425.5+
Socket (see socket, electric)		
Soldering	219	129
Iron	219	245+
Iron design	D08	30
With pressure	219	85.1

Figure 8.3

The search results for all our descriptive terms are summarized in Figure 8.4. For the general terms "car," "automobile," and "vehicle," the most relevant class/subclass appears to be Class 340, subclass 425.5+ (Figure 8.3). The more specific terms "turn signal," "turn," and "signal" are related to Class 116, subclass 28R+ (Signals & Indicators). Finally, the most specific terms, "timer" and "electrical," again lead to Class 340, subclass 425.5+. Clearly, Classes/subclasses 116/28R+ and 340/425.5+ warrant further examination.

Search Results from Cross-Referenced List of Inventions

General Terms Used for Cars: Car, Automobile and Vehicle

Subject Area	Class	Subclass
Land Vehicle	280	
Vehicle Mounted	340	425.5+

More Specific Terms Pertaining to Turn Signals:
Turn Signal, Turn and Signal

Subject Area	Class	Subclass
Signals & Indicators	116	28R+

Terms Pertaining to the Type of Turn Signal: Timer and Electrical

Subject Area	Class	Subclass
Electrical	340	425.5+

Figure 8.4

Manual of Classification

We have now proceeded as far as we can in the *Index*. Now, we turn to the *Manual of Classification*. This manual has an indented list of all the subclasses to be found under each main class. The classes are listed in numerical order. Each class is covered by its own page or group of pages. Here you can easily look up each of the class/subclass numbers found in the *Index*.

Why look up the class/subclass numbers in this manual? Don't we already have our class/subclass information from the *Index*? Well, yes and no. What we have so far are a few individual class/subclass combinations. By using the *Manual of Classification*, we can see all of the subclasses within each major class. Moreover, this listing of subclasses is indented and provides a visual aid for understanding how the various subclasses are related. By reviewing the indented list of subclasses, you may find further classifications of interest.

```
425.5   LAND VEHICLE ALARMS OR INDICATORS
426     .Of burglary or unauthorized use
427     ..Of motorcycles or bicycles
428     ..Responsive to changes in voltage or current in a vehicle
          electrical system
429     ..Responsive to inertia, vibration, or tilt
430     ..With entrance/exit time delay
431     .For trailer
432     .For bicycle
433     .For school bus
434     .For taxi
435     .Of relative distance from an obstacle
436     .Of collision or contact with external object
437     ..Curb
438     .Internal alarm or indicator responsive to a condition of the
         vehicle
439     ..Operation efficiency (e.g., engine performance, driver
          habits)
440     ..Tilt, imbalance, or overload

441     ..Speed of vehicle, engine, or power train
442     ..Tire deflation or inflation
443     ...By indirect detection means (e.g., height measurement)
444     ....Relative wheel speed
445     ...With particular telemetric coupling
```

Figure 8.5

Figure 8.5 is a page from the *Manual of Classification* for Class 340. The figure shows a partial listing of the indented list of subclasses under the subclass 425.5—LAND VEHICLE ALARMS OR

INDICATORS. The dots or periods to the left of the subclass title indicate the specificity of the subclass. That is, the more dots, the more specific the subclass. For example, subclass 442 has two dots to the left of the title and refers to tire deflation or inflation. Subclass 443 has three dots to the left and refers to a particular measurement means of deflation or inflation—namely, tire height.

From a close examination of the indented list of subclasses, it would appear that subclass 465, Turning or steering, would be most relevant for the turn-signal-canceling invention.

Figure 8.6 shows the appropriate section from the indented list of subclasses. Here we see that subclass 463 refers to the general topic of "External alarms or indicators of movement." Subclass 465 limits those movements to turning or steering.

```
463       .External alarm or indicator of movement
464       ..Plural indications (e.g., go, slow, stop)
465       ..Turning or steering
466       ..Speed
467       ..Acceleration or deceleration
```

Figure 8.6

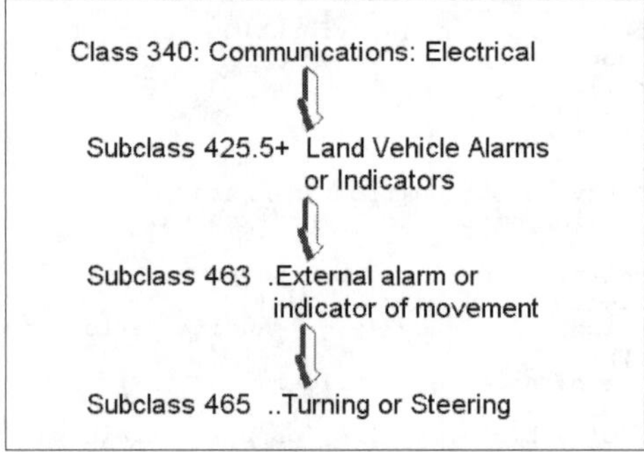

Figure 8.7

As noted, the process of finding the appropriate subclass moves from the general to the specific. Figure 8.7 summarizes this process for Class 340, subclass 465. First, our search starts with the general topic "Communications: Electrical." Then it proceeds to electrical communications that are used for "Land Vehicle Alarms or Indicators." Then it further limited the topic to "external alarm or indicator of movement." Finally, the patents issued under subclass 465 are limited to electrical signals that are used on land vehicles for the purpose of external indicators of "Turning or Steering."

Classification Definitions

The third manual we discuss, *Classification Definitions*, contains a written description for every class and subclass used by the PTO. This is where you can look up each class/subclass number and determine its relevance.

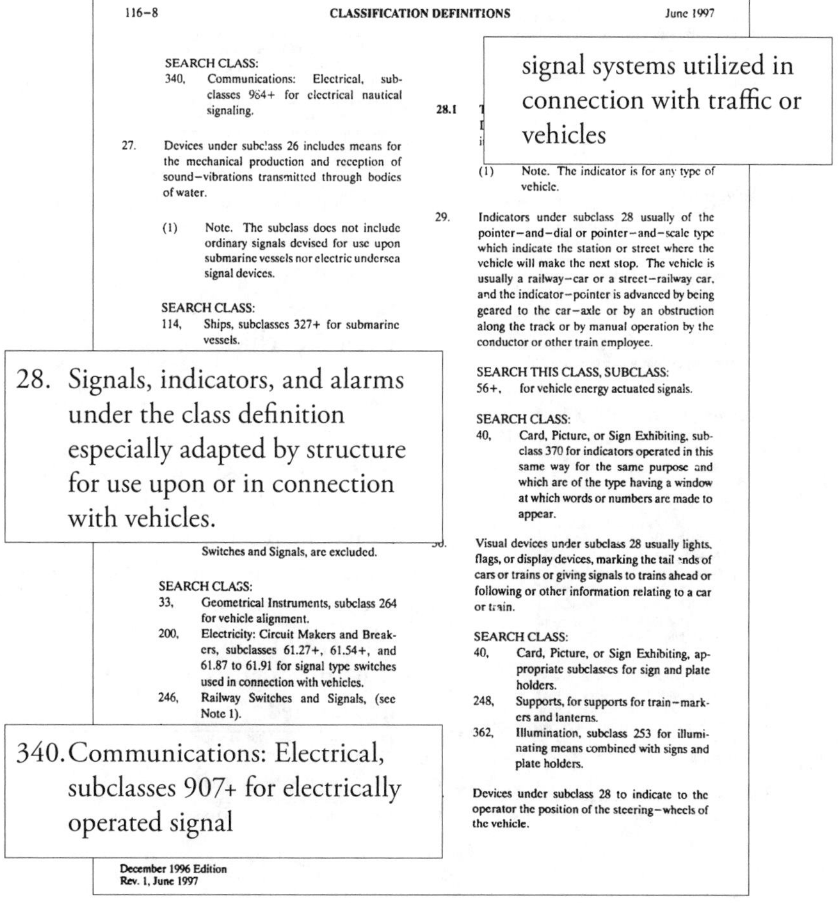

116-8 **CLASSIFICATION DEFINITIONS** June 1997

SEARCH CLASS:
340, Communications: Electrical, subclasses 984+ for electrical nautical signaling.

27. Devices under subclass 26 includes means for the mechanical production and reception of sound-vibrations transmitted through bodies of water.

(1) Note. The subclass does not include ordinary signals devised for use upon submarine vessels nor electric undersea signal devices.

SEARCH CLASS:
114, Ships, subclasses 327+ for submarine vessels.

28. Signals, indicators, and alarms under the class definition especially adapted by structure for use upon or in connection with vehicles.

Switches and Signals, are excluded.

SEARCH CLASS:
33, Geometrical Instruments, subclass 264 for vehicle alignment.
200, Electricity: Circuit Makers and Breakers, subclasses 61.27+, 61.54+, and 61.87 to 61.91 for signal type switches used in connection with vehicles.
246, Railway Switches and Signals, (see Note 1).

340. Communications: Electrical, subclasses 907+ for electrically operated signal

28.1 signal systems utilized in connection with traffic or vehicles

(1) Note. The indicator is for any type of vehicle.

29. Indicators under subclass 28 usually of the pointer-and-dial or pointer-and-scale type which indicate the station or street where the vehicle will make the next stop. The vehicle is usually a railway-car or a street-railway car, and the indicator-pointer is advanced by being geared to the car-axle or by an obstruction along the track or by manual operation by the conductor or other train employee.

SEARCH THIS CLASS, SUBCLASS:
56+, for vehicle energy actuated signals.

SEARCH CLASS:
40, Card, Picture, or Sign Exhibiting, subclass 370 for indicators operated in this same way for the same purpose and which are of the type having a window at which words or numbers are made to appear.

30. Visual devices under subclass 28 usually lights, flags, or display devices, marking the tail ends of cars or trains or giving signals to trains ahead or following or other information relating to a car or train.

SEARCH CLASS:
40, Card, Picture, or Sign Exhibiting, appropriate subclasses for sign and plate holders.
248, Supports, for supports for train-markers and lanterns.
362, Illumination, subclass 253 for illuminating means combined with signs and plate holders.

Devices under subclass 28 to indicate to the operator the position of the steering-wheels of the vehicle.

December 1996 Edition
Rev. 1, June 1997

Figure 8.8

Figure 8.8 shows page 116-118 of the *Classification Definitions*—that is, this is the eighth page for Class 116. About halfway down the left-hand column is the description for subclass 28 (boxed). Reading the definition, you can see that this subclass pertains to signals that are especially adapted for use upon, or in connection with, vehicles.

Below each subclass definition is a Search Class reference that contains a listing of additional classes that are related to the subject matter. In the figure, we see that Class 340 is referenced for signal systems utilized in connection with traffic or vehicles.

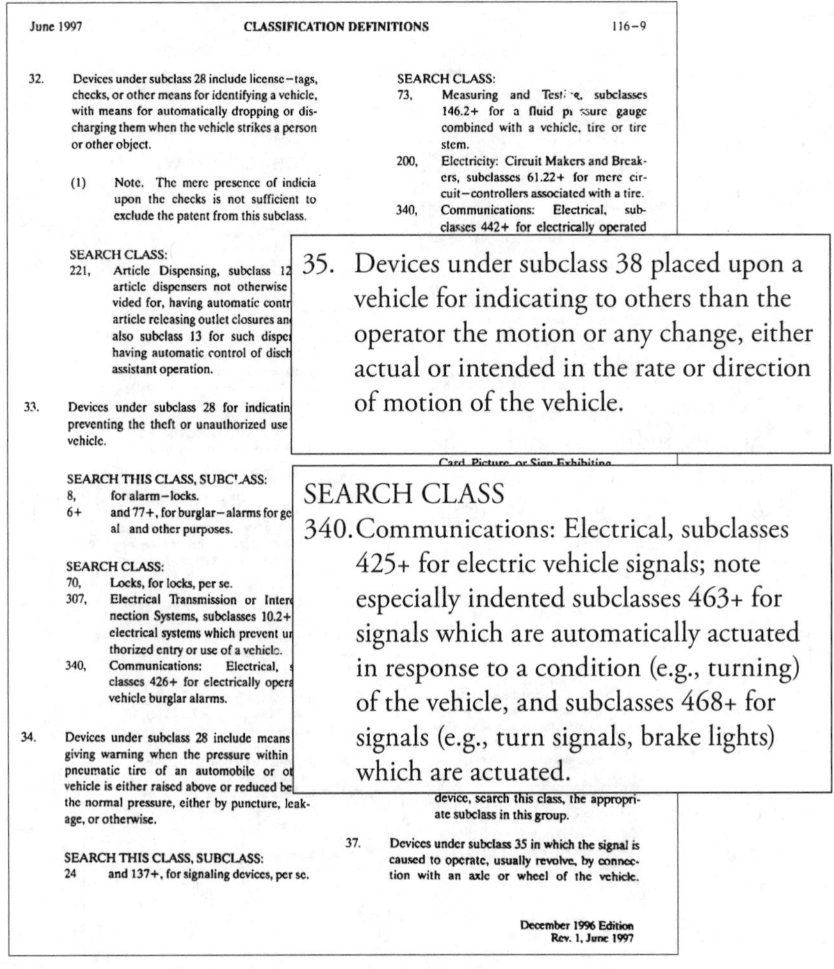

June 1997 | CLASSIFICATION DEFINITIONS | 116-9

32. Devices under subclass 28 include license-tags, checks, or other means for identifying a vehicle, with means for automatically dropping or discharging them when the vehicle strikes a person or other object.

(1) Note. The mere presence of indicia upon the checks is not sufficient to exclude the patent from this subclass.

SEARCH CLASS:
221, Article Dispensing, subclass 12 article dispensers not otherwise vided for, having automatic contr article releasing outlet closures an also subclass 13 for such dispe having automatic control of disch assistant operation.

33. Devices under subclass 28 for indicatin preventing the theft or unauthorized use vehicle.

SEARCH THIS CLASS, SUBCLASS:
8, for alarm-locks.
6+ and 77+, for burglar-alarms for ge al and other purposes.

SEARCH CLASS:
70, Locks, for locks, per se.
307, Electrical Transmission or Inter nection Systems, subclasses 10.2+ electrical systems which prevent un thorized entry or use of a vehicle.
340, Communications: Electrical, s classes 426+ for electrically oper vehicle burglar alarms.

34. Devices under subclass 28 include means giving warning when the pressure within pneumatic tire of an automobile or ot vehicle is either raised above or reduced be the normal pressure, either by puncture, leakage, or otherwise.

SEARCH THIS CLASS, SUBCLASS:
24 and 137+, for signaling devices, per se.

SEARCH CLASS:
73, Measuring and Testing, subclasses 146.2+ for a fluid pressure gauge combined with a vehicle, tire or tire stem.
200, Electricity: Circuit Makers and Breakers, subclasses 61.22+ for mere circuit-controllers associated with a tire.
340, Communications: Electrical, subclasses 442+ for electrically operated

35. Devices under subclass 38 placed upon a vehicle for indicating to others than the operator the motion or any change, either actual or intended in the rate or direction of motion of the vehicle.

Card Picture or Sign Exhibiting

SEARCH CLASS
340. Communications: Electrical, subclasses 425+ for electric vehicle signals; note especially indented subclasses 463+ for signals which are automatically actuated in response to a condition (e.g., turning) of the vehicle, and subclasses 468+ for signals (e.g., turn signals, brake lights) which are actuated.

device, search this class, the appropriate subclass in this group.

37. Devices under subclass 35 in which the signal is caused to operate, usually revolve, by connection with an axle or wheel of the vehicle.

December 1996 Edition
Rev. 1, June 1997

Figure 8.9

Figure 8.9 shows page 116-119 from the *Classification Definitions.* Here, we see that Class 116, subclass 35 relates to "Devices under subclass 28 placed upon a vehicle for indicating to others than the operator, the motion of any change, either actual or intended, in the rate or direction of the motion of the vehicle." This definition tells us that subclass 28 is for signaling devices used only on vehicles and only for the purpose of indicating a change of direction (a turn) or a change in rate of travel (brake lights) to persons other than the driver.

Below this definition, in the search class cross-reference, we again see a reference to Class 340. Clearly, Class 340, along with the referenced subclass 463, is highly relevant to vehicle turn signals.

Figure 8.10 displays page 340-23 from the *Classification Definitions.* Subclass 463 includes signals for turning, braking, and backing. However, subclass 465 (boxed) is specifically limited to electronic signals used to indicate vehicle turning—"Subject matter under subclass 463 in which the external signal indicates that the vehicle is executing a turning movement."

As you can see after using these three databases, Class 340, subclass 465 is a highly likely place to find patents related to turn signals for vehicles. In addition, Class/subclass 340/465 is a good place to check to see if the idea for an automatic turn-signal-canceling device has been anticipated. Figure 8.11 shows, in flow-chart format, the process for using the classification manuals.

June 1996 **CLASSIFICATION DEFINITIONS** 340–23

362, Illumination, subclasses 61+ for vehicle mounted illumination devices which may include fault, or position (e.g., aiming) indicators.

459. Plural conditions:
Subject matter under subclass 438 incl
systems or devices which combine two or
automatic alarms or indicators, or in wh
single alarm or indicator serves two or
diverse functions.

SEARCH THIS CLASS, SUBCLASS:
439+, for alarms or indicators which res
to a combination of two or more re
conditions which measure engine
ciency.

460. With voice warning:
Subject matter under subclass 459 in whic
alarm or indicator includes a recorde
synthesized voice signal.

461. With particular display means:
Subject matter under subclass 459 wh
plural diverse indicators share a common h
ing or mounting.

462. Digital:
Subject matter under subclass 461 wherein one or more of the indicators is a digital display.

463. External alarm or indicator of movement:
Subject matter under subclass 425.5 including external signalling systems which automatically respond to a state of motion (e.g., turning, acceleration, deceleration, backing) of the vehicle and which communicate with persons outside the vehicle (e.g., other drivers, pedestrians).

(1) Note. The state of motion may be sensed directly, as by an accelerometer, or it may be sensed by devices responsive to the activation of a system which causes the movement (e.g., the steering linkage or the transmission gear selector).

464. Plural indications (e.g., go, slow, stop):
Subject matter under subclass 463 in which two or more diverse motion indicators are combined.

465. **Turning or steering:**

Subject matter under subclass 463 in which the external signal indicates that the vehicle is executing a turning movement.

SEARCH THIS CLASS, SUBCLASS:

475+ for systems which are manually set to indicate the operator's intention to initiate a turning movement and may be automatically cancelled upon completion of the turn.

Subject matter under subclass 463 in which the external signal indicates a change in the speed of the vehicle.

(1) Note. External signal lights which are actuated by: (a) an inertial sensor, (b) a switch associated with the accelerator pedal, or (c) a device which senses changes in engine vacuum are classified here. Brake lights, which are actuated by a switch associated with the brake pedal, are provided for in this class (340), subclass 479.

SEARCH CLASS:
180, Motor Vehicles, subclasses 282+ for systems or devices which directly control a vehicle subsystem (e.g., an ignition circuit) in response to an acceleration or deceleration.

December 1996 Edition
Rev. 1, June 1997

Figure 8.10

Classification Manual Flowchart

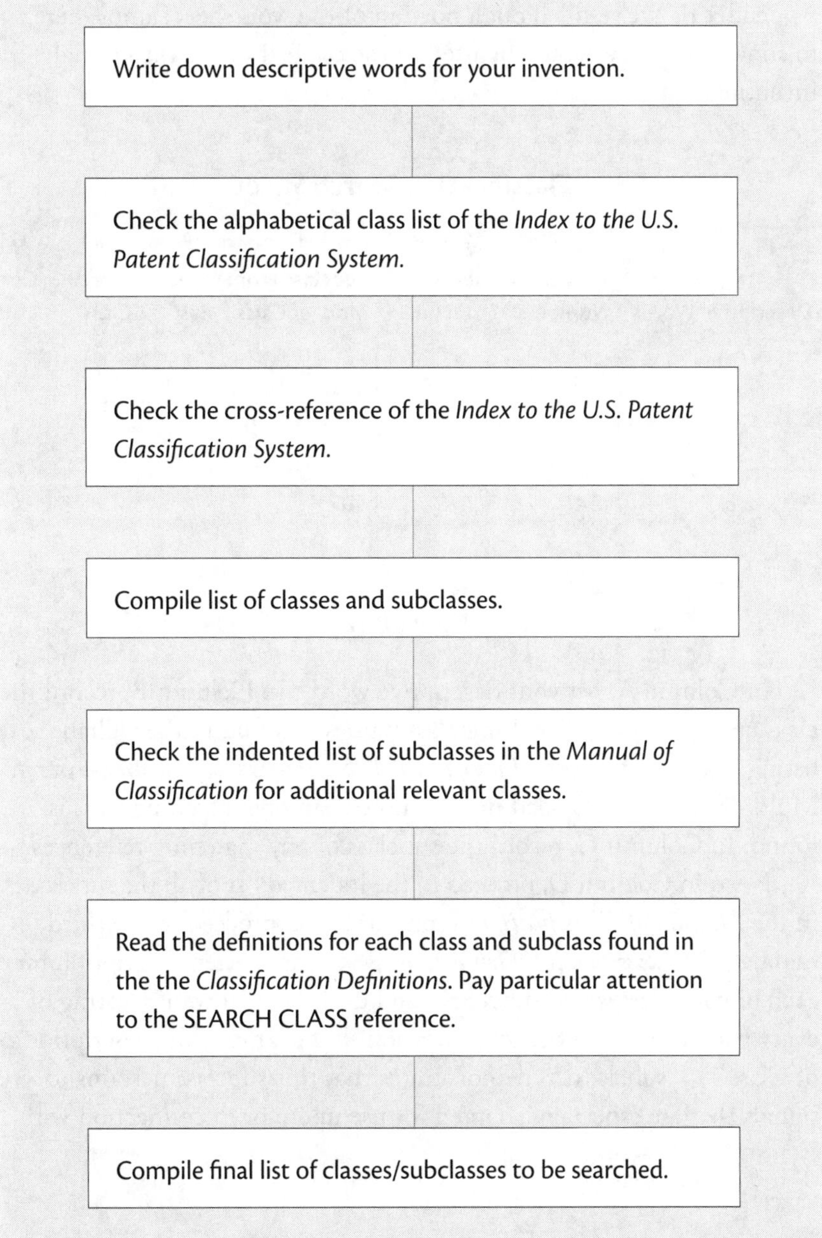

Write down descriptive words for your invention.
Check the alphabetical class list of the *Index to the U.S. Patent Classification System*.
Check the cross-reference of the *Index to the U.S. Patent Classification System.*
Compile list of classes and subclasses.
Check the indented list of subclasses in the *Manual of Classification* for additional relevant classes.
Read the definitions for each class and subclass found in the the *Classification Definitions*. Pay particular attention to the SEARCH CLASS reference.
Compile final list of classes/subclasses to be searched.

Figure 8.11

We have created a classification search worksheet (Figure 8.12) that you can use when searching classes. You'll find blank worksheets in Appendix B. We've filled out a portion of the worksheet sample here to show you how it would be used in the context of the turn signal invention.

Classification Search Sheet

A	B	C	D	E	F	G
Descriptive Words	Class Numbers	Subclass From Index	Subclass From *Man. of Class.*	Get List	Search Class	Get List
1. Turn Signal	116	28		X	340	
		35		X	340	
2. Vehicle	340	425.5+	465	X	340/475	X

Figure 8.12

In Column A, list your descriptive words. In Column B, record the class numbers of any matching class names you find in the alphabetical listing of classes from the *Index to the U.S. Patent Classification System.* Multiple rows are provided in case more than one matching class is found. In Column C, record the subclass of any matching references.

Next, in Column D, proceed to the indented list of all the subclasses in the *Manual of Classification*. From here, you proceed to the third manual, the *Classification Definitions.* Read the written description for each of your classes and subclasses and decide if you want a listing of every patent issued in that classification. For example, the description of Class 116, subclass 28 demonstrates that this subclass pertains to signals that are especially adapted for use upon, or in connection with, vehicles. So we marked an "X" in Column E, the "Get List" column next to subclass 28, which reminds us to get a list of patents issued in that class/subclass.

The search class cross-reference for subclass 28 (right below the subclass definition—Figure 8.9) contained a reference to Class 340. So, in our example, that's noted in the Search Class column, Column F.

Finally, since Class 340, subclass 465—Turning or Steering—appears relevant to the turn signal invention, an "X" is placed in Column G (the corresponding Get List column). The search class cross-reference for subclass 465 (Figure 8.10) contained a reference to subclass 475, so we note that in Column F and mark the Get List column, Column G, for this subclass as well.

The classification search worksheet is helpful because as you proceed from left to right, filling out the sheet, you can see exactly where you found your classification information. Also, referencing the search class information (far left column) helps in two ways. First, as discussed previously, it leads you to other places to search. Second, it gives you a feel for the quality of the search results.

Finding the correct classifications for your invention is the key to a successful patent search. Once you have identified a given class, it is relatively simple to create a listing of every issued patent within that class. This technique is superior to randomly searching the text of patents for matching keywords because keyword-searching results depend entirely on the terms used. If different words are used to describe similar, patented inventions, you will miss many related patents.

Since relevant prior art is often missed by inexperienced patent searchers who fail to identify the appropriate categories, we have prepared a visual tool—the Class Finder Tool—to help you choose the correct words to describe your invention (Figure 8.13). (Blank copies of the Class Finder Tool are included in Appendix B.)

Class Finder Tool:

General Field or
Application of Invention

Invention Itself or
Device Applied to

Invention Attributes

Figure 8.13

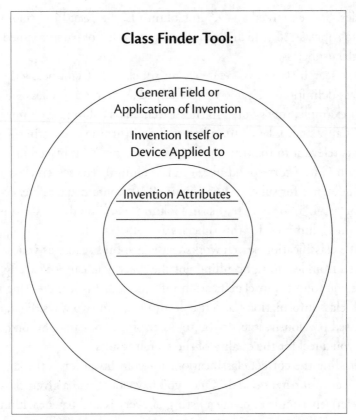

The outer circle of the Class Finder Tool represents the general field or application of the invention. You can think of it as all the relevant factors surrounding your idea. The inner circle represents the invention itself. Try to find words that will encompass the most general aspects of your invention. If the invention is a new application applied to an existing device, then the inner circle is the device that the invention is directly applied to. The blank lines within the inner circle are where you write down the specific attributes of the invention.

Figure 8.14 is an example of the Class Finder Tool filled out for our turn-signal-canceling device. In our example, we originally thought turn signals applied only to cars. However, the circle around the turn signal device reminds us that there are other devices that use turn signals.

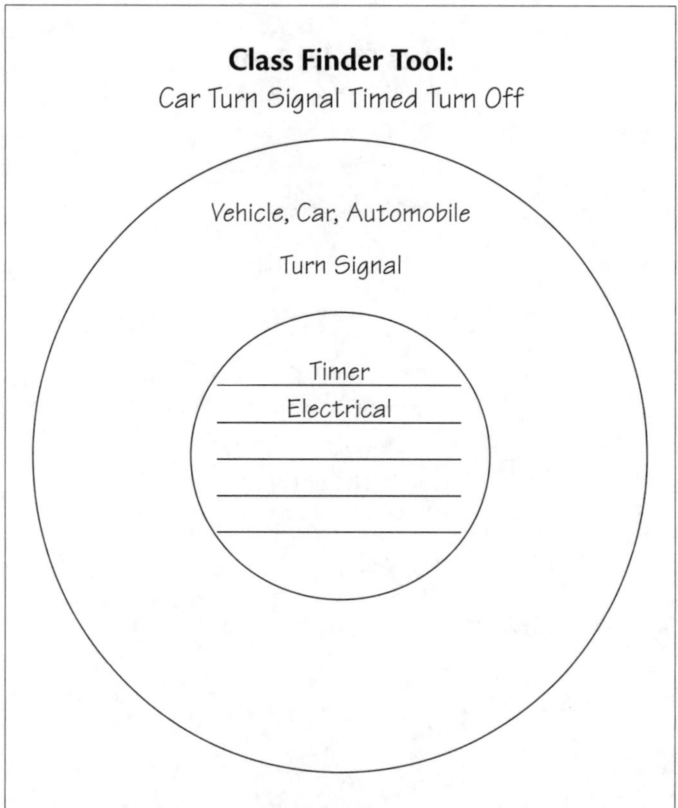

Figure 8.14

As a further example, Figure 8.15 shows the Class Finder Tool filled out for the bathroom nightlight invention that we discussed in Chapter 3. Here, the major aspect of the invention is a lamp/nightlight which uses a standard light bulb. Since there are many ways to cast light (for example, fireplaces, arc lamps, and reflected sunlight), the general field is illumination. Finally, the specific attributes include a flexible support and use in the bathroom.

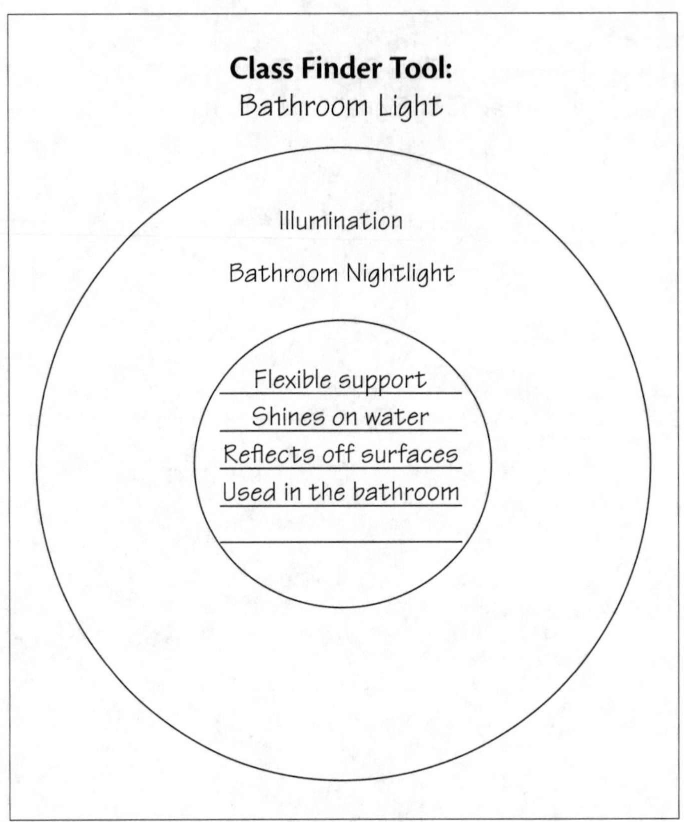
Class Finder Tool:
Bathroom Light
Illumination
Bathroom Nightlight
Flexible support
Shines on water
Reflects off surfaces
Used in the bathroom

Figure 8.15

CHAPTER

9

Using CASSIS

The PTO stores a great deal of patent and trademark information in DVD format and has developed a special computer search program to retrieve this information. This system, known as the Classification and Search Support Information System (CASSIS), is available at every PTDL. These PTDLs also have personnel to help you get started. If you plan on using CASSIS, it's a good idea to call ahead to the PTDL and make an appointment.

The CASSIS DVD Database

Each DVD in the CASSIS series is devoted to a certain topic. Below is a breakdown of a few of these DVDs.

Welcome to CASSIS2

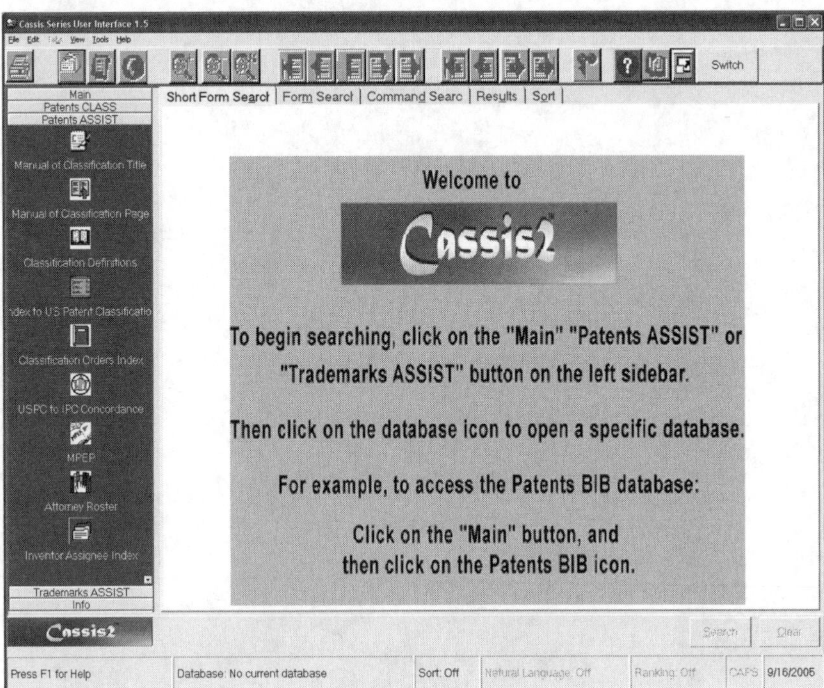

Figure 9.1

CASSIS DVDs	
Title	**DVD Contents**
Patents BIB	Bibliographical data for utility patents issued from the year 1969 to the present. This includes the date of issue, state/country of first-listed inventor's residence, assignee at time of issue, patent status (withdrawn, expired, etc.), current classifications, and patent title.
Patents CLASS	Current classification of all utility, design, and plant patents issued from the first U.S. patent to the present.
Patents ASSIST	An electronic version of the *Index to the U.S. Patent Classification System, Manual of Classification* and the *Classification Definitions.* Other electronic manuals on the DVD include the *Classification Orders Index* (provides a list of classifications abolished and established since 1976, with corresponding classification order number and effective date), the *IPC-USPC Concordance* (the *U.S. Patent Classification System to International Patent Classification Concordance* is a guide for relating the U.S. Patent Classification System to the International Patent Classification System, published by the World Intellectual Property Organization), the *Manual of Patent Examining Procedure* (provides patent examiners and patent applicants with a reference work on the practices and procedures related to prosecution of patent applications in the U.S. Patent and Trademark Office), a listing of attorneys and agents registered to practice before the PTO, and the *Patentee-Assignee Index* (shows ownership at time of issue for utility patents 1969 to present, for other types of patents 1977 to present, and inventors' names from 1975 to present).
USAApp	Facsimile images of patent application publications filed on or after November 29, 2000.
USAPat	Facsimile images of U.S. patents from 1994 to the present. The operative word here is DVDs. The current USAPat back-file project is capturing the image data for all patent grants since 1790 on a set of approximately 400 DVD-ROMs.

CASSIS is currently in its second version (CASSIS2) (Figure 9.1). The CASSIS databases are grouped in four divisions: Main, Patents CLASS, Patents ASSIST, and Trademarks ASSIST. To access the data on a particular CASSIS DVD, select one of the buttons on the left side of the Web page. Near the top navigation bar are a series of tabs: Short Form Search, Form Search, Command Search, Results, and Sort.

Index to the U.S. Patent Classification System

Let's start with the CASSIS version of the *Index to the U.S. Patent Classification System* (found on the "Patents ASSIST" DVD). If you click on the Patents ASSIST button (as shown in Figure 9.1), and then click on the *Index* icon (about halfway down the figure), a popup window will display the content information for the DVD loaded into the computer.

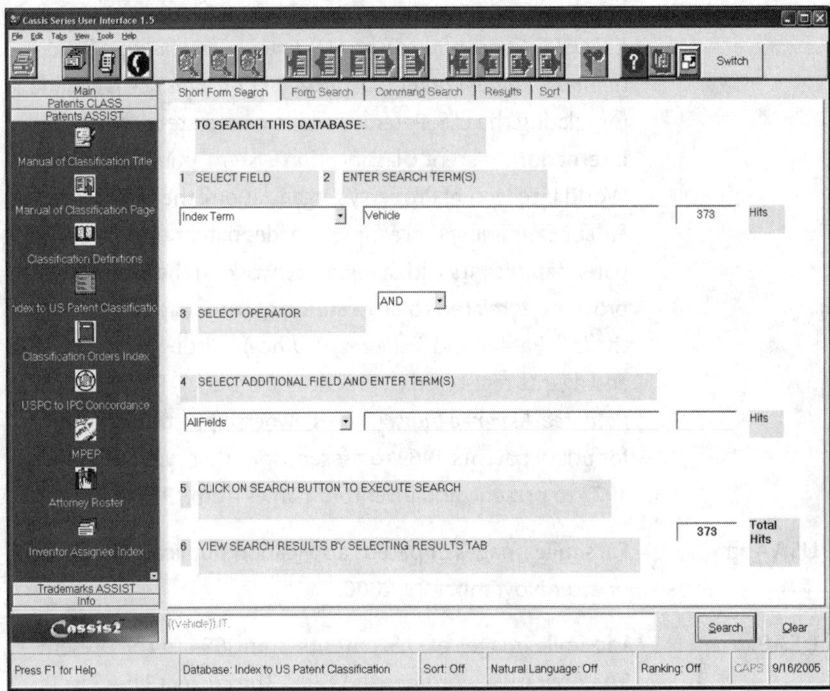

Figure 9.2

After clicking OK, you will see the screen shown in Figure 9.2. This is the Short Form Search page. Here you can search for class titles that match your descriptive keywords. For example, Figure 9.2 displays a search for an *Index* term that matches the word "vehicle." The total hits for this search are 373 (as you can see in the lower-right corner of Figure 9.2). To review these hits, click on the Results tab (the fourth tab below the navigation bar on the top of the page)

The Results screen displays two windows. The upper window shows an alphabetical cross-referenced listing of invention subject areas based on "vehicle." If you want to see how the search term is referenced in any given invention subject area, click on that subject area. Figure 9.3 displays what happens if you scroll to "Turn Indicators" and click on the adjacent selection box.

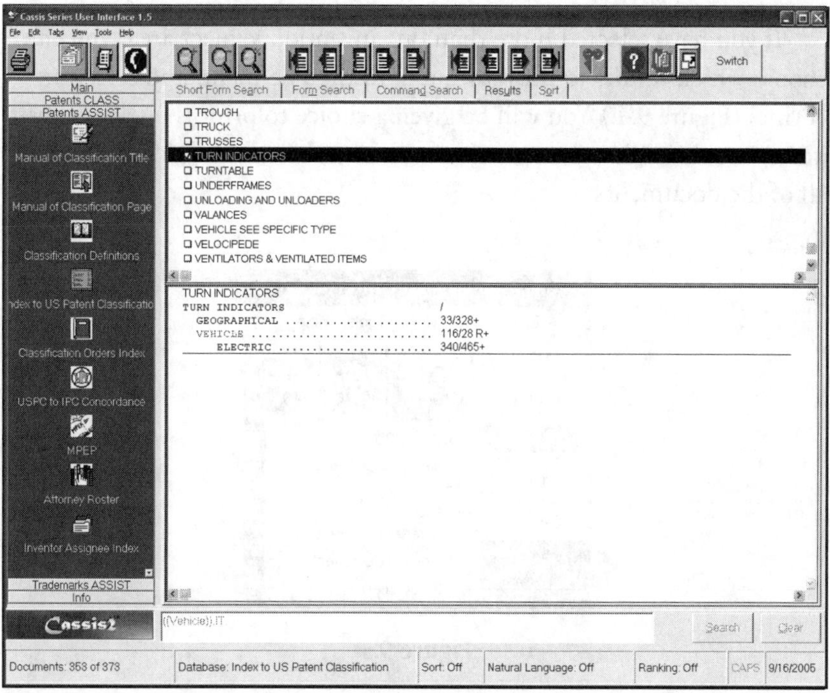

Figure 9.3

The lower display window on Figure 9.3 shows that Class 166, subclass 28R+ is referenced. Note that this is the same result we obtained from our manual search of the *Index* in Chapter 7. You can get a printout of the display by clicking on the printer icon in the upper-left corner.

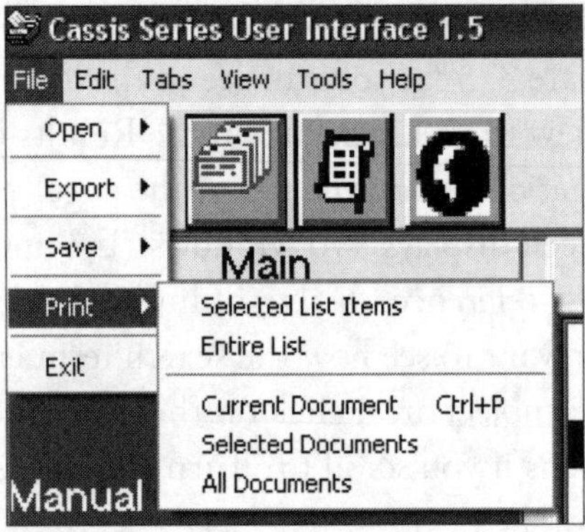

Figure 9.4

If you have selected more than one invention subject area, you can choose which results to print by going to the File menu and selecting "Print" (Figure 9.4.) You will be given a choice to print the selected list items, the entire list, the current document, the selected documents, or all of the documents.

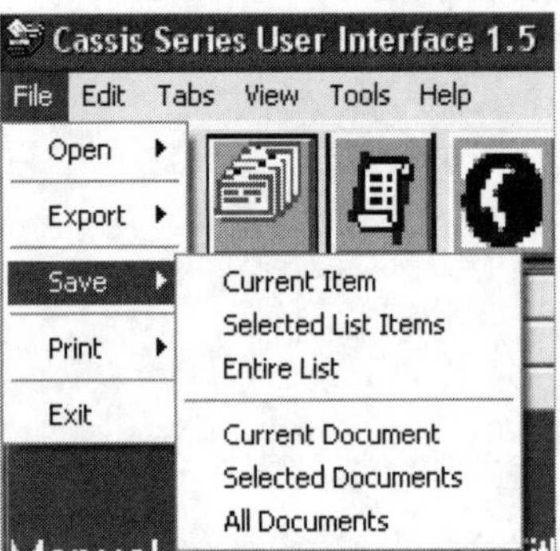

Figure 9.5

To save your search results, click on the File menu and select "Save" (Figure 9.5). You are given the choice of saving the current item from the results list, selected list items, the entire list, the current document, selected documents, or all of the documents.

TIP

Unbelievable as it may seem, you will need a 3.5-inch formatted floppy disk (remember those) in order to save your results to the CASSIS computer. (And obviously, your personal computer will have to be capable of reading floppy disks as well.)

Manual of Classification

Our next CASSIS reference volume, the *Manual of Classification*, can be viewed by clicking on the "*Manual of Classifications* Page" icon, (as seen on the left side of Figure 9.3). The basic search screen for the *Manual of Classification* is shown in Figure 9.6, where we have set the system to search for Class Number 340. (The Total Hits—one—are shown in the bottom-right corner.)

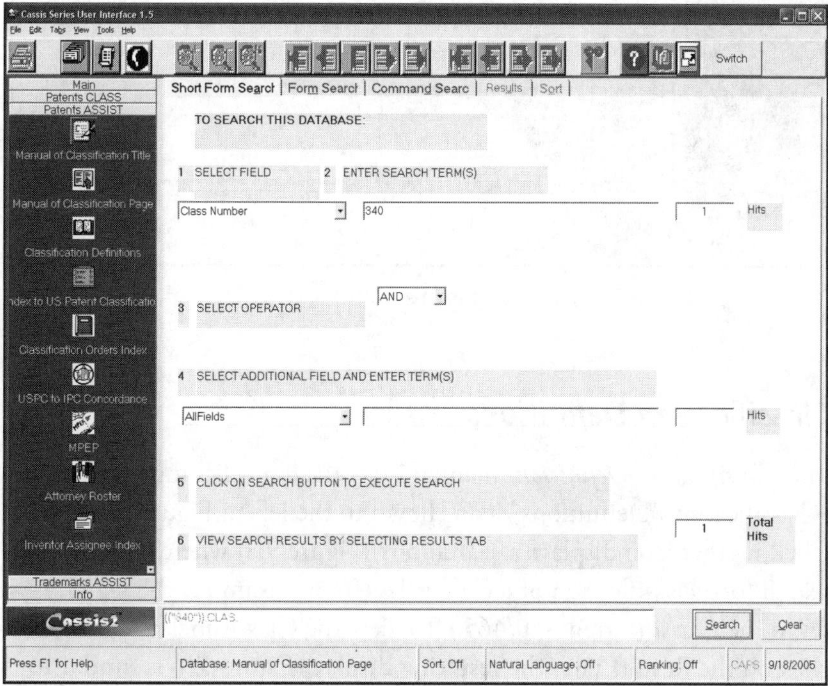

Figure 9.6

Figure 9.7 displays what you will see if you click on the Results tab. This is similar to the Results screen obtained from the search of the *Index of the U.S. Patent Classification System*, as shown in Figure 9.2. In Figure 9.2, there were 373 occurrences of the search term "vehicle."

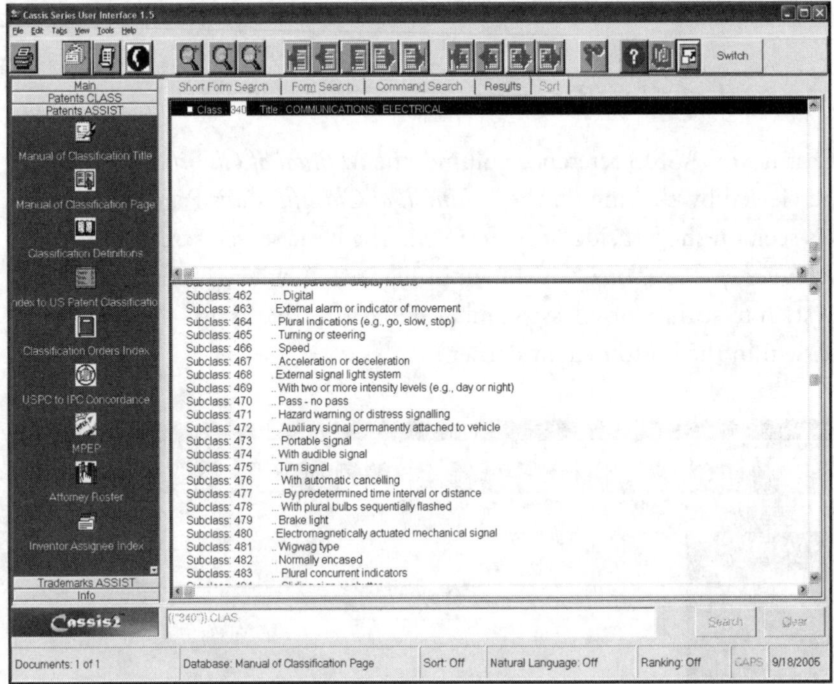

Figure 9.7

Classification Definitions

The *Classification Definitions* manual is accessed by clicking on the "Classifications Definitions" icon shown to the left in Figure 9.7. Clicking that icon displays a search box (Figure 9.8) where you can search for a classification or a class title. (In our example, the search is set to the Classification 340/465.) To view the Class/subclass definition, click on the Results tab. The resulting display (Figure 9.9) is similar to the indented list shown in Chapter 7.

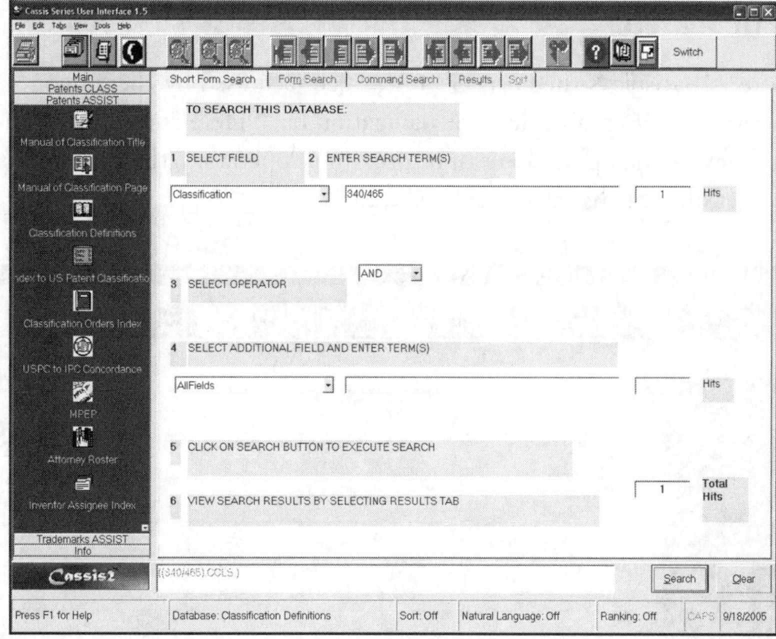

Figure 9.8

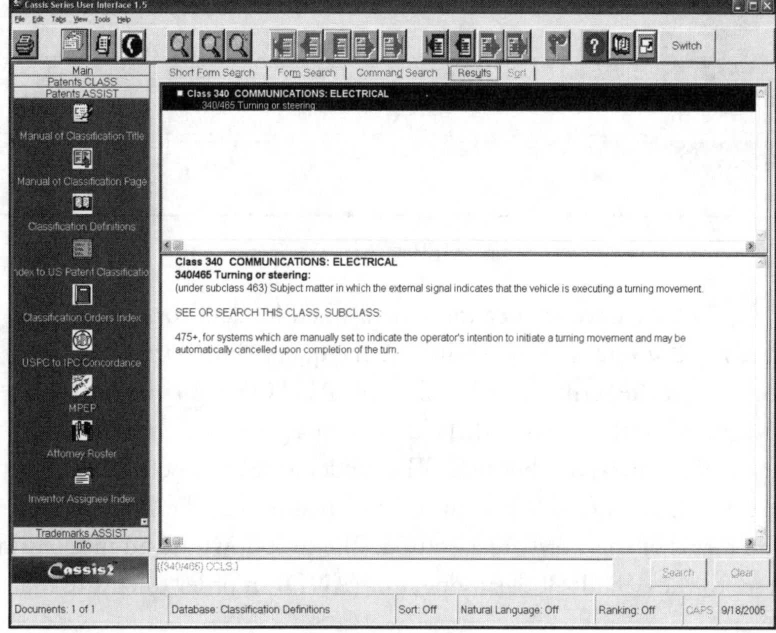

Figure 9.9

Form Search

Figure 9.10 displays the Form Search screen (accessed by clicking on the corresponding tab below the navigation bar). Here you can type in search terms and apply Boolean or proximity operators (these are terms that measure the distance between words).

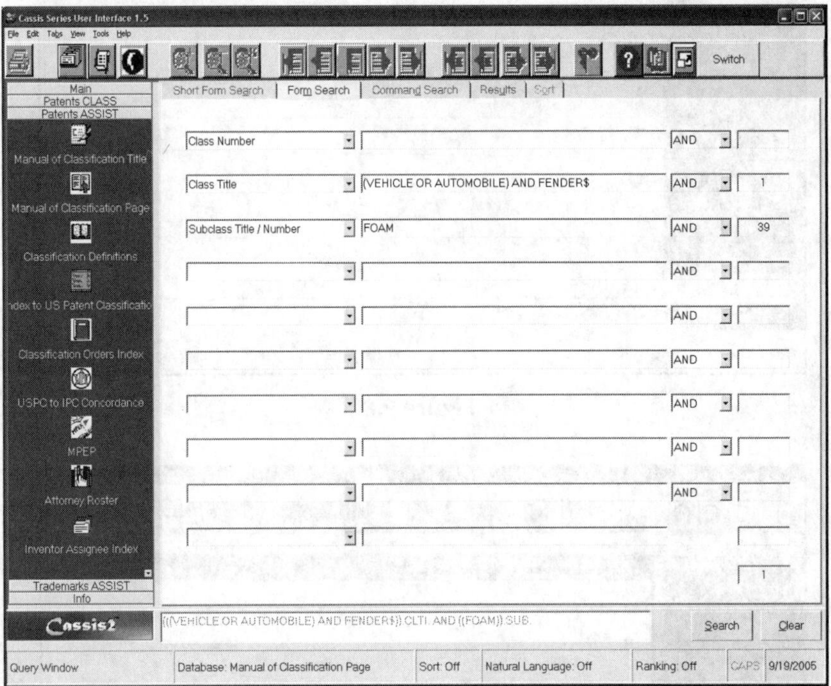

Figure 9.10

Suppose we have an idea for a foam-filled fender. To search the *Manual of Classification,* we could use the query shown in Figure 9.10, searching for the terms "(VEHICLE OR AUTOMOBILE) AND FENDER$" in the Class Title field, as well as the term "FOAM" in the Subclass Title/Number field. The wildcard ($) has been used for the search term "FENDER$" in order to insure that the singular and plural forms of the word are captured. The dropdown menu in Column 3 is set to the default Boolean operator (AND) in order to ensure that both the Class Title and Subclass Title/Number search results match our queries for a hit to be returned. The system has located one Class/subclass definition in its search (Figure 9.11).

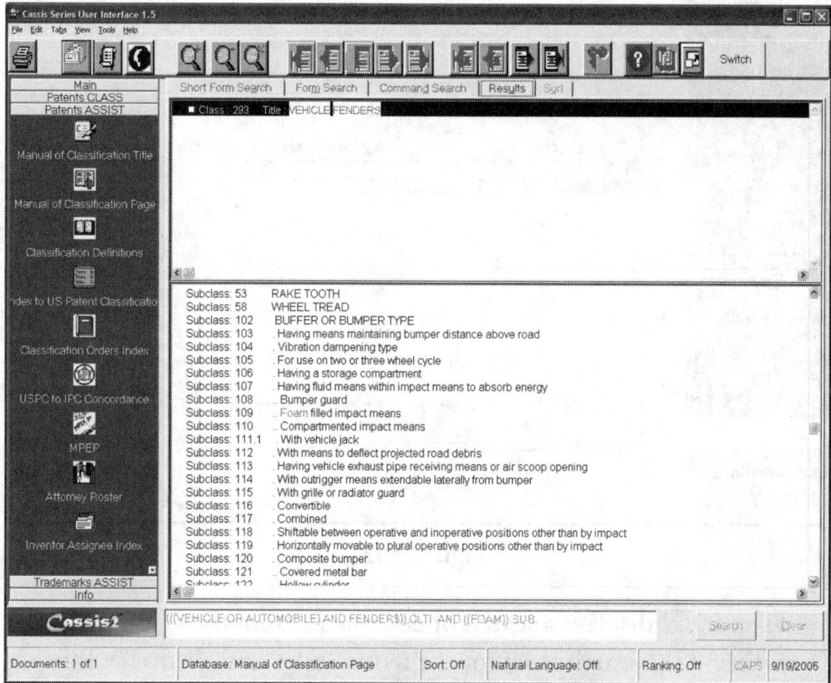

Figure 9.11

Clicking the Results tab (Figure 9.11), reveals the upper window displaying Class 293—Vehicle Fenders. The lower window displays the class breakdown. Toward the middle of this window is Subclass 109—Foam-filled impact means.

Command Search

The Command Search screen (Figure 9.12), accessed by clicking the third tab below the navigation bar, provides additional flexibility in combining information from different search fields using Boolean and proximity operators, wildcards, and phrases.

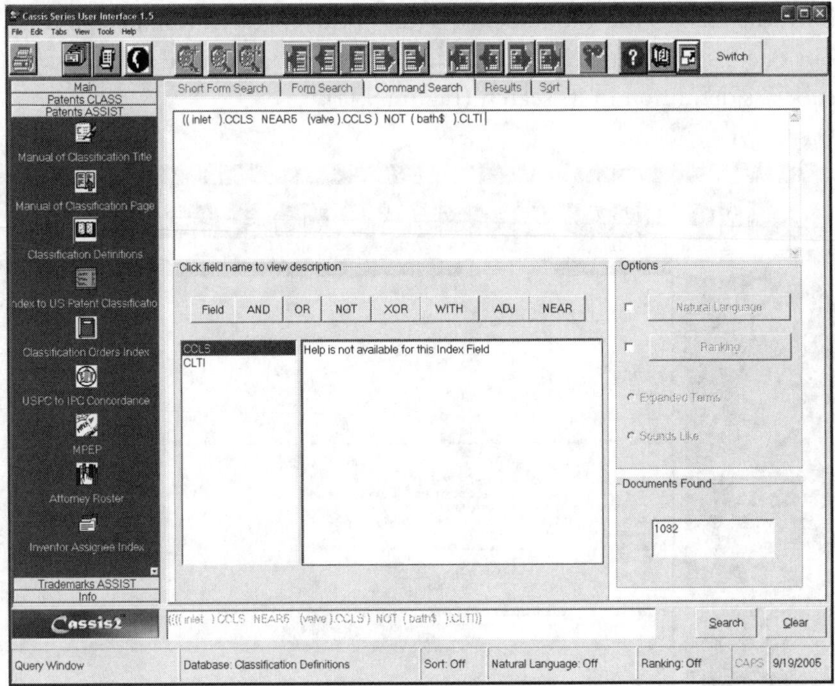

Figure 9.12

Figure 9.12 displays a search of documents from the *Classification Definitions.* (The search is set for the terms "inlet" and "valve.") This search demonstrates the use of proximity operators. For example, if you want to find any documents that had "vehicle" within five words of "engine," you would type "vehicle NEAR5 engine" and the results would show documents with the two search terms within five words of each other, in any order. (Note that the search also specifies that the term "bath$" cannot occur in the classification title of the search result. This is useful for excluding bathroom applications.)

Proximity Operators		
Operator	**Description**	**Examples**
ADJ	Indicates that the search terms must appear next to each other in the order specified. Additional separation can be allowed by including an optional number.	Inline ADJ Skate Inline ADJ5 Skate
NEAR	Indicates that the search terms can appear in either order with up to one word between. Additional separation can be allowed by including an optional number.	Inlet NEAR valve Inlet NEAR5 valve
WITH	Indicates that the search terms must appear in the same sentence. The search terms can appear in any order.	Valve WITH fluid

Additional CASSIS Features

Additional features of the CASSIS system include natural language searching (that is, searching without Boolean operators); customized displays; saving and loading frequently used search queries; and searching for a listing of all the patents issued within a given Class/subclass (Patents CLASS DVD).

CHAPTER

10

EAST Meets WEST

If you visit the PTO public search facility in Alexandria, Virginia, you can use computer workstations that provide access to the EAST and WEST search systems. The search system used with these databases is referred to as the BRS search engine language (BRS is named after the former search company Bibliographic Retrieval Services). Both EAST and WEST use a proprietary software system to convert users' search commands into a form that the BRS search engine understands.

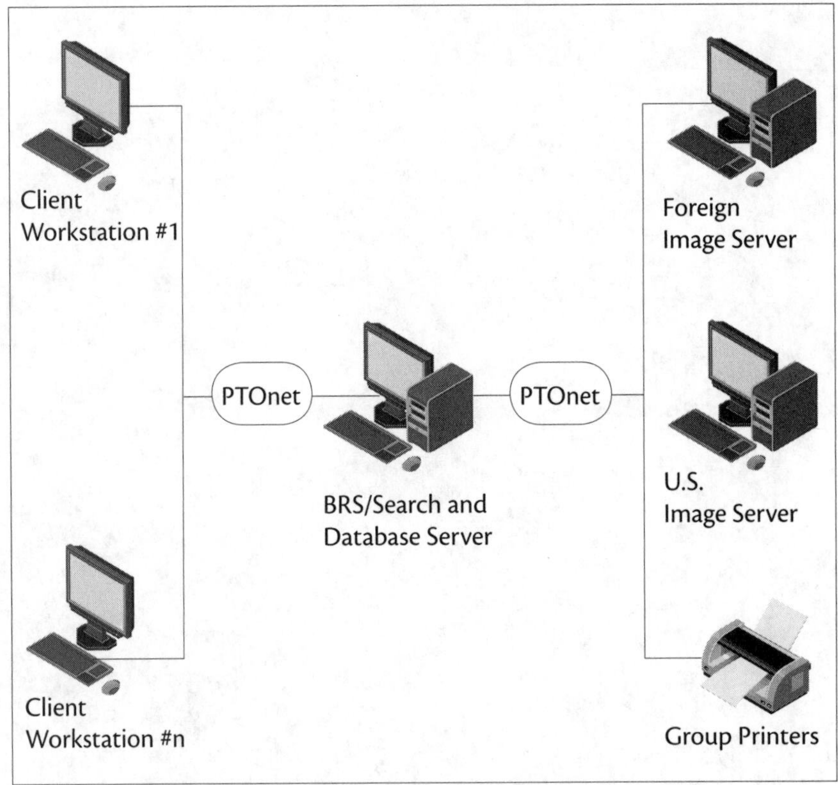

Figure 10.1 (Source: EAST Training Manual—USPTO)

Web-based Examiner Search Tool (WEST)

Freeform Search

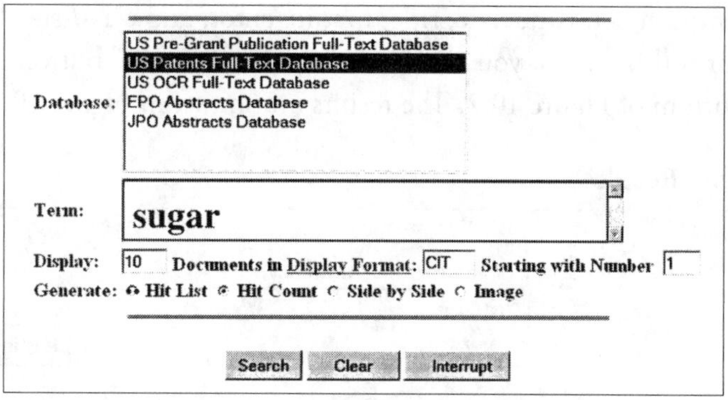

Figure 10.2 (Source: WEST Training Manual—USPTO)

In order to use the WEST search interface, you will need assistance from PTO personnel who will log you in with a user ID and password. Once you are logged in, WEST displays a default freeform search window (Figure 10.2). One of the major advantages to using WEST is the wealth of searchable patent data. A summary of the searchable databases is shown in the table below.

The WEST Databases	
Database	**Contents**
USPT	Bibliographic information (patent number, publication date, and current classification information) for patents from the 1790s to the present
USOCR	Scanned image file of patents issued from 1920 to 1970 with minimal index information, such as patent number, title (utility), publication date, and current classification information. No text editing performed.
PGPub	Utility patent applications that have been pending for 18 months
JPAB	English-language abstracts of unexamined Japanese patent applications starting with October 1976
EPAB	Published documents from the EPO and selected member countries

As an example, a simple search for the keyword "sugar" is shown in Figure 10.2 using the default U.S. Patents Full-Text Database. The output is displayed in the CIT (Citation) format. This format includes the patent number, issue date, title, first inventor, and class/ subclass. To perform this search, you would click on the "Search" button shown at the bottom of Figure 10.2. The results are shown in Figure 10.3.

Hit Screen Results

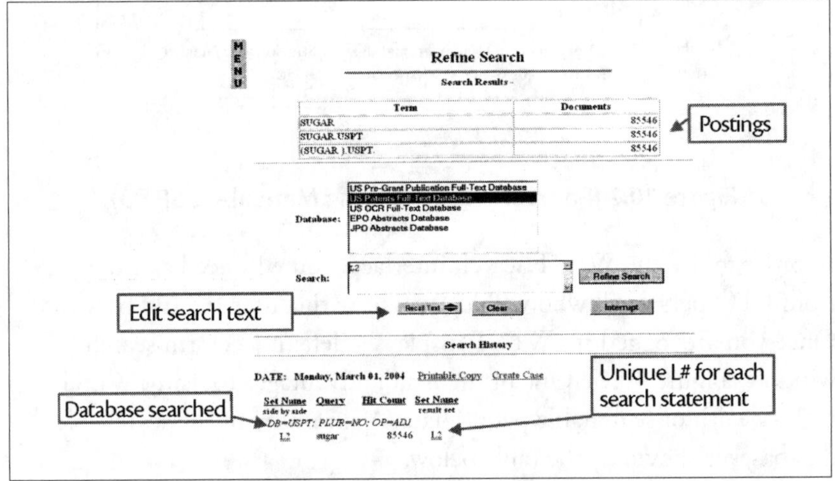

Figure 10.3 (Source: WEST Training Manual—USPTO)

The results of a WEST search are often referred to as a "posting." A posting consists of:

- the term(s) searched
- the total number of records containing the search terms, and
- a unique L-number label applied to each search result answer set.

In Figure 10.3, you can see, for example, that there are 85,546 hits for the keyword "sugar." This group of results makes up what is called an "answer set." To the right of our answer set is the L-number (bottom of Figure 10.3). These L-numbers increase sequentially throughout your search session, ranging from 1 to 999. Using WEST, multiple search words can be combined with Boolean search terms as shown. (See Chapter 2 for a detailed discussion of Boolean searching.)

Multiple search words can also be combined with proximity operators. The variety of proximity operators are shown in the table below. Note that:

- All The proximity operators can be combined with NOT.
- The ADJ and NEAR operators can be followed by a number (1–99) that represents the maximum number of "words apart."
- The default separation of one is used if no number is specified.

Some examples of proximity searches are:

- electrical NOT with wire
- electrical ADJ wire (by default, the BRS system will interpret "wire" as being separated from "electrical" by one term), and
- electrical NEAR wire.

Hit List Results

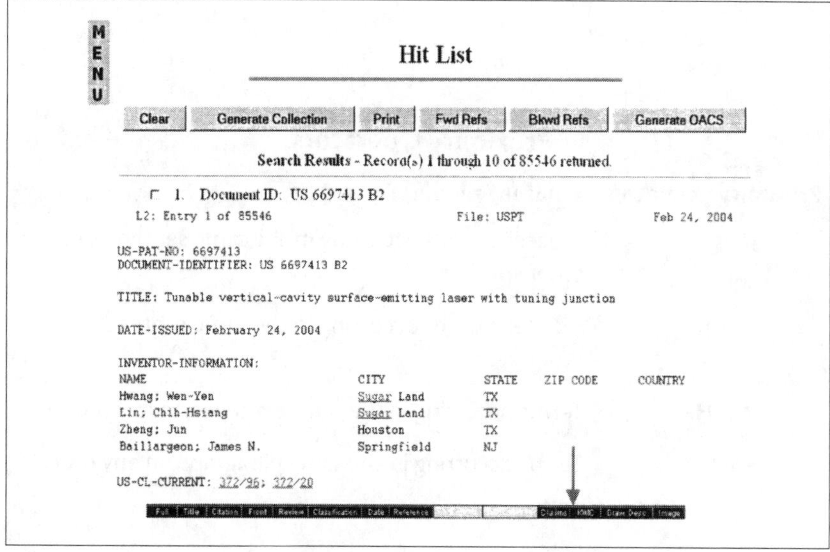

Figure 10.4 (Source: WEST Training Manual—USPTO)

If you click on the L-number that was generated as a result of your search, the Hit List is displayed (Figure 10.4). The patents are numbered and listed based on the issue date, with the most recently issued displayed first.

Boolean Operators	
Boolean Operator	**What It Searches For**
AND	Documents that contain both of the specified search terms with no restriction as to where the terms are found in relation to one another
OR	Documents that contain one or more specified search terms with no restriction as to where the terms are found in relation to one another
NOT	Documents that contain the first term you specify, but NOT the second term
XOR	Documents that contain EITHER the first term or the second term, but NOT both terms

Proximity Operators	
Proximity Operator	**What It Searches For**
ADJ	Adjacent terms occurring in the same sentence, in the order specified
NEAR	Adjacent terms occurring in the same sentence, in any order
WITH	Terms occurring in the same sentence, in any order
SAME	Terms occurring in the same paragraph, in any order

To see how the search keyword is used in the context of the patent, click on the "KWIC" (KeyWord In Context) button indicated by the arrow at the bottom of Figure 10.4. By clicking on the KWIC button, the entire paragraph that each search term is located in will be displayed (Figure 10.5).

As you can see, the search term is also highlighted and underlined, indicating that it is a clickable link that directs the computer to the next occurrence of the search term.

KWIC in Text

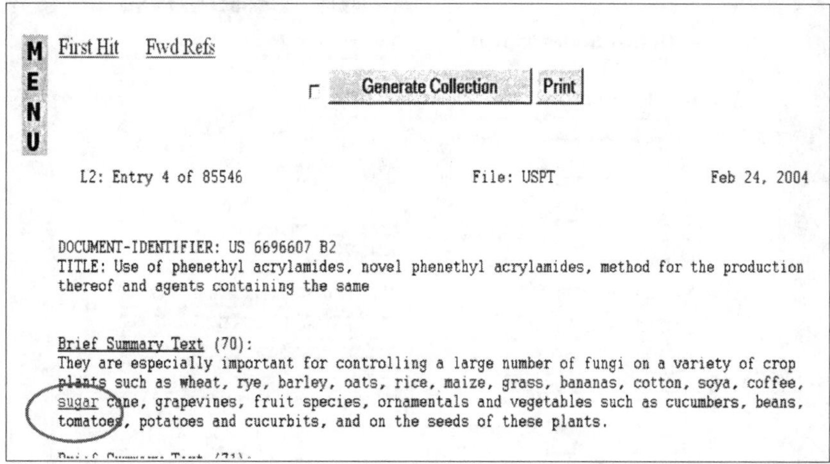

Figure 10.5 (Source: WEST Training Manual—USPTO)

Images of the patent document can also be viewed using WEST. At the extreme lower right of Figure 10.4 is a clickable button labeled "Image." To view an image of the displayed patent, click on this link (Figures 10.6 and 10.7).

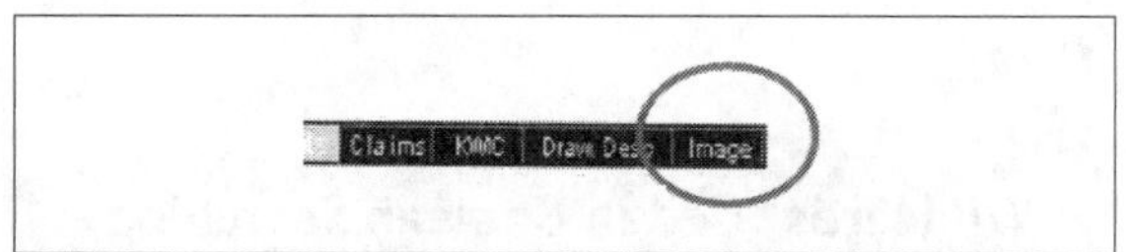

Figure 10.6 (Source: WEST Training Manual—USPTO)

Wildcard (truncation) characters are also allowed in WEST search queries to replace character(s) within a search term or keyword. A table of available wildcards is shown below.

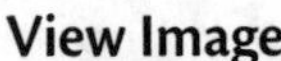

View Image

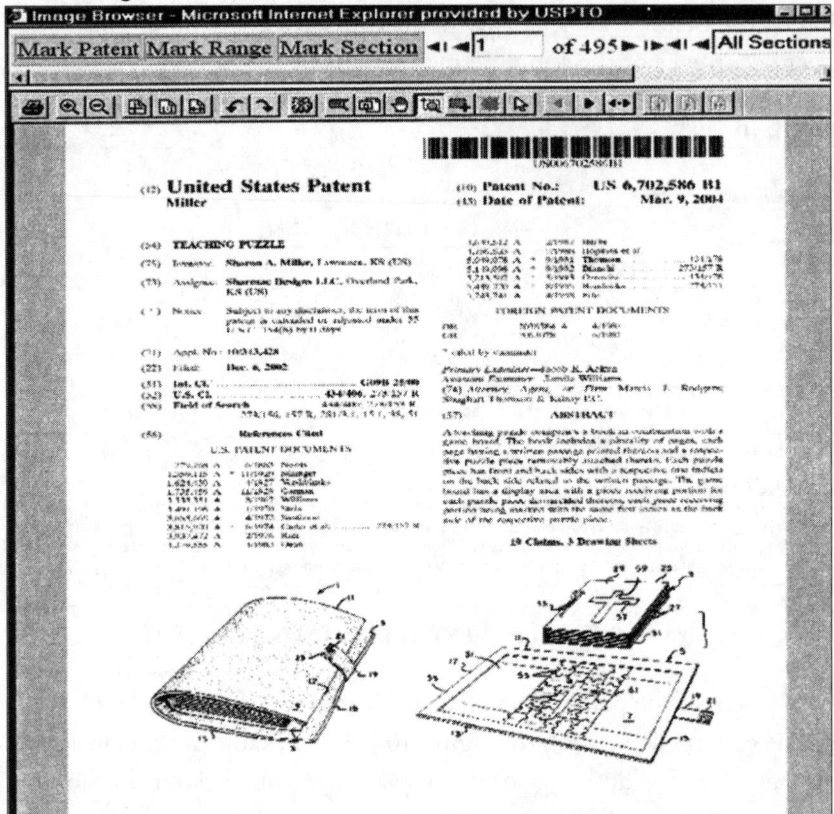

Figure 10.7 (Source: WEST Training Manual—USPTO)

Wildcards Used in Boolean Searching	
Wildcard	**What It Does**
$	Replaces any number (including 0) of characters—for example, "wast$" would find waste, wasted, wasteful, and wasteland.
$n	Specifies the definite number of wildcard characters to be replaced—for example, "wast$"4 would locate wasteful, but not wasted and wasteland.
?	Replaces exactly one (1) character—for example, "w?sh" would find wish and wash.

Examiner Automated Search Tool (EAST)

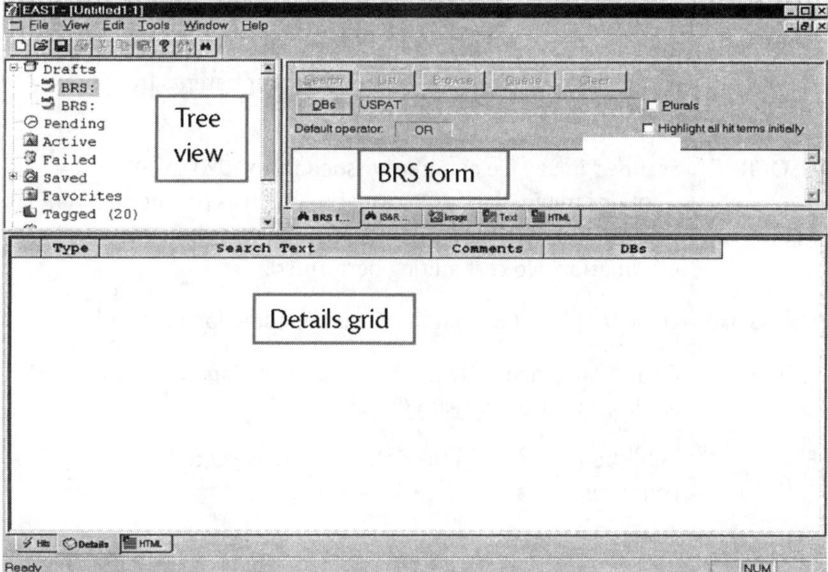

Figure 10.8 (Source: EAST Training Manual—USPTO)

The EAST search system—also available at the PTO facility in Alexandria, Virginia—uses the same search operators and wildcards as the WEST system. In order to use EAST, you will need PTDL personnel to log you in with a user ID and password. Once logged in, EAST opens up in the default workspace shown in Figure 10.8. A workspace is a window of an application that has subwindows within it.

The default EAST workspace has three frames (subwindows):

- the tree view, which contains various folders associated with the active session
- the BRS form window, where you enter your search queries, and
- the details grid, which displays the results of your search.

The searchable databases available with EAST are virtually identical to those available with WEST, but the names are different. Also, there is the caveat that the USOCR database cannot be combined with other databases while performing multiple database file searching. A summary of the searchable databases is shown in the table below.

EAST Databases	
Database	**Contents**
USPAT	Bibliographic information (patent number, publication date, and current classification information) for patents from the 1790s to the present
USOCR	Scanned image file of patents issued from 1920 to 1970. Contains minimal index information, such as patent number, title (utility), publication date, and current classification information. No text editing performed.
US-PGPUB	Utility applications that have been pending for 18 months
JPO	English-language abstracts of unexamined Japanese patent applications starting with October 1976
EPO	Published documents from the EPO and selected member countries

To select a database to search, click on the DBs button shown in Figure 10.9. Available databases are added or deleted by selecting the appropriate check box. Click "OK" to confirm the database selection.

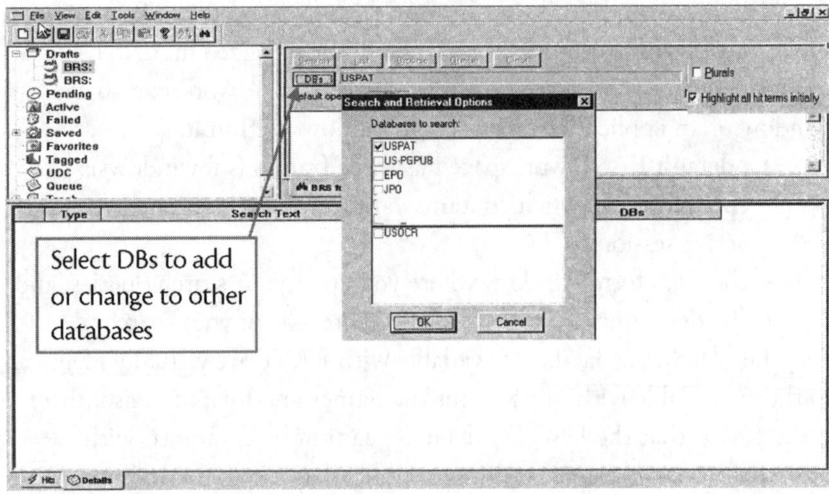

Figure 10.9 (Source: EAST Training Manual—USPTO)

EAST processing can be monitored via the tree view. The most relevant folders in the tree view (as displayed in the upper left of Figure 10.8) are:

- **Drafts.** When you type in a search statement, the words appear here.
- **Pending.** This contains queries that have been submitted to the BRS server for processing.
- **Active.** This contains search results.
- **Failed.** If a query encounters an error during a search or the search is aborted, the query will be marked with a red icon.
- **Saved.** Search collections from the Active folder are saved here.
- **Tagged.** This allows users to easily identify all patents having a user-defined tag.
- **Queue.** Draft queries can be placed in this folder for execution at a later time.
- **Trash.** Deleted items are moved here.

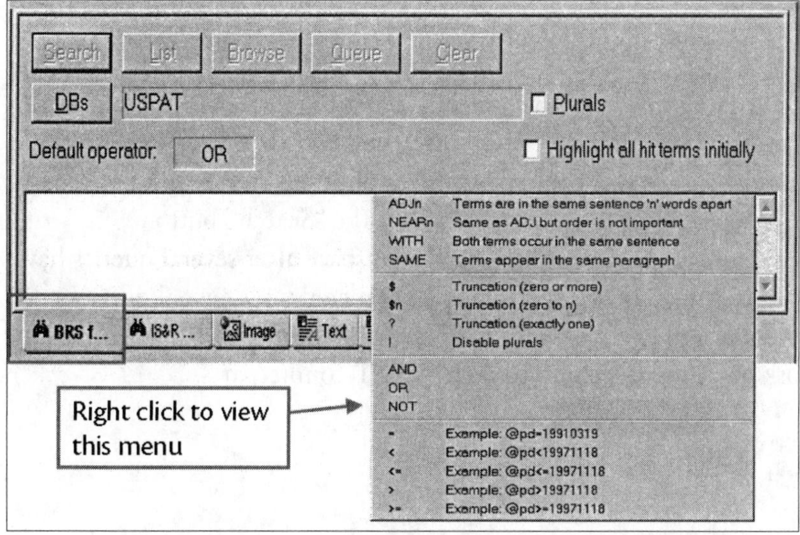

Figure 10.10 (Source: EAST Training Manual—USPTO)

The BRS form window is shown in Figure 10.10. The BRS form permits the user to enter simple and complex searches. When composing a search, right-click inside the window to get the dropdown menu shown in Figure 10.10. Then simply select the desired operator with your mouse to add it to the search query you are constructing.

Selecting a Button for Text Searching

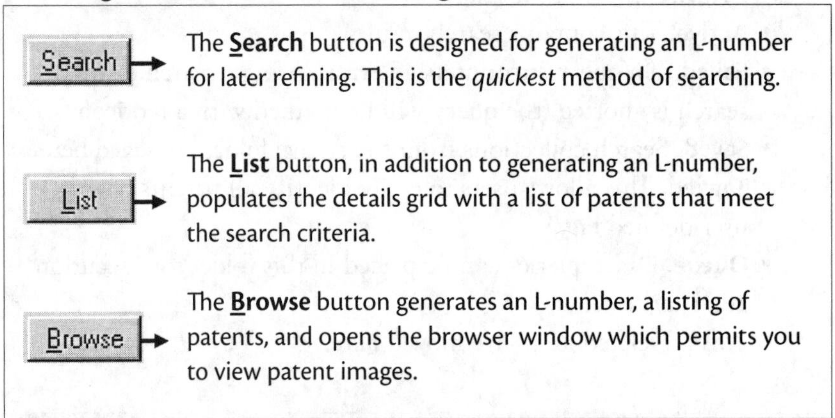

Search
The Search button is designed for generating an L-number for later refining. This is the quickest method of searching.
List
The List button, in addition to generating an L-number, populates the details grid with a list of patents that meet the search criteria.
Browse
The Browse button generates an L-number, a listing of patents, and opens the browser window which permits you to view patent images.

Figure 10.11 (Source: EAST Training Manual—USPTO)

There are five clickable buttons that are grayed out in Figure 10.10. Once you begin entering your search query, these buttons will become active. A summary of the most relevant buttons is shown in Figure 10.11. To perform a quick search, click the "Search" button.

Figure 10.12 shows the EAST workspace after several queries have been executed. The Active folder is populated with several queries and the details grid is filled with L-labeled search results. These L-labels work in a similar fashion to their WEST counterparts.

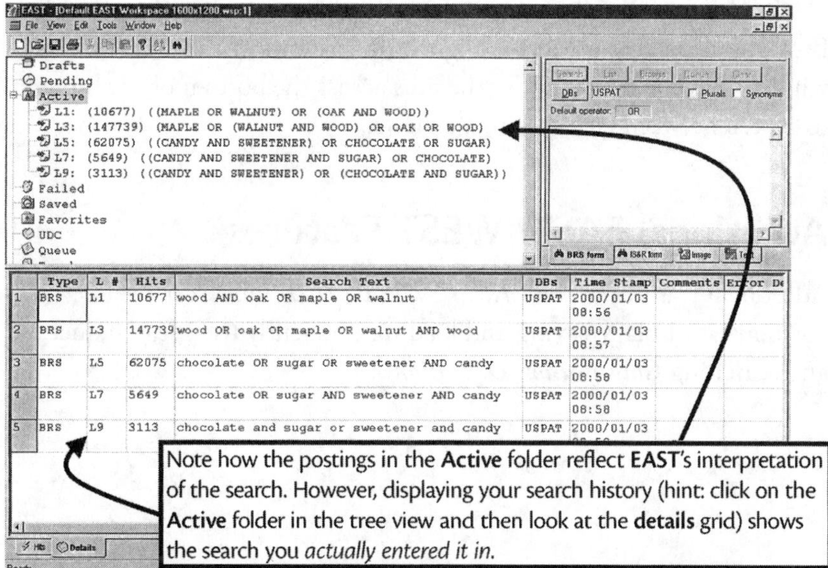

Figure 10.12 (Source: EAST Training Manual—USPTO)

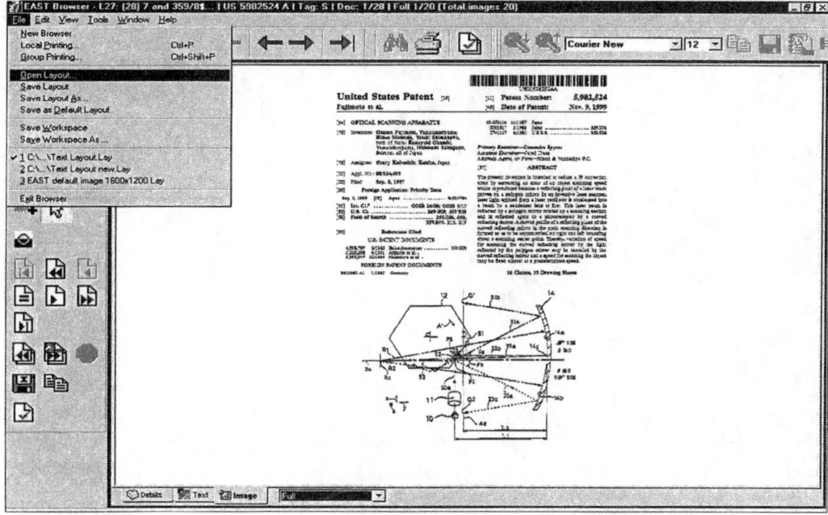

Figure 10.13 (Source: EAST Training Manual—USPTO)

In order to view the text or image results of your search, select the Browse button (Figure 10.11). Figure 10.13 shows an example browser window view of a patent. Use the tabs across the bottom of the browser to switch between text and image views.

Additional EAST/ WEST Features

Additional features of the EAST/ WEST search interfaces include customized displays, saving and loading frequently used search queries, and searching *Classification Definitions.*

Glossary

abstract a concise, one-paragraph summary of the patent. It details the structure, nature, and purpose of the invention. The abstract is used by the PTO and the public to quickly determine the gist of what is being disclosed.

ANDed search commands the process of combining multiple keywords in a Boolean argument together with AND operators. An example would be: Fire AND Protection AND (Building OR Structure), where Fire, Protection, and the keywords within the parentheses are ANDed.

Boolean logic logic used to combine keywords into more powerful searches. There are four Boolean logical operators that we need to understand: AND, OR, XOR, and ANDNOT.

CASSIS Classification And Search Support Information System.

class and subclass categories that the PTO uses to classify or sort the various types of inventions.

Class Finder Tool visual aid used for finding the relevant classes of an invention.

compositions of matter items such as chemical compositions, conglomerates, aggregates, or other chemically significant substances that are usually supplied in bulk (solid or particulate), liquid, or gaseous form.

conception the mental part of inventing, including how an invention is formulated or how a problem is solved.

copyright the legal right to exclude others, for a limited time, from copying, selling, performing, displaying, or making derivative versions of a work of authorship, such as a writing, music, or artwork.

date of invention the earliest of the following dates: (a) the date an inventor filed the patent application (provisional or regular), (b) the date an inventor can prove that the invention was built and tested in the United States, or a country that is a member of North American Free Trade Association (NAFTA) or the World Trade Organization (WTO), or (c) the date an inventor can prove that the invention was conceived in a NAFTA or WTO country, provided the inventor can also prove diligence in building and testing it or filing a patent application on it.

deposit date the date the PTO receives a patent application.

design patent covers the unique, ornamental, or visible shape or design of a non-natural object.

Doctrine of Equivalents (DoE) a form of patent infringement that occurs when an invention performs substantially the same function in substantially the same manner and obtains the same result as the patented invention. A court analyzes each element of the patented invention separately. As a result of a Supreme Court decision, the DoE must be applied on an element-by-element basis to the claims.

experimental use doctrine a rule excusing an inventor from the one-year bar provided that the alleged sale or public use was primarily for the purpose of perfecting or testing the invention.

field codes characters that precede a keyword at the PTO website. The characters are used to limit the search for that keyword to certain sections of the patent.

first Office Action (sometimes called an *official letter* or *OA*) response from the patent examiner after the initial examination of the application. It is very rare that an application is allowed in the first Office Action. More often, the examiner rejects some or all of the claims.

first sale doctrine (also known as the *exhaustion doctrine*) once a patented product (or product resulting from a patented process) is sold or licensed, the patent owner's rights are exhausted and the owner has no further rights as to the resale of that particular article.

hit match reported by a computer search program between a keyword and a database. The document that the word occurred in and sometimes the location of the word are returned to the user.

infringement an invention is infringing if it is a literal copy of a patented invention, or if it performs substantially the same function in substantially the same manner and obtains the same result as the patented invention (see *doctrine of equivalents*).

interference a costly, complex PTO proceeding that determines who will get a patent when two or more applicants are claiming the same invention. It is basically a method of sorting out priority of inventorship. Occasionally, an interference may involve a patent that has been in force for less than one year.

invention any new article, machine, composition, process, or new use developed by a human.

keyword search search process carried out by a computer program where entered keywords are matched with words stored in a database. When the program finds a match, the program will report back the document in which the word was found, and in some cases, the location of the word within the document.

lab notebook a system of documenting an invention that usually includes: descriptions of the invention and novel features; procedures used in the building and testing of the invention; drawings, photos, or sketches of the invention; test results and conclusions; discussions of any known prior art references; and additional documentation, such as correspondence and purchase receipts.

literal infringement occurs if a defendant makes, sells, or uses the invention defined in the plaintiff's patent claim. In other words, the infringing product includes each and every component, part, or step in the patented invention. It is a literal infringement because the defendant's device is actually the same invention in the patent claim.

machine a device or things used for accomplishing a task; usually involves some activity or motion performed by working parts.

manufactures (sometimes termed *articles of manufacture*) items that have been made by human hands or by machines; may have working or moving parts as prime features.

means-plus-function clause (or *means for* clause) a provision in a patent claim in which the applicant does not specifically describe the structure of one of the items in the patent and instead describes the function of the item. Term is derived from the fact that the clause usually starts with the word "means."

new matter any technical information, including dimensions, materials, and so on, that was not present in the patent application as originally filed. An applicant can never add new matter to an application (PTO Rule 118).

new-use invention a new and unobvious process or method for using an old and known invention.

nonobviousness a standard of patentability. In 1966, the U.S. Supreme Court established the steps for determining unobviousness in the case of *Graham v. John Deere*, 383 US 1 (1966).

Notice of Allowance a document issued when the examiner is convinced that the application meets the requirements of patentability. An issue fee is due within three months.

Office Action (*OA*, also known as *Official Letter* or *Examiner's Action)* correspondence (usually including forms and a letter) from a patent examiner that describes what is wrong with the application and why it cannot be allowed. Generally, an OA will reject claims, list defects in the specifications or drawings, raise objections, or cite and enclose copies of relevant prior art demonstrating a lack of novelty or nonobviousness.

on-sale bar prevents an inventor from acquiring patent protection if the application is filed more than one year from the date of sale, use, or offer of sale of the invention in the United States.

one-year rule a rule that requires an inventor to file a patent application within one year after selling, offering for sale, or commercially or publicly using or describing an invention. If an inventor fails to file within one year of such occurrence, the inventor is barred from obtaining a patent.

patent a grant from a government that confers upon an inventor the right to exclude others from making, using, selling, importing, or offering an invention for sale for a fixed period of time.

patent application a set of papers that describe an invention and that are suitable for filing in a patent office in order to apply for a patent on the invention.

Patent Application Declaration (PAD) a declaration that identifies the inventor or joint inventors and provides an attestation by the applicant that the inventor understands the contents of the claims and specification and has fully disclosed all material information. The PTO provides a form for the PAD.

patent pending (also known as the *pendency period*) time between filing a patent application (or PPA) and issuance of the patent. The inventor has no patent rights during this period. However, when and if the patent later issues, the inventor will obtain the right to prevent the continuation of any infringing activity that started during the pendency period. If the application has been published by the PTO during the pendency period and the infringer had notice, the applicant may later seek royalties for these infringements during the pendency period. It's a criminal offense to use the words "patent applied for" or "patent pending" (they mean the same thing) in any advertising if there's no active, applicable, regular or provisional patent application on file.

patent prosecution the process of shepherding a patent application through the PTO.

Patent Rules of Practice administrative regulations located in Volume 37 of the Code of Federal Regulations (37 CFR § 1).

pendency period (see *patent pending*).

plant patent covers plants that can be reproduced through the use of grafts and cuttings (asexual reproduction).

preferred embodiment "best guess" version of the invention configuration at the time the patent application was written.

prior art the state of knowledge existing or publicly available either before the date of an invention or more than one year prior to the patent application date.

process (sometimes referred to as a *method*) a way of doing or making things that involves more than purely mental manipulations.

Provisional Patent Application (PPA) an interim document that clearly explains how to make and use the invention. The PPA is equivalent to a reduction to practice (see below). If a regular patent application is filed within one year of filing the PPA, the inventor can use the PPA's filing date for the purpose of deciding whether a reference is prior art. In addition to an early filing date, an inventor may claim patent pending status for the one-year period following the filing of PPA. You can file a PPA using Nolo Now, Nolo's online legal document service, at www.nolo.com.

reduction to practice the point at which the inventor can demonstrate that the invention works for its intended purpose. Reduction to practice can be accomplished by building and testing the invention (actual reduction to practice), or by preparing a patent application or provisional patent application that shows how to make and use the invention and that it works (constructive reduction practice). In the event of a dispute or a challenge at the PTO, invention documentation is essential in order to prove the "how and when" of conception and reduction to practice.

repair doctrine affirmative defense based on the right of an authorized licensor of a patented device to repair and replace unpatented components. It also includes the right to sell materials used to repair or replace a patented invention. The defense does not apply for completely rebuilt inventions, unauthorized inventions, or items that are made or sold without authorization of the patent owner.

search class cross-reference listing of additional classes that are related to the current subject matter. Located below the current subclass definition in the *Classification Definitions*.

Small Entity Status a status that enables small businesses, independent inventors, and nonprofit companies to pay a reduced application fee. To qualify, an independent inventor must either own all rights or have transferred—or be obligated to transfer—rights to a small business or nonprofit organization. Nonprofit organizations are defined and listed in the Code of Federal Regulations and usually are educational institutions or charitable organizations. A small entity business is one with fewer than 500 employees. The number of employees is computed by averaging the number of full- and part-time employees during a fiscal year.

specification a patent application disclosure made by the inventor and drafted so that an individual skilled in the art to which the invention pertains could, when reading the patent, make and use the invention without needing further experiment. A specification is constructed of several sections. Collectively, these sections form a narrative that describes and distinguishes the invention. If it can later be proved that the inventor knew of a better way (or "best mode") and failed to disclose it, that failure could result in the loss of patent rights.

statutory subject matter an invention that falls into one of the five statutory classes: process (method), machine, article of manufacture, composition, or a "new use" of one of the first four.

utility patent the main type of patent, which covers inventions that function in a unique manner to produce a utilitarian result.

wildcard an asterisk (*), a dollar sign ($), or a question mark (?) that can be used to replace one or more characters (letters) in a keyword.

APPENDIX A

Reference Collection of U.S. Patents Available for Public Use in Patent and Trademark Depository Libraries

The following libraries, designated as Patent and Trademark Depository Libraries (PTDLs), receive patent and trademark information from the U.S. Patent and Trademark Office. Many PTDLs have on file patents issued since 1790, trademarks published since 1872, and select collections of foreign patents. All PTDLs receive both the patent and trademark sections of the *Official Gazette* of the U.S. Patent and Trademark Office and numerical sets of patents in a variety of formats. Patent and trademark search systems in the CASSIS optical disk series are available at all PTDLs to increase access to that information. It is through the optical disk systems and other depository materials that preliminary patent and trademark searches may be conducted through the numerically arranged collections.

Each PTDL offers reference publications that outline and provide access to the patent and trademark classification systems, as well as other documents and publications that supplement the basic search tools. PTDLs provide technical staff assistance in using all materials.

All information is available for use by the public free of charge. However, there may be charges associated with the use of online systems, photocopying, and related services.

Since there are variations in the scope of patent and trademark collections among the PTDLs, and their hours of service to the public vary, anyone contemplating use of these collections at a particular library is urged to contact that library in advance about its collections, services, and hours.

For the latest copy of this list, or for Web links to each PTDL, go to the PTO's *Official Gazette* site at www.uspto.gov/web/offices/com/sol/og. Then go to the latest *Official Gazette* and open "Patent and Trademark Depository Libraries."

List of Patent and Trademark Depository Libraries		
State	**Name of Library**	**Telephone**
Alabama	Auburn University Libraries ◆	334-844-1737
	Birmingham Public Library	205-226-3620
Alaska	Anchorage: Z.J. Loussac Public Library	907-562-7323
Arizona	Tempe: Noble Library, Arizona State University ◆	480-965-7010
Arkansas	Little Rock: Arkansas State Library ◆	501-682-2053
California	Los Angeles Public Library ◆	213-228-7220
	Sacramento: California State Library	916-654-0069
	San Diego Public Library	619-236-5813
	San Francisco Public Library ◆	415-557-4500
	Sunnyvale Center for Innovation (has APS Image terminals) ◆ * ▲	408-730-7290
Colorado	Denver Public Library	720-865-1711
Connecticut	Hartford Public Library	860-543-8628
	New Haven Free Public Library	203-946-8130
Delaware	Newark: University of Delaware Library	302-831-2965
DC	Washington: Howard University Library	202-806-7252
Florida	Fort Lauderdale: Broward County Main Library ◆	954-357-7444
	Miami: Dade Public Library ◆	305-375-2665
	Orlando: University of Central Florida Libraries	407-823-2562
	Tampa: Campus Library, University of South Florida	813-974-2726
Georgia	Atlanta: Price Gilbert Memorial Library, Georgia Institute of Technology	404-894-4508

◆ WEST (Web-based Examiner Search Tool) subscriber.

* Also does fee-based patent searching.

▲ EAST (Examiner Assisted Search Tool) subscriber.

List of Patent and Trademark Depository Libraries (cont'd)

State	Name of Library	Telephone
Hawaii	Honolulu: Hawaii State Public Library System◆	808-586-3477
Idaho	Moscow: University of Idaho Library	208-885-6235
Illinois	Chicago Public Library	312-747-4450
	Springfield: Illinois State Library	217-782-5659
Indiana	Indianapolis: Marion County Public Library	317-269-1741
	West Lafayette: Siegesmond Engineering Library	765-494-2872
Iowa	Des Moines: State Library of Iowa	515-242-6541
Kansas	Wichita: Ablah Library, Wichita State University◆	800-572-8368
Kentucky	Louisville Free Public Library	502-574-1611
Louisiana	Baton Rouge: Troy H. Middleton Library, Louisiana State University	225-578-8875
Maine	Orono: Raymond H. Fogler Library, University of Maine	207-581-1678
Maryland	College Park: Engineering and Physical Sciences Library, University of Maryland	301-405-9157
Massachusetts	Amherst: Physical Sciences Library, University of Massachusetts	413-545-1370
	Boston Public Library◆	617-536-5400 Ext. 265
Michigan	Ann Arbor: Media Union Library, University of Michigan	734-647-5735
	Big Rapids: Abigail S. Timme Library, Ferris State University	231-592-3602
	Detroit Public Library (has APS Image Terminals)◆▲	313-833-3379

◆ WEST (Web-based Examiner Search Tool) subscriber.

* Also does fee-based patent searching.

▲ EAST (Examiner Assisted Search Tool) subscriber.

List of Patent and Trademark Depository Libraries (cont'd)		
State	**Name of Library**	**Telephone**
Minnesota	Minneapolis Public Library and Information Center◆	612-630-6120
Mississippi	Jackson: Mississippi Library Commission	601-961-4111
Missouri	Kansas City: Linda Hall Library◆	816-363-4600
	St. Louis Public Library◆	314-241-2288 Ext. 390
Montana	Butte: Montana College of Mineral Science & Technology Library	406-496-4281
Nebraska	Lincoln: Engineering Library, University of Nebraska◆	402-472-3411
Nevada	Las Vegas: Clark County Library	702-507-3421
	Reno: University of Nevada-Reno Library	702-784-6500 Ext. 257
New Hampshire	Concord: New Hampshire State Library	603-271-2239
New Jersey	Newark Public Library	973-733-7779
	Piscataway: Library of Science & Medicine, Rutgers University	732-445-2895
New Mexico	Albuquerque: University of New Mexico General Library	505-277-4412
New York	Albany: New York State Library	518-474-5355
	Buffalo and Erie County Public Library	716-858-7101
	New York Public Library (The Research Libraries)	212-592-7000
	Rochester Public Library	716-428-8110
	Stony Brook: Engineering Library, State University of New York	631-632-7148

◆ WEST (Web-based Examiner Search Tool) subscriber.

* Also does fee-based patent searching.

▲ EAST (Examiner Assisted Search Tool) subscriber.

List of Patent and Trademark Depository Libraries (cont'd)

State	Name of Library	Telephone
North Carolina	Raleigh: D.H. Hill Library, N.C State University ◆	919-515-2935
North Dakota	Grand Forks: Chester Fritz Library, University of North Dakota	701-777-4888
Ohio	Akron: Summit County Public Library	330-643-9075
	Cincinnati and Hamilton County, Public Library of	513-369-6971
	Cleveland Public Library ◆	216-623-2870
	Columbus: Ohio State University Library	614-292-3022
	Dayton: Paul Laurence Dunbar Library, Wright State University	937-775-3521
	Toledo/Lucas County Public Library ◆	419-259-5209
Oklahoma	Stillwater: Oklahoma State University Center for Trade Development ◆	405-744-7086
Oregon	Portland: Paul L. Boley Law Library, Lewis & Clark College	503-768-6786
Pennsylvania	Philadelphia, The Free Library of ◆	215-686-5331
	Pittsburgh, Carnegie Library of	412-622-3138
	University Park: Pattee Library, Pennsylvania State University	814-865-6369
Puerto Rico	Bayamón: University of Puerto Rico	787-786-5225
	Mayaguez General Library, University of Puerto Rico	787-832-4040 Ext. 2022
Rhode Island	Providence Public Library	401-455-8027
South Carolina	Clemson University Libraries	864-656-3024
South Dakota	Rapid City: Devereaux Library, South Dakota School of Mines & Technology	605-394-1275

◆ WEST (Web-based Examiner Search Tool) subscriber.

* Also does fee-based patent searching.

▲ EAST (Examiner Assisted Search Tool) subscriber.

List of Patent and Trademark Depository Libraries (cont'd)		
State	**Name of Library**	**Telephone**
Tennessee	Nashville: Stevenson Science Library, Vanderbilt University	615-322-2717
Texas	Austin: McKinney Engineering Library, University of Texas at Austin	512-495-4500
	College Station: Sterling C. Evans Library, Texas A & M University◆ ▲	979-845-5745
	Dallas Public Library◆	214-670-1468
	Houston: The Fondren Library, Rice University◆	713-348-5483
	Lubbock: Texas Tech University	806-742-2282
	San Antonio Public Library	210-207-2500
Utah	Salt Lake City: Marriott Library, University of Utah◆	801-581-8394
Vermont	Burlington: Bailey/Howe Library, University of Vermont	802-656-2542
Virginia	Richmond: Virginia Commonwealth University◆	804-828-1104
Washington	Seattle: Engineering Library, University of Washington◆	206-543-0740
West Virginia	Morgantown: Evansdale Library, West Virginia University◆	304-293-4695 Ext. 5113
Wisconsin	Madison: Kurt F. Wendt Library, University of Wisconsin, Madison	608-262-6845
	Milwaukee Public Library	414-286-3051
Wyoming	Cheyenne: Wyoming State Library	307-777-7281

◆ WEST (Web-based Examiner Search Tool) subscriber.

* Also does fee-based patent searching.

▲ EAST (Examiner Assisted Search Tool) subscriber.

APPENDIX

B

Forms

Classification Search Sheet

A	B	C	D	E	F	G
Descriptive Words	Class Numbers	Subclass From *Index*	Subclass From *Man. of Class.*	Get List	Search Class	Get List

Classification Search Sheet

A	B	C	D	E	F	G
Descriptive Words	Class Numbers	Subclass From *Index*	Subclass From *Man. of Class.*	Get List	Search Class	Get List

Classification Search Sheet

A	B	C	D	E	F	G
Descriptive Words	Class Numbers	Subclass From *Index*	Subclass From *Man. of Class.*	Get List	Search Class	Get List

Classification Search Sheet

A	B	C	D	E	F	G
Descriptive Words	**Class Numbers**	**Subclass From *Index***	**Subclass From *Man. of Class.***	**Get List**	**Search Class**	**Get List**

Classification Search Sheet

A	B	C	D	E	F	G
Descriptive Words	Class Numbers	Subclass From *Index*	Subclass From *Man. of Class.*	Get List	Search Class	Get List

Classification Search Sheet

A	B	C	D	E	F	G
Descriptive Words	Class Numbers	Subclass From *Index*	Subclass From *Man. of Class.*	Get List	Search Class	Get List

Classification Search Sheet

A	B	C	D	E	F	G
Descriptive Words	Class Numbers	Subclass From *Index*	Subclass From *Man. of Class.*	Get List	Search Class	Get List

Classification Search Sheet

A	B	C	D	E	F	G
Descriptive Words	Class Numbers	Subclass From *Index*	Subclass From *Man. of Class.*	Get List	Search Class	Get List

Classification Search Sheet

A	B	C	D	E	F	G
Descriptive Words	Class Numbers	Subclass From *Index*	Subclass From *Man. of Class.*	Get List	Search Class	Get List

Classification Search Sheet

A	B	C	D	E	F	G
Descriptive Words	Class Numbers	Subclass From *Index*	Subclass From *Man. of Class.*	Get List	Search Class	Get List

Classification Search Sheet

A Descriptive Words	B Class Numbers	C Subclass From *Index*	D Subclass From *Man. of Class.*	E Get List	F Search Class	G Get List

Classification Search Sheet

A	B	C	D	E	F	G
Descriptive Words	Class Numbers	Subclass From *Index*	Subclass From *Man. of Class.*	Get List	Search Class	Get List

Class Finder Tool:

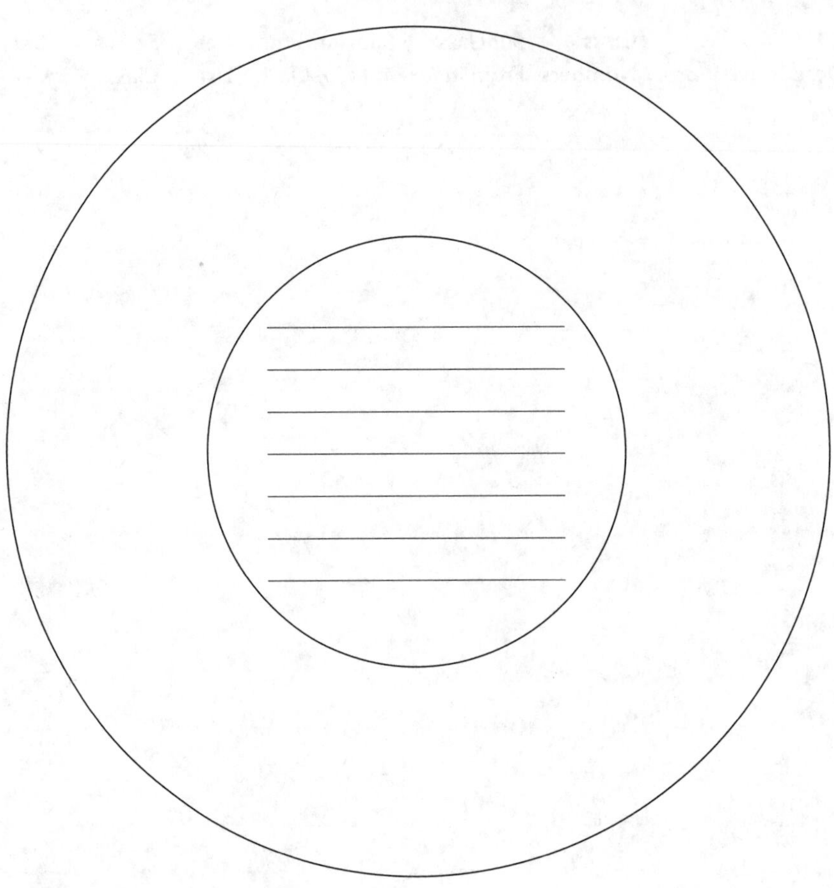

Class Finder Tool:

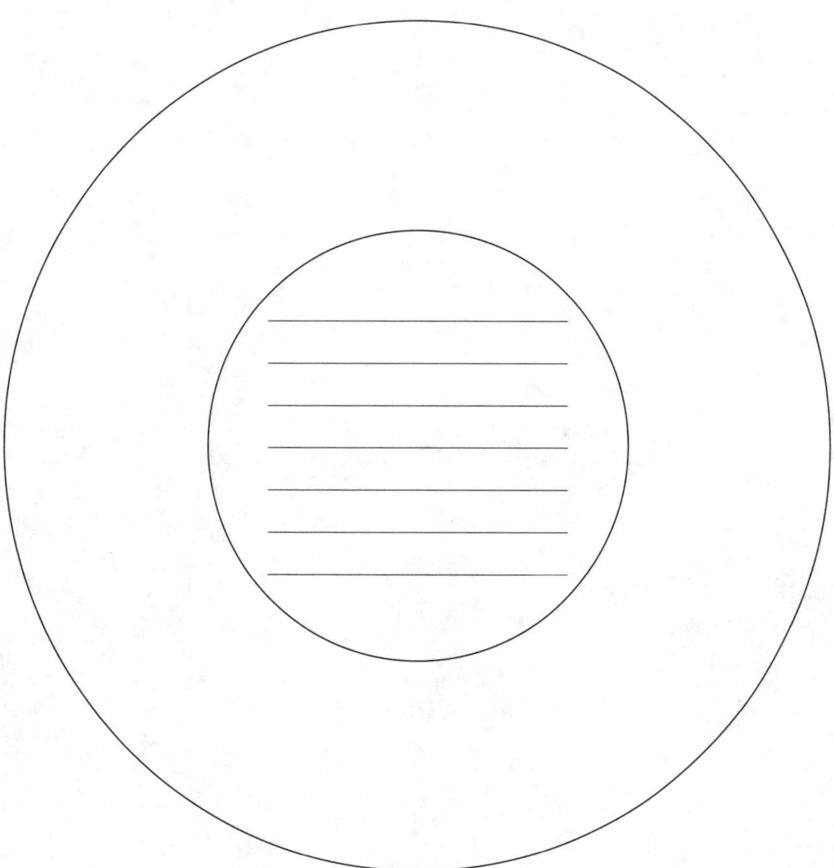

Class Finder Tool:

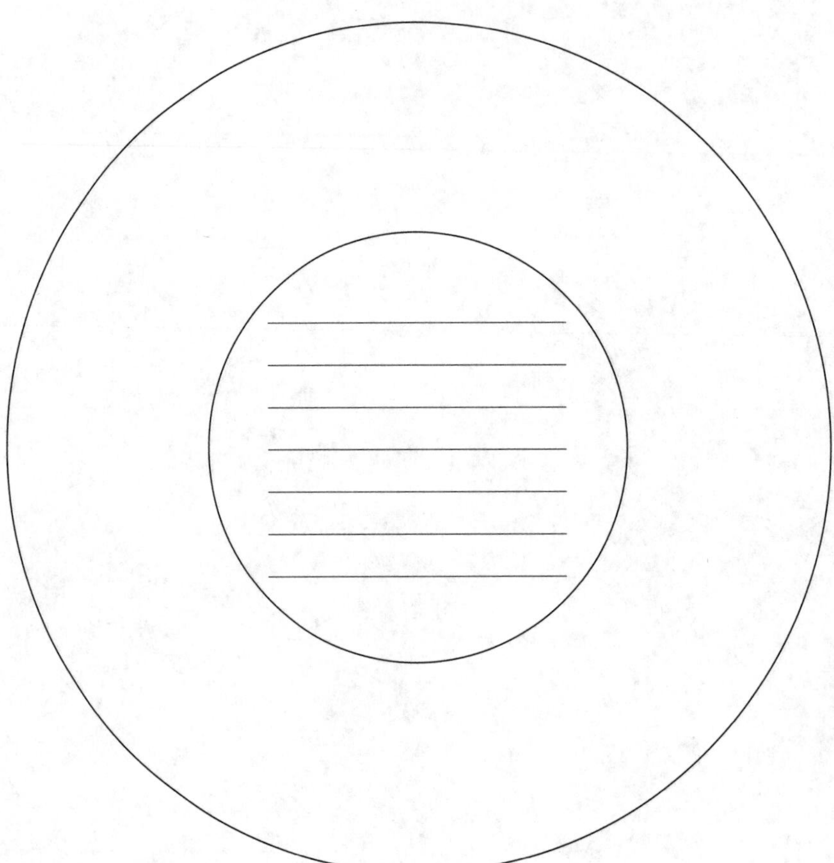

Class Finder Tool:

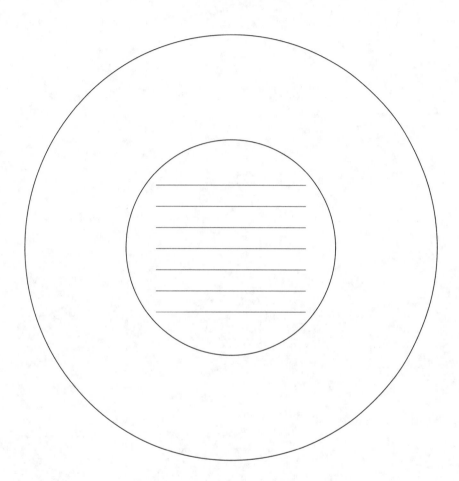

Class Finder Tool:

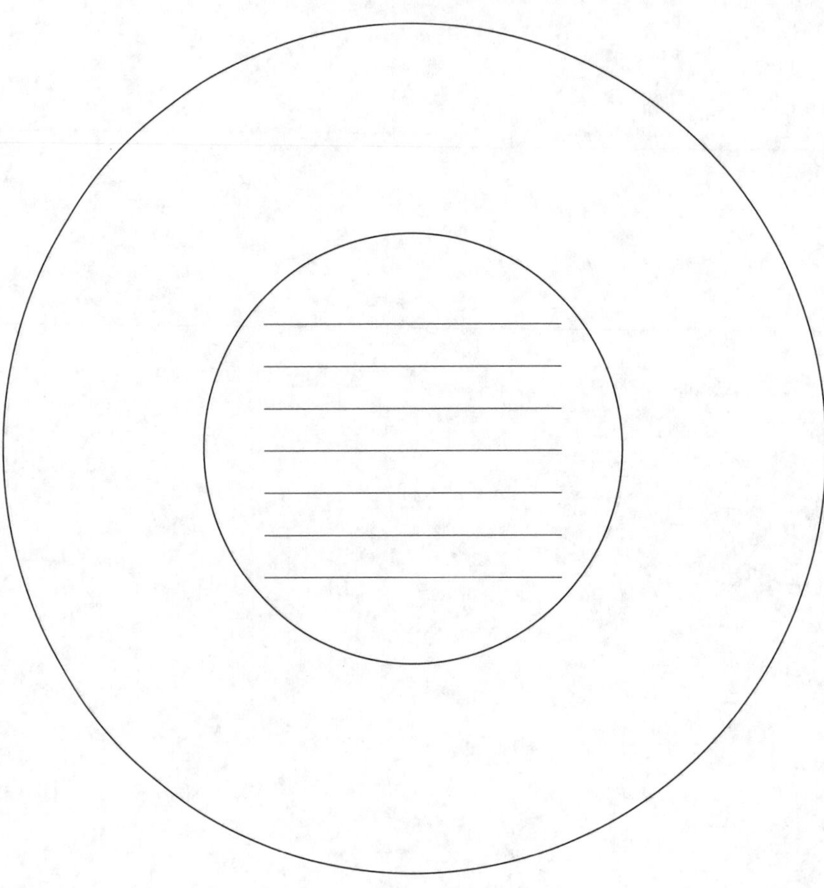

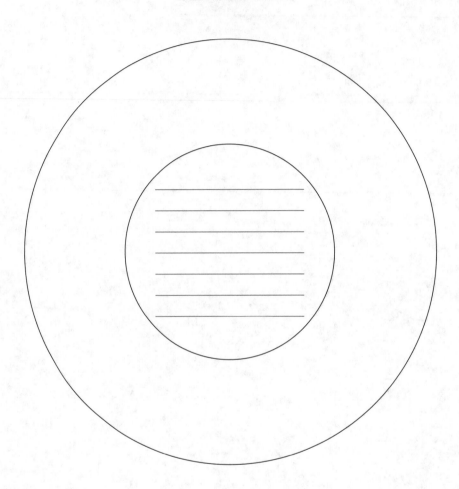

Class Finder Tool:

Class Finder Tool:

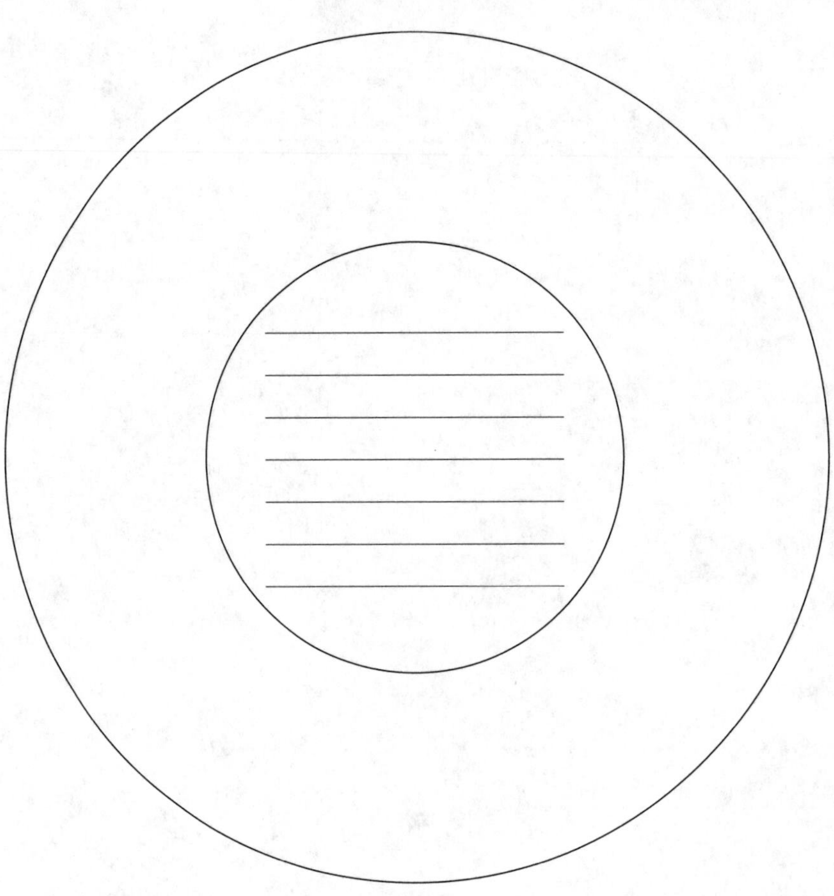

Class Finder Tool:

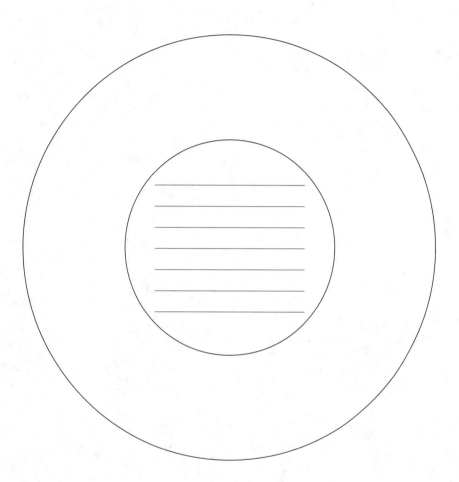

Class Finder Tool:

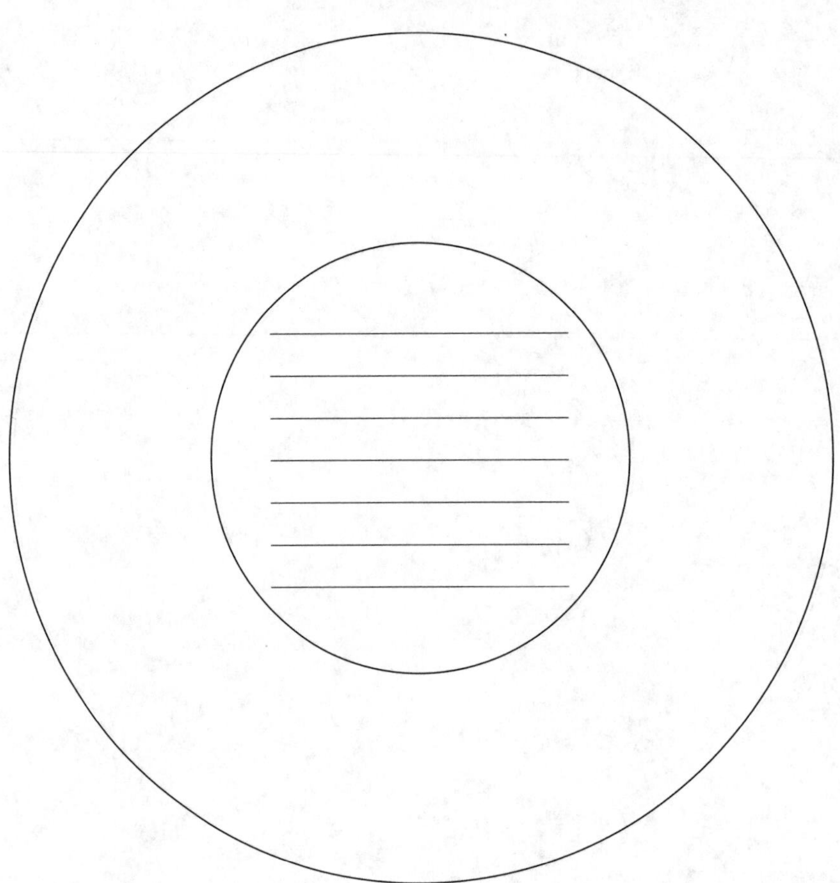

Class Finder Tool:

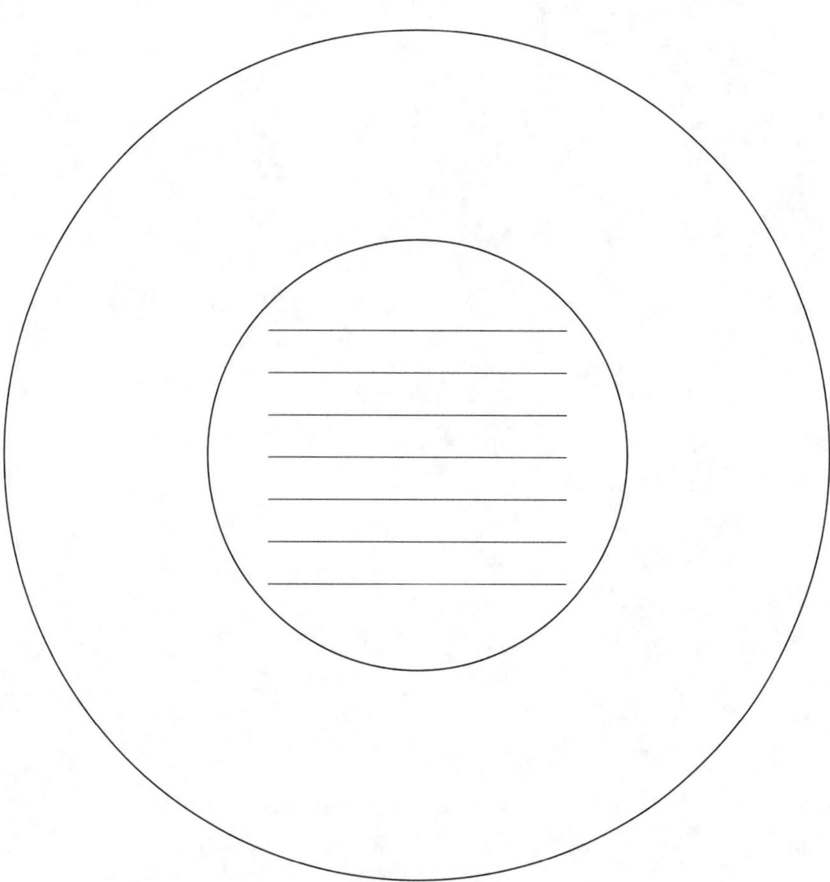

Class Finder Tool:

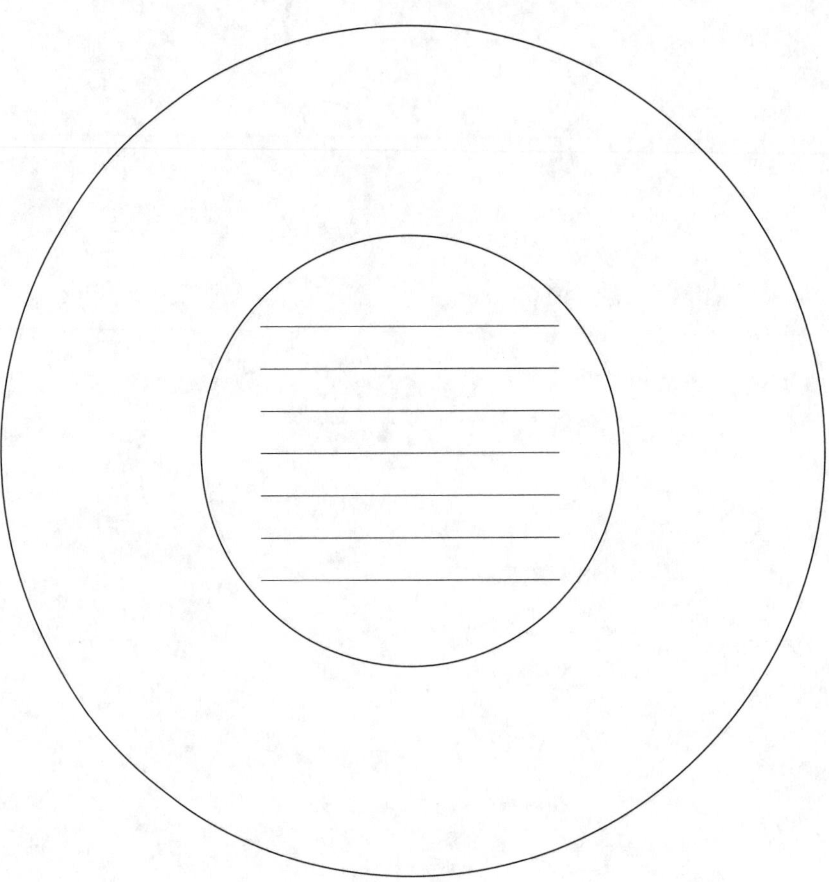

Index

D

E

F

G

K

L

M

N

Q

R

S

U

Get the Latest in the Law

Nolo's Legal Updater
We'll send you an email whenever a new edition of your book is published! Sign up at **www.nolo.com/legalupdater**.

Updates at Nolo.com
Check **www.nolo.com/update** to find recent changes in the law that affect the current edition of your book.

Nolo Customer Service
To make sure that this edition of the book is the most recent one, call us at **800-728-3555** and ask one of our friendly customer service representatives (7:00 am to 6:00 pm PST, weekdays only). Or find out at **www.nolo.com**.

4 **Complete the Registration & Comment Card ...**
... and we'll do the work for you! Just indicate your preferences below:

Registration & Comment Card

NAME DATE

ADDRESS

CITY STATE ZIP

PHONE EMAIL

COMMENTS

WAS THIS BOOK EASY TO USE? (VERY EASY) 5 4 3 2 1 (VERY DIFFICULT)

☐ Yes, you can quote me in future Nolo promotional materials. *Please include phone number above.*

☐ Yes, send me **Nolo's Legal Updater** via email when a new edition of this book is available.

Yes, I want to sign up for the following email newsletters:

- ☐ **NoloBriefs** (monthly)
- ☐ **Nolo's Special Offer** (monthly)
- ☐ **Nolo's BizBriefs** (monthly)
- ☐ **Every Landlord's Quarterly** (four times a year)

PATSE5

☐ Yes, you can give my contact info to carefully selected partners whose products may be of interest to me.

Send to: **Nolo** 950 Parker Street Berkeley, CA 94710-9867, Fax: (800) 645-0895, or include all of the above information in an email to regcard@nolo.com with the subject line "PATSE5."

NOLO Catalog

BUSINESS	PRICE	CODE
Business Buyout Agreements (Book w/CD-ROM)	$49.99	BSAG
The California Nonprofit Corporation Kit (Binder w/CD-ROM)	$69.99	CNP
California Workers' Comp	$34.99	WORK
The Complete Guide to Buying a Business (Book w/CD-ROM)	$24.99	BUYBU
The Complete Guide to Selling a Business (Book w/CD-ROM)	$34.99	SELBU
Consultant & Independent Contractor Agreements (Book w/CD-ROM)	$34.99	CICA
The Corporate Records Handbook (Book w/CD-ROM)	$69.99	CORMI
Create Your Own Employee Handbook (Book w/CD-ROM)	$49.99	EMHA
Dealing With Problem Employees	$44.99	PROBM
Deduct It! Lower Your Small Business Taxes	$34.99	DEDU
The eBay Business Start-Up Kit (Book w/CD-ROM)	$24.99	EBIZ
Effective Fundraising for Nonprofits	$24.99	EFFN
The Employer's Legal Handbook	$49.99	EMPL
The Essential Guide to Family & Medical Leave (Book w/CD-ROM)	$49.99	FMLA
The Essential Guide to Federal Employment Laws	$44.99	FEMP
The Essential Guide to Workplace Investigations (Book w/CD-ROM)	$39.99	NVST
Every Nonprofit's Guide to Publishing	$29.99	EPNO
Form a Partnership(Book w/CD-ROM)	$39.99	PART
Hiring Your First Employee: A Step-by-Step Guide	$24.99	HEMP
Form Your Own Limited Liability Company (Book w/CD-ROM)	$44.99	LIAB
Home Business Tax Deductions: Keep What You Earn	$34.99	DEHB
How to Form a Nonprofit Corporation (Book w/CD-ROM) —National Edition	$49.99	NNP
How to Form a Nonprofit Corporation in California (Book w/CD-ROM)	$49.99	NON
How to Form Your Own California Corporation (Binder w/CD-ROM)	$59.99	CACI
How to Form Your Own California Corporation (Book w/CD-ROM)	$39.99	CCOR
How to Run a Thriving Business: Strategies for Success & Satisfaction	$19.99	THRV

BUSINESS

Title	PRICE	CODE
How to Write a Business Plan (Book w/CD-ROM)	$34.99	SBS
Incorporate Your Business (Book w/CD-ROM)—National Edition	$49.99	NIBS
Investors in Your Backyard (Book w/CD-ROM)	$24.99	FINBUS
The Job Description Handbook (Book w/CD-ROM)	$29.99	JOB
Legal Guide for Starting & Running a Small Business	$34.99	RUNS
Legal Forms for Starting & Running a Small Business (Book w/CD-ROM)	$29.99	RUNSF
LLC or Corporation?	$24.99	CHENT
The Manager's Legal Handbook	$39.99	ELBA
Marketing Without Advertising	$20.00	MWAD
Music Law: How to Run Your Band's Business (Book w/CD-ROM)	$39.99	ML
Negotiate the Best Lease for Your Business	$24.99	LESP
Nolo's Crash Course in Small Business Basics (Audiobook on 5 CDs)	$34.99	ABBIZ
Nolo's Quick LLC	$29.99	LLCQ
Nonprofit Meetings, Minutes & Records (Book w/CD-ROM)	$39.99	NORM
The Performance Appraisal Handbook (Book w/CD-ROM)	$29.99	PERF
The Progressive Discipline Handbook (Book w/CD-ROM)	$34.99	SDHB
Retire—And Start Your Own Business (Book w/CD-ROM)	$34.99	BOSS
Small Business in Paradise: Working for Yourself in a Place You Love	$19.99	SPAR
The Small Business Start-Up Kit (Book w/CD-ROM)—National Edition	$29.99	SMBU
The Small Business Start-Up Kit for California (Book w/CD-ROM)	$29.99	OPEN
Smart Policies for Workplace Technologies: Email, Blogs, Cell Phones & More (Book w/CD-ROM)	$29.99	TECH
Starting & Building a Nonprofit: A Practical Guide (Book w/CD-ROM)	$29.99	SNON
Starting & Running a Successful Newsletter or Magazine	$29.99	MAG
Tax Deductions for Professionals	$34.99	DEPO
Tax Savvy for Small Business	$36.99	SAVVY
The Work From Home Handbook	$19.99	USHOM
Wow! I'm in Business	$21.99	WHOO
Working for Yourself: Law & Taxes for Independent Contractors, Freelancers & Consultants	$39.99	WAGE
Working With Independent Contractors (Book w/CD-ROM)	$34.99	HICI
Your Limited Liability Company (Book w/CD-ROM)	$49.99	LOP
Your Rights in the Workplace	$29.99	YRW

CONSUMER

	PRICE	CODE
How to Win Your Personal Injury Claim	$34.99	PICL
Nolo's Encyclopedia of Everyday Law	$29.99	EVL
Nolo's Guide to California Law	$34.99	CLAW
Your Little Legal Companion (Hardcover)	$9.95	ANNIS

ESTATE PLANNING & PROBATE

8 Ways to Avoid Probate	$21.99	PRAV
The Busy Family's Guide to Estate Planning (Book w/ CD)	$24.99	FAM
Estate Planning Basics	$21.99	ESPN
Estate Planning for Blended Families: Providing for Your Spouse & Children in a Second Marriage	$34.99	SMAR
The Executor's Guide: Settling a Loved One's Estate or Trust	$39.99	EXEC
Get It Together: Organize Your Records (Book w/CD-ROM)	$21.99	GET
How to Probate an Estate in California	$49.99	PAE
Make Your Own Living Trust (Book w/CD-ROM)	$39.99	LITR
Nolo's Simple Will Book (Book w/CD-ROM)	$36.99	SWIL
Plan Your Estate	$44.99	NEST
Quick & Legal Will Book (Book w/CD-ROM)	$21.99	QUIC
Special Needs Trusts: Protect Your Child's Financial Future (Book w/CD-ROM)	$34.99	SPNT

FAMILY MATTERS

Always Dad: Being a Great Father During & After a Divorce	$16.99	DIFA
Building a Parenting Agreement That Works	$24.99	CUST
The Complete IEP Guide: How to Advocate for Your Special Ed Child	$34.99	IEP
Divorce & Money: How to Make the Best Financial Decisions During Divorce	$34.99	DIMO
Divorce Without Court: A Guide to Mediation & Collaborative Divorce	$34.99	DWCT
Do Your Own California Adoption (Book w/CD-ROM)	$34.99	ADOP
Every Dog's Legal Guide: A Must-Have for Your Owner	$19.99	DOG
The Guardianship Book for California	$34.99	GB

FAMILY MATTERS	PRICE	CODE
A Judge's Guide to Divorce (Book w/CD-ROM)	$24.99	JDIV
A Legal Guide for Lesbian & Gay Couples (Book w/CD-ROM)	$34.99	LG
Living Together: A Legal Guide for Unmarried Couples (Book w/CD-ROM)	$34.99	LTK
Nolo's Essential Guide to Divorce	$24.99	NODV
Nolo's IEP Guide: Learning Disabilities	$29.99	IELD
Parent Savvy	$19.99	PRNT
Prenuptial Agreements (Book w/CD-ROM)	$34.99	PNUP

GOING TO COURT

Becoming a Mediator	$29.99	BECM
Beat Your Ticket: Go to Court & Win—National Edition	$21.99	BEYT
The Criminal Law Handbook: Know Your Rights, Survive the System	$39.99	KYR
Everybody's Guide to Small Claims Court—National Edition	$29.99	NSCC
Everybody's Guide to Small Claims Court in California	$29.99	CSCC
Fight Your Ticket & Win in California	$29.99	FYT
How to Change Your Name in California (Book w/CD-ROM)	$34.99	NAME
Legal Research: How to Find & Understand the Law	$39.99	LRES
Nolo's Deposition Handbook	$34.99	DEP
Nolo's Plain-English Law Dictionary	$29.99	DICT
Represent Yourself in Court: How to Prepare & Try a Winning Case	$39.99	RYC
Win Your Lawsuit: A Judge's Guide to Representing Yourself in California Superior Court	$39.99	SLWY

HOMEOWNERS, LANDLORDS & TENANTS

Buying a Second Home (Book w/CD-ROM)	$24.99	SCND
The California Landlord's Law Book: Evictions (Book w/CD-ROM)	$44.99	LBEV
The California Landlord's Law Book: Rights & Responsibilities (Book w/CD-ROM)	$44.99	LBRT
California Tenants' Rights	$29.99	CTEN
Deeds for California Real Estate	$27.99	DEED
The Essential Guide for First-Time Homeowners	$19.99	USOWN
Every Landlord's Guide to Finding Great Tenants (Book w/CD-ROM)	$24.99	FIND

MONEY MATTERS	PRICE	CODE
Nolo's Guide to Social Security Disability (Book w/CD-ROM)	$29.99	QSS
The Sharing Solution: How to Prosper by Sharing Resources, Simplifying Your Life & Building Community	$24.99	SHAR
Solve Your Money Troubles: Debt, Credit & Bankruptcy	$24.99	MT
Stand Up to the IRS	$29.99	SIRS
Stopping Identity Theft: 10 Easy Steps to Security	$19.99	USID
Surviving an IRS Tax Audit	$24.95	SAUD

RETIREMENT & SENIORS		
Get a Life: You Don't Need a Million to Retire Well	$24.99	LIFE
IRAs, 401(k)s & Other Retirement Plans: Taking Your Money Out	$34.99	RET
Long-Term Care: How to Plan & Pay for It	$24.99	ELD
Nolo's Essential Retirement Tax Guide	$24.99	RTAX
Retire Happy: What You Can Do Now to Guarantee a Great Retirement	$19.99	USRICH
Social Security, Medicare & Goverment Pensions	$29.99	SOA
Work Less, Live More: The Way to Semi-Retirement	$17.99	RECL
The Work Less, Live More Workbook (Book w/ CD)	$19.99	RECW

PATENTS AND COPYRIGHTS		
All I Need Is Money: How to Finance Your Invention	$19.99	FINA
The Copyright Handbook: What Every Writer Needs to Know (Book w/CD-ROM)	$39.99	COHA
Getting Permission: How to License & Clear Copyrighted Material Online & Off (Book w/CD-ROM)	$34.99	RIPER
How to Make Patent Drawings	$29.99	DRAW
The Inventor's Notebook	$24.99	INOT
Legal Guide to Web & Software Development (Book w/CD-ROM)	$44.99	SFT
Nolo's Patents for Beginners	$29.99	QPAT
Patent, Copyright & Trademark: An Intellectual Property Desk Reference	$39.99	PCTM
Patent It Yourself	$49.99	PAT
Patent Pending in 24 Hours	$34.99	PEND

Order anytime at WWW.NOLO.COM
Call 800-728-3555 • Mail or fax the order form in this book

PATENTS AND COPYRIGHTS

	PRICE	CODE
Patent Savvy for Managers: Spot & Protect Valuable Innovations in Your Company	$29.99	PATM
Patent Searching Made Easy	$39.99	PATSE
Patenting Art & Entertainment	$39.99	PATAE
Profit From Your Idea (Book w/CD-ROM)	$34.99	LICE
The Public Domain	$34.99	PUBL
Trademark: Legal Care for Your Business & Product Name	$39.99	TRD
What Every Inventor Needs to Know About Business & Taxes (Book w/CD-ROM)	$21.99	ILAX

SOFTWARE

Call or check our website at www.nolo.com for special discounts on Software!

LLC Maker—Windows	$89.99	LLP1
PatentEase Deluxe 6.0—Windows	$349.00	PEAS
Quicken Legal Business Pro 2009—Windows	$109.99	SBQB9
Quicken WillMaker Plus 2009—Windows	$89.99	WQP9

Special Upgrade Offer

Save 35% on the latest edition of your Nolo book

Because laws and legal procedures change often, we update our books regularly. To help keep you up-to-date, we are extending this special upgrade offer. Cut out and mail the title portion of the cover of your old Nolo book and we'll give you 35% off the retail price of the New Edition of that book when you purchase directly from Nolo. This offer is to individuals only. Prices and offer subject to change without notice.

Order anytime at WWW.NOLO.COM

Call 800-728-3555 • Mail or fax the order form in this book

Order Form

Name	
Address	
City	
State, Zip	
Daytime Phone	
E-mail	

Our "No-Hassle" Guarantee

Return anything you buy directly from Nolo for any reason and we'll cheerfully refund your purchase price. No ifs, ands or buts.

☐ Check here if you do not wish to receive mailings from other companies

Item Code	Quantity	Item	Unit Price	Total Price

Method of payment

☐ Check ☐ VISA

☐ American Express

☐ MasterCard

☐ Discover Card

Subtotal	
Add your local sales tax (California only)	
Shipping: RUSH $12, Basic $6 (See below)	
"I bought 2, ship it to me FREE!" (Ground shipping only)	
TOTAL	

Account Number

Expiration Date

Signature

Shipping and Handling

Rush Delivery—Only $12

We'll ship any order to any street address in the U.S. by UPS 2nd Day Air* for only $12!

* Order by 9:30 AM Pacific Time and get your order in 2 business days. Orders placed after 9:30 AM Pacific Time will arrive in 3 business days. P.O. boxes and S.F. Bay Area use basic shipping. Alaska and Hawaii use 2nd Day Air or Priority Mail.

Basic Shipping—$6

Use for P.O. Boxes, Northern California and Ground Service.

Allow 1-2 weeks for delivery.

U.S. addresses only.

For faster service, use your credit card and our toll-free numbers

Call our customer service group Monday thru Friday 7am to 6pm PST

Phone
1-800-728-3555

Fax
1-800-645-0895

Mail
Nolo
950 Parker St.
Berkeley, CA 94710

Order 24 hours a day @ www.nolo.com